GENDER, SONG, AND SENSIBILITY

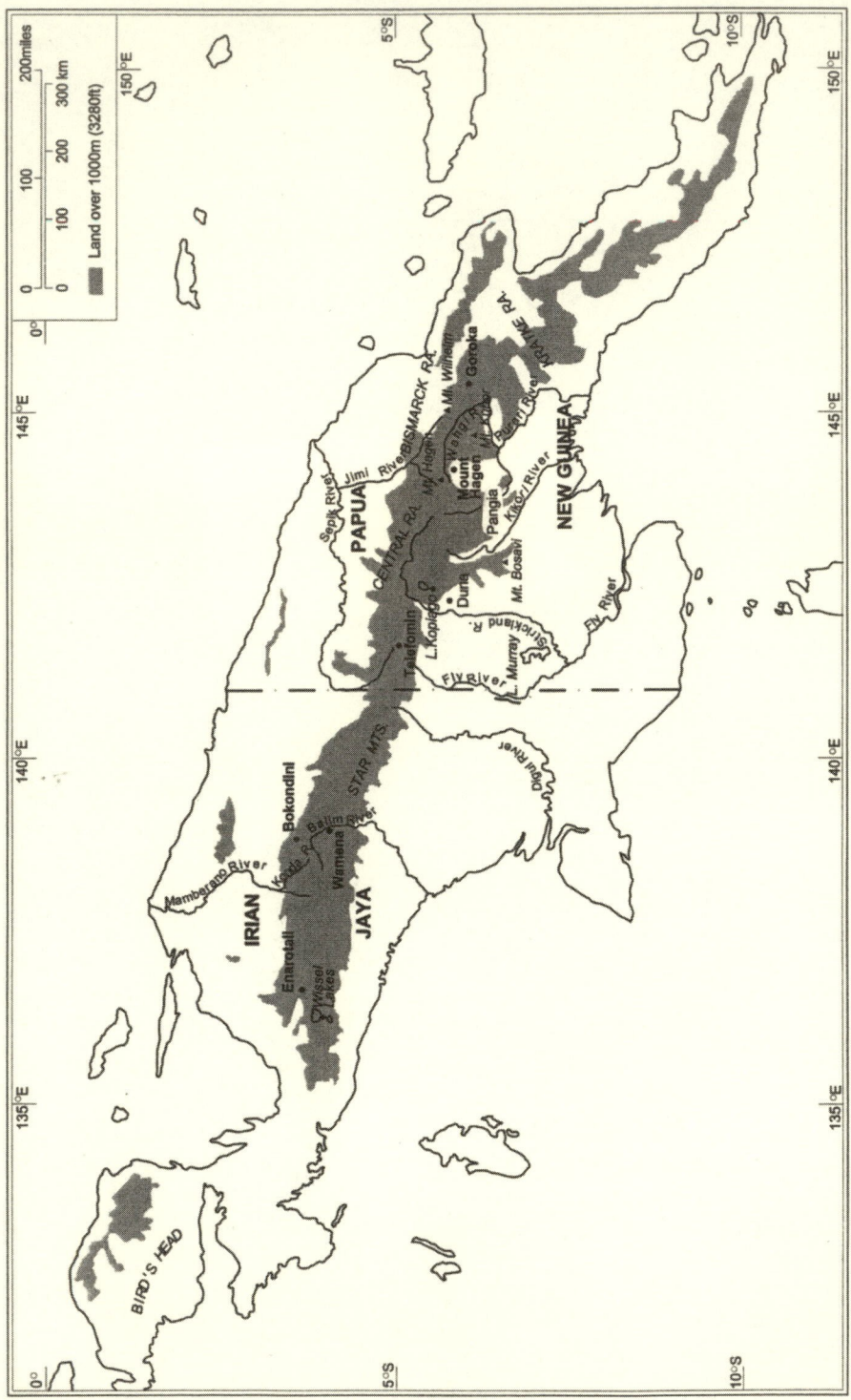

GENDER, SONG, AND SENSIBILITY

*Folktales and Folksongs
in the Highlands of New Guinea*

Pamela J. Stewart and Andrew Strathern

PRAEGER

Westport, Connecticut
London

Library of Congress Cataloging-in-Publication Data

Stewart, Pamela J.
    Gender, song, and sensibility : folktales and folksongs in the highlands of New Guinea /
Pamela J. Stewart and Andrew Strathern.
      p. cm.
    Includes bibliographical references and index.
    ISBN 0-275-97792-7 (alk. paper)
    1. Ethnology—Papua New Guinea. 2. Man-woman relationships—Papua New Guinea.
3. Tales—Papua New Guinea. 4. Folk songs—Papua New Guinea. 5. New Guinea—
Social life and customs. I. Strathern, Andrew. II. Title.
GN671.N5S776 2002
306'.09953—dc21   2002025313

British Library Cataloguing in Publication Data is available.

Library of Congress Catalog Card Number: 2002025313
ISBN: 0-275-97792-7

First published in 2002

Praeger Publishers, 88 Post Road West, Westport, CT 06881
An imprint of Greenwood Publishing Group, Inc.
www.praeger.com

Printed in the United States of America

The paper used in this book complies with the
Permanent Paper Standard issued by the National
Information Standards Organization (Z39.48–1984).

10 9 8 7 6 5 4 3 2 1

Copyright Acknowledgments

The authors and publisher gratefully acknowledge permission for use of the following material:

Excerpts from Stewart, Pamela J., and Andrew Strathern. 1997. "Netbags Revisited: Cultural
Narratives from Papua New Guinea." *Pacific Studies*, 20(2): 1–30.

Excerpts from Stewart, Pamela J., and Andrew Strathern. 2000. *Remaking the World: Myth,
Mining, and Ritual Change among the Duna of Papua New Guinea*. Washington, D.C.:
Smithsonian Institution Press.

To the humanity of expression that sits in the quiet corners of imagination.

Contents

Photo essay follows page 119.

Acknowledgments

We wish to record here our thanks to the government and people of Papua New Guinea for relevant research permissions and for collaboration over the years, including the songs and folk tales we present in the text. For a few specific quotations from our book *Remaking the World: Myth, Mining, and Ritual Change among the Duna of Papua New Guinea* (P.J. Stewart and A. Strathern, 2002), we thank the Smithsonian Institution Press for their permission to use these passages. We also thank Dale Robertson, Editor of *Pacific Studies* for the right to use certain passages and materials from our article on "Netbags Revisited: Cultural Narratives from New Guinea," which appeared in *Pacific Studies* 20(2): 1–30, 1997. Chapter 7 contains extracts from two of our unpublished conference papers: Stewart and Strathern (2000), "Power and Placement in Blood Practices," presented at the 2000 AAA meetings session "Blood Mysteries"; and Strathern and Stewart (1999), "Cults, Closures, and Collaborations," presented at the 1999 ASAO meeting session, "Women in Male Rituals of New Guinea."

Our research work in the field has been supported by grants from the American Philosophical Society, the Pitcairn-Crabbe fund of the Department of Religious Studies, University of Pittsburgh, and by the Office of the Dean, Faculty of Arts and Sciences, University of Pittsburgh; also by the Department of Anthropology, James Cook University of North Queensland, Australia. For a specific grant to assist with photographic materials for this book, we are especially grateful to the Richard D. and Mary Jane Edwards Endowed Publications Fund, administered by Dean N. John Cooper, FAS,

University of Pittsburgh. We wish to also acknowledge the cooperation and input of Greenwood Publications, through their Acquisitions Editor Jane Garry and Production Editor Lori Ewen, as well as the copyeditor for the manuscript. All shortcomings in the final product remain ours.

Chapter 1

Introduction: Sensibilities and Sexuality

Anthropologists writing about the New Guinea Highlands have tended to characterize the societies of this region in certain ways. These social groups have therefore acquired a kind of regional stereotype that constitutes a general problem for cross-cultural generalization and comparison as Arjun Appadurai has pointed out (Appadurai 1996). Aspects of these generalizations are repeated from author to author until they become canonical and unquestioned. The stereotype includes features such as warfare, male initiation, male domination over females, ideas concerning menstrual "pollution," which is seen as an instrument for male domination, and patterns of male polygyny that express male hegemony in general. Particularly with regard to notions of pollution, the stereotype also includes the supposed denigration of sexual activity, and patterns of avoidance, separation, and antagonism between men and women. One of our purposes in writing this book is to reexamine the terms of this stereotype and to build up a rather different overall picture, one that gives room for what we may recognize as a more positive view of gendered relations in these societies and takes into fuller consideration the nuanced expressiveness and ingenuity of the New Guinea Highlands people. For example, in one area of the Highlands of Papua New Guinea, Mount Hagen, the Female Spirit (Amb Kor) was said to reveal herself to a chosen man by the presence of menstrual blood on grass near his home. The blood was seen as one sign of the powers of fertility she could confer on the whole group through her coming in this way—as a bride to the cult leader and his followers. Ethnographic evidence of this kind has suggested to us another side to ideas about relations between men and women, one that emphasizes the positive values of sexual alliance and fertility, as opposed to the themes of sexual separation and taboo. In actuality it is important to see how such ideas are balanced together, and how taboos and separation themselves may be expressing notions of alliance. In order to argue for this view, it is necessary to take a detailed look at the ethnography itself. Equally, it is imperative to realize that a great deal of ethnography is itself an interpretation of materials rather than an uncomplicated presentation of data or facts.

Our aim here is not, however, entirely to subvert previous pictures of ethnographic "realities" in the Highlands. To argue for positive aspects of social relations is not to deny the existence of conflict, domination, exploitation, violence, and the like. It is, rather, to try to see another side of social life or attitudes, one that will enable us to get a balanced view of it. Such a project can contribute to what Bruce Knauft has called the development of a critically humanistic sensibility in anthropological discourse (Knauft 1996): a sensibility that valorizes cultural diversity while still critiquing forms of inequality. In the same way, our previously proposed "Collaborative Model" of gender relations in no way asserts that these relations are simply harmonious or egalitarian (Stewart and Strathern 1999a). It does suggest, however, that we pay attention to collaborative elements in interactions and in symbolic constructions that may be neglected in analyses concentrating primarily on domination and antagonism.

The Highlands areas of New Guinea were explored by outsiders from the 1930s onward. The discovery that they were populated by many thousands of vigorous agricultural peoples with relatively high population densities, elaborate social systems, and flamboyant forms of ritual displays and exchanges, as well as bouts of intense fighting between groups, attracted a stream of colonial government officials, missionaries, anthropologists, and business people (traders and plantation owners). In the Highlands of Papua New Guinea the newcomers were largely Australian, but anthropological work was also carried out by American and German Catholic and Lutheran missionaries, and by research students from a number of different countries working in anthropology programs that incorporated the current theories of social process and social structure. Inevitably, the work of all these observers was strongly imbued with the prevalent ideas of the time, and also with the historical context itself, including the projection of notions about "the primitive world," which was seen as contrasting with the world of "civilization." Ideas of the extreme difference from the world of the observers, along with the partly unconscious projection onto the world of the Highlanders of themes present in the observers' own cultures, entered into the mix of observation and interpretation. Disentangling these threads, and replacing them with current perspectives, is understandably a complex enterprise. Indeed, within anthropology itself, there has been an ongoing debate about gender relations in New Guinea, a debate that has shifted its perspectives over time in the light of changing theories.

Ethnographically, a stream of writings from early on pointed out that there were empirical differences between the various Highlands societies themselves. Following the initial discovery and exploration, these observations tended to be constructed on an east-west axis, an orientation that has remained even though it has obscured some cross-cutting similarities and complications and left out altogether certain regions such as the Ok and Strickland-Bosavi areas, for which separate traditions of analysis have been built. For instance, Richard Salisbury, writing about the Siane people of the Eastern Highlands, argued that the economic, calculating aspects of Siane Pig Feasts were outweighed in importance "by the need to initiate a new group of boys and to obtain ancestral blessing." He suggested that "a significant contrast" could be made with the festivals of the Mae Enga and Hagen peoples "to the west . . . where economic considerations appear to be primary" (Salisbury 1962: 93). In the same passage, Salisbury suggested further that while Siane feasts were organized largely on a corporate basis, "to the west the accumulation and distribution of property is on an individual basis" (p. 93). Generalizations of this kind, which may have appeared valid at the time, did not take into account the complex interplays of social concerns that inform festivals throughout the Highlands or indeed New Guinea generally. Nevertheless, there certainly are important regional differences. Michael Allen (1967) pointed to some of these in the context of ritual practices and social structure, arguing for the primacy of descent, male initiation, and warfare in the east, compared to alliance, exchange, and fertility cults in the west. Daryl Feil (1987) systematized a large body of data into a scheme of this kind, correlating it with the historical intensification of agricultural practices in the west and the corresponding elaboration of exchange festivals. In this book, we will accept the validity of parts of this comparative framework, particularly with regard to our theme of gender relations, and our own examples are drawn predominantly from those societies that fell within the category of "the west" in these earlier analyses. We are not, therefore, attempting simply to overturn the comparisons and distinctions that have been made previously; although we will be suggesting that some modifications of analyses of the Eastern Highlands cases need to be made.

There are, in addition, some recent general trends in anthropological thinking, which were not available to earlier writers, that have influenced our thinking. These have to do with our way of approaching the topic of gender relations and sensibilities, including sexuality. Discussions of sexual practices tend to present these forms of behavior as a discrete, analyzable sphere of human activity that can be picked out for special treatment on its own. This may be perfectly valid for some analytical or practical purposes. It does not, however, suit our purpose here nor is it the best approach, outside of certain specialized studies. Our orientation to the topic derives, rather, from two different sources. One is old: the tradition of holism in anthropological writing, inspired in quite different ways by Franz Boas and Bronislaw Malinowski. Malinowski's own account of sexual practices among the Trobrianders of Papua New Guinea stressed both their extensive and intensive embedding within the cycles of production and exchange in the society at large, and also the cultural specificity of certain erotic acts, such as the biting off of eyelashes as a mark of endearment (Malinowski 1929: 297, 334, 342–43, 472).

The second source of our approach lies in the analyses of embodiment that have come to form a significant part of anthropological theorizing at least since the 1990s (and have their roots further back [see A. Strathern 1996 and Strathern and Stewart 1999a for more on this topic]). Pioneers in this field of study, such as Mary Douglas, stressed the importance of the body as a source of productive metaphors for social life, that is, as a "natural symbol" (Douglas 1970). Others, such as John Blacking, emphasized the sensuous and dynamic qualities of bodily activities themselves as constituent elements of social processes, for example, in dancing (Blacking 1977). Thomas Csordas (e.g., 1990, 1994), in an extensive and influential series of writings, drew these threads together in a general contrast between approaches that tend to see the body as a passive register of social imprints and those that see it as a source of activity, agency, and sensuous self-expression. He argued further that embodiment, the fact of our being embodied persons, should be taken as the very existential ground of culture and self-definition, rather than these being grounded in a kind of mentalistic psychology. In synthetic terms it seems important to bear both of these aspects in mind, since they coexist empirically (see, e.g., Bryan Turner 1992).

The approach of Csordas, Turner, and many others is influenced by a broader philosophical trend that draws its inspiration partly from existentialism and phenomenology, adding to these viewpoints a concentration on aspects of the body itself and how these can be seen as the living roots of expressions that are metaphorical. George Lakoff and Mark Johnson have contributed definitively to this trend, summed up in their work *Philosophy in the Flesh* (1999). Their discussions of the embodied mind not only challenge, in a by now familiar fashion, the Cartesian postulate of an essential split between body and mind as a part of the Western philosophical tradition, but go on to examine what an embodied philosophy itself would be. One of their principal concerns is to stress that "because concepts and reason both derive from, and make use of, the sensorimotor system, the mind is not separate from or independent of the body. Therefore classical faculty psychology is incorrect" (1999: 555). They argue, as they also did in earlier works, that certain metaphors derived from bodily experiences importantly shape conceptual areas of experience itself such as courtship, citing here the idea that "love is a journey" (pp. 63–69).

The implications of this argument are twofold: the body is in the mind, but the mind is also in the body. They form a complex whole. It follows then that when we speak about activities that in the ideological form of thought shaped by the Pauline traditions of Christianity are labeled as bodily by comparison with those that are mental or spiritual, we have to remember that these activities are equally mental and bodily. Not only are mental states influenced by bodily derived "image schemata," in Lakoff and Johnson's terms, but bodily states are also influenced by mental ones, in short by the imagination. Since sex and sexual activity are one of the dimensions of life often seen as bodily, along with other "acts of the flesh," it is clear that we have to apply this argument to them also. Sexual activities are accompanied by, even defined by, imaginative schemes of thought and feeling that greatly influence not only the meanings of these activities but also their practical course in the broad context of life. It is not surprising, then, that sexual activities are ordinarily surrounded by rosters of culturally expressive forms such as songs, dances, myths and folk tales, rituals, magical spells, and religious invocations that serve the dual purpose of directing or channeling people's actions and of creating meanings for those actions that make them attractive. These rosters in turn define what we call cultural sensibilities. Sexual activity, like any other activity, takes place within the framework of these sensibilities, and these in turn touch on deep realms of being such as senses of personhood, self, and the emotions. It is these realms that are created and expressed in cultural genres to which people endlessly add their variations and their particular structures of feeling. This is the reason why in this book we place stress on these genres of expression. We also do so because, in the earlier literature at least, such genres were relatively neglected or referred to only briefly when gender relations were discussed. Categories of action such as courtship, marriage, reproduction, and illicit sexual actions could therefore be represented without a sense of the underlying ethos or aesthetic impulses that tend to go with them. While not denying the significance of formal social analysis, still less the importance of conflict and actions defined by the societies under study as deviant and liable to have negative consequences for the group at large, we argue that such modes of analysis do need to be set against the positive backdrop of expressive culture, and it is this backdrop that we intend to explore. In fact, to make our point, we will foreground it, converting it from a vague backdrop to a major contextualizing feature.

"Sensibility" is a useful term for our study here, because it mediates between the worlds of the mental and the sensory. It encompasses conscious thought and action while being clearly informed and directed in various ways by the unconscious psyche and developed notions about gender relations (see Damasio 1999 for further discussion on consciousness and action). Sen-

sibility includes the senses, and it is the senses that are often evoked in songs
and dances. It also incorporates the idea of the culturally appropriate or
habitual behavior. A certain Trobriand cultural sensibility framed the practice of erotic eyelash biting. The Trobrianders found the act exciting in
sensory terms, partly because of the erotic connotations of the eyes themselves as the seat of desire (Malinowski 1929: 166, 169, 296–97). Not all
New Guineans would share this idea. For some Highlanders, for example,
the ingestion of another person's hair can be seen as dangerous. What trig-
gers a certain emotion, therefore, differs from case to case. At the same time
what the Trobrianders said about the eyes obviously finds cross-cultural sensory parallels. Hageners, for instance, of the Western Highlands Province of
Papua New Guinea say that a sign of sexual interest is evident when two
people's eyes meet and "fight" (*mong rakl el etembil*).

Along with the interest in embodiment, and consonant with it, there has
been a growth of analysis in the anthropology of the senses, and also the
emotions generally, in ways that fit within the parameters of our book. Diane
Ackerman wrote *A Natural History of the Senses* in 1990, exploring in turn
smell, touch, taste, hearing, vision, and synesthesia. The titles of her sections
reveal a constant moving backward and forward between the physical and
the imaginative, for example, on smell, "buckets of light," "an offering to
the Gods," and "the oceans inside us"; or on touch, "the inner climate,"
"adventures in the touch dome," and "the skin has eyes." Her discussions
play also on parts of the body. In one example reminiscent of our remarks
above about Trobriand ideas, she notes that "giving one's lover a lock of
hair to wear in a small locket around his neck used to be a moving and
tender gesture, but also a dangerous one, since . . . a tuft of someone's hair
could be used to cast a spell against them" (Ackerman 1990: 84). In the
same passage Ackerman mentions the anecdote of "a medieval knight [who]
wore a lock of his lady's pubic hair into battle," thus taking with him a
portion of her protective life-force (Ackerman 1990: 84). Such ideas would
be recognizable enough to the New Guinea Highlanders whom we know,
both in their elementary form (the association of hair with life-force) and
in their particular imaginative expression (the use of body parts as marks of
attraction and affection, also of memory and grief). These expressions link
body and person together by way of synecdoche, and refer to the fact that
body parts may outlast the life of the person and so come to stand for the
person. We may recall here the poet John Donne's lines in "The Relique,"
with its reference to "a bracelet of bright hair about the bone," the sign of
a loving couple lying together in a grave, and their thought that this could
be a way to make their souls meet again at the time of the Resurrection of
the dead. As is typical in Donne's poetry, the complex weaving together of
spiritual and physical themes in the context of sexual love itself powerfully
conveys a certain sensibility, expressed in his couplet in the poem "The
Extasie": "Loves mysteries in soules doe grow/But yet the body is his

booke" (Donne 1970: 80–81, 77). Donne's philosophical reflections turn on the body/soul dichotomy in Christian metaphysics, a distinction that is not paralleled with any exactitude in Highlands New Guinea notions; yet his invocation of the symbiotic relationship between the different parts of the person certainly would resonate with Hagen ideas of the *noman*, or mind (see Stewart and Strathern 2001a: 113–38). For the Hageners both desires and thought begin or meet in the *noman*, and the state of the skin, or outer body, reflects that of the *noman*. Decoration, for the Hageners and for the neighboring Wahgi people, reveals the *noman*, and hence it is possible, in Michael O'Hanlon's phrase, to "read the skin" (O'Hanlon 1989). For them, too, then, as for John Donne, the body becomes "love's book" or "visualized desires."

Constance Classen has summed up matters of this sort in her own book *Worlds of Sense* (1993). She explores a range of certain ethnographic cases from the point of view of a specific sense, paying particular attention to odor and olfaction. One of her chapters concerns words and speech. Essentially she stresses the embodied characteristics of performance in language use. She also traces the sense-based origins of words that classify cognitive qualities in the English language, noting their metaphorical transfer from a physical to a mental domain in a way that fits with Lakoff and Johnson's work. This kind of domain also shows cross-cultural similarities that are bodily based. The English term "sharp," referring to intelligence, comes from a root meaning to cut. In Melpa, the Hagen language, an analogous usage of the word *nengena*, or sharp edge, is also applied to persons of keen intelligence. Classen also points out that particular senses are the foci of cultural interest for different peoples. For the Ongee of Little Andaman Island in the Bay of Bengal, a small hunting and gathering population, "smell is the fundamental cosmic principle." Living beings are said to be made of smell, and "the most concentrated form of odour according to the Ongee are bones, believed to be solid smell. . . . An inner spirit is said to reside within the bones of living beings. While one is sleeping, this internal spirit gathers all the odours one has scattered during the day and returns them to the body, making continued life possible" (Classen 1993: 127). Perhaps such a philosophy is particularly appropriate for a hunting and gathering people who depend on smell to a high degree in their quest for food within their environment. For the Hageners, blood and "grease" are considered to be highly important elements in living creatures, including people, and the bones are said to contain *ombil tiköm*, a form of grease or *kopong* that gives people strength and is akin to the substance of the brain, *peng koya* (Stewart and Strathern 2001a: 113–38). While they do not privilege any one sense over the others they have a strongly humoral view of the human body that intersects with their philosophy of the *noman*, as mind or person, and gives that philosophy its embodied foundation in a way analogous to the Ongee people's deployment of ideas about smell.

Classen's approach is exemplified further and complemented by the contributors to David Howes's edited volume, *The Varieties of Sensory Experience* (Howes 1991a). Michael Lambek's introductory remarks to this collection agree with Lakoff and Johnson: "all metaphor is sense based" (Lambek 1991: x). As Lambek also notes, understanding this point is itself "to engage in an act of imagination" (p. xi), and thus to recognize the multiple acts of imagination by which cultural expressions built on the senses have been created. In one of his contributions to the volume, Howes proposes a sensorial anthropology that deals with the combinatory qualities of perceived sense experiences in different cultural contexts, as well as with particular cultural foci. He proposes that a stress on the visual goes with individuality, on aurality with the communal. He also suggests that there is a politics of sensory orders; citing Anthony Seeger's work in the volume, he notes that among the Suya, women are restricted to expressing themselves through odor, which for the Suya is anti-social, and through taste, which is regarded with indifference, whereas high value is accorded to the speech of males and their singing (Howes 1991b: 167–91). While not all of Howes's suggested generalizations and interpretations carry over to the Highlands of New Guinea (to which he has also applied them), his general arguments in favor of a sensorial anthropology are certainly valuable and tie in well with other well known approaches (as found in, e.g., Stoller 1989, 1997; Jackson 1989).

But how do we move from a sensorial anthropology to the concept of sensibility? The pathway is shown quite clearly by the idea of sensory orders, which Howes argues may also constitute political orders. We can broaden this further by saying that the world of the senses is always infused with worlds of morals, that is, with a general social orientation toward others. This is why we so often find a synaesthetic effect in sensory expressions, so that a sense-apprehension comes to stand for an emotional state. Emotional states belong to the universe of sociality and culture as much as to internally experienced feelings. In one Highlands society, Pangia in the Southern Highlands Province of Papua New Guinea, the term for a bad smell, such as of rotting food or feces, is *korimi*. The same term is used for anger, in a usage exactly comparable to the English expression "made a stink," and anger is also held to emerge from the nose. A certain attitude toward anger is shown in this expression. Anger is unpleasant. It may be justified, but it makes others feel awkward. It requires that the "air be cleared," that is, that the conflict that is causing it be resolved. The problem may have to be "flushed away." The attitude involved has its roots in a sensory impression, but it expresses more than the impression itself, drawing it into service in social life. It is this combination of sensory impression and moral or social stance rooted in cultural attitudes that we call a sensibility.

Sensibilities operate across the board. In this regard what we are calling sensibility resembles Pierre Bourdieu's concept of the habitus (Bourdieu

1977) as a durably installed set of predispositions out of which social practice is generated. However, we do not intend to make our concept work as hard as Bourdieu requires for the habitus, that is, we are not making it into a master concept or final explanatory tool. We see it rather as a term to capture an aspect of overall behavior and conduct, one that enables us to get closer to the nuances of lived conduct and to enter further into the culturally situated phenomenological experiences of persons (see also Leavitt 2001).

None of the chapters in Howes's collection on sensory experience concentrates on questions dealing with sexual practices. One, however, touches on them in passing, while discussing taste. Joel Kuipers, writing on the Weyewa people of Sumba in Indonesia, tells us that in ritual speech an opposition between bitter and bland tastes prevails and things that are consumable in ritual are classified as bland if they are available for use and bitter if they are not. This category of "things" includes, in fact, persons, that is, marriageable women. A familiar equation between sexual activity and eating is thus set up, and "a girl may be declared *poddu* [bitter] if her father, in his great joy at begetting a daughter, promises a spectacular feast in gratitude to the ancestors, and then later reneges on his commitment. The girl is considered *poddu* (bitter, prohibited) until her father makes good his promise" (Kuipers 1991: 122). The association of ideas involved here deters people from marrying the girl, since bitter tastes are disliked. In English also the expressions of "being bitter" about something, "bitter disappointment," and "bitter regret" draw on an analogous sense of the term.

Kuipers's example leads us to a further point. He was referring to a context he describes as ritual. A classification appropriate to contexts of ritual consumption of foods was carried over into the context of marriage. No doubt this was appropriate also because marriages are occasions for feasts and they require the blessings of the ancestors. There is a seamless transition from a sensory expression of taste generally to a specific context of a feast and then to the domain of sex impinging on the daily life of a girl who was not supposed to receive suitors until her father's promise to his ancestors was fulfilled. The example shows us the enchainment of factors linking together ritual and everyday life, and thereby demonstrates that we should not make too sharp a demarcation between these domains. Naturally, in so far as ritual has to do with making ideal statements about relations, which by definition are not always attained outside of the ritual context, we cannot simply equate or collapse the two. The actual gap between ritual and everyday life patterns may be great or small, and this often depends on patterns of historical change in the society concerned. But for our purposes here it is sufficient to establish a different point: that there is feedback or influence between these domains and that they therefore merge into one another in certain ways. Instead of seeing ritual and everyday contexts necessarily as being in a dichotomous relationship, therefore, we can see them as expressing a continuum of meanings. Again, this does not mean that we should simply equate the two contexts. Ritual heightens and solemnizes patterns of action in order to bring humans into alignment with more overarching principles or concerns. As Victor Turner argued (e.g., Turner 1977), it sets up its own special conditions and creates its own structural framework. It is in some ways set apart from ordinary life. And its prescriptions are not always fulfilled in practice, either in people's perceptions or in historical fact. Promises made in ritual contexts are not always kept. Ritual may also reflect the ideology of those in power and may be, from some analytical perspectives, an instrument to impress that power on others, thus denying or suppressing other forms of "reality" or meaning (Bloch 1989; Rappaport 1999).

Nevertheless, several further considerations apply that support our contention or preference for regarding ritual and everyday contexts as interconnected. First, if ritual is a part of religious action and religion creates powerful and enduring moods and attitudes among people, as Clifford Geertz maintained (Geertz 1965), these powerful moods must extend beyond the moments of ritual action itself through memory of the cognitive images presented in ritual contexts (Whitehouse 2000). This observation fits with the formulations of earlier anthropologists who saw rituals as having cathartic functions for the individuals participating in them, thus impacting the conscious recognition of relationships between people and their environment, including the world of spirits and dead ancestors, in such a way as to perpetuate ritually prescribed modes of interaction in the day-to-day context. Second, rituals of various sorts are interwoven with details of other activities and come to form a part of the everyday, as for example when rituals are performed as a regular part of garden making among various peoples. These ritual practices may be highly gender specific with the individual routine being defined by further notions of gendered history through myth and indigenous religious practice. Leach (1954: 12) likened these to aesthetic practices that symbolically announce the status and identity of the garden makers, seeing ritual therefore as a statement about social structure. From another viewpoint we may argue that ritual is itself seen as just as much instrumental and technical as the physical acts of clearing, tilling, and planting crops. Within the traditions of Christian thought there is the notion that everything happens through God's will, as expressed in the hymn lines: "We plow the fields and scatter/The good seed on the land/But it is fed and watered/By God's almighty hand." Hence we see the necessity from this viewpoint to perform the ritual of praying to God in order for the garden to grow. With New Guinea ancestors the same need existed.

Leach himself goes further than we have done here and argues that Durkheim's distinction between the sacred and the profane is untenable, and that ritual can be seen as referring to aspects of acts, not classes of acts set apart from others. The effect of such a view would be to collapse the difference between ritual and everyday contexts, just as we have noted that the distinction between technical and ritual acts can from one viewpoint be collapsed (Leach 1954: 12). Leach had a penchant for making strong statements, designed to jolt his readers out of accustomed ways of thinking, and we intend, by citing him, to administer a small jolt of this sort. For convenience, we can still preserve the idea of some ritual contexts being set apart from other contexts of life, such as in the Spirit Cults we talk about later in the book. But being set apart does not mean that they are unconnected with social life generally, since they inform the participants with ideological values that penetrate the daily behavior of persons and they are also structured to some degree by the daily social interactions between groups that participate in such a ritual performance.

This fits with the orthodox view, which Leach repeats, that ritual acts make statements about social structure. But there is another reason, at the organizational level, why we need to see ritual and everyday events as connected, and this is that the preparations for ritual events often take up long periods of time. This is true for all the major ritual festivals in Highlands societies. It has also been strikingly shown by Laurence Carucci in his study of the year-round activities connected with *Kūrijmōj* (Christmas) celebrations on the Enewetak and Wūjlan atolls in Micronesia (Carucci 1997). Many "everyday" activities over a period of months are infused with preparations, anticipations, work, debates, and struggles over the timing of such festivals in the Highlands of Papua New Guinea. Everyday life gains much of its meaning from the ritual cycle itself. Indeed, the same is true for the introduced Christian religion, in which efforts are made by its proponents to make it encompass life as a whole in the way the old rituals did, especially in strengthening political alliances.

Summing up our argument here, we can say that special forms of action and statements found in ritualized contexts may not be directly translated into other spheres of life. They do, however, inform those spheres, and may be a part of them, and they act to give identity to people and provide senses of meaning in themselves. Hence, in looking at people's sexual practices it is worthwhile to do as we will do in this book, that is, look at ritual contexts and expressive genres of behavior that surround and inform these practices. We do not propose that a category of "everyday life" exactly reproduces a category of "ritual action." No anthropologist would wish to undertake such an exercise, since it is quite clear that insofar as ritual makes ideal statements or exaggerated representations these may not always be observed in practice. We do argue, however, for the relevance of evidence from ritual practices that throws light on people's cultural sensibilities in general and hence also on the domain of sexual life.

There are several reasons we emphasize this point, when it might appear to be obvious as we have stated it. The first is that the point is not at all obvious to those who see ritual and everyday life as separate, even opposed, domains. We have cited Leach to indicate that insofar as such a view is derived from Durkheim it is contestable. But Durkheim also clearly thought that ritual produced results in social life outside of the ritual contexts themselves. Our second reason has to do with the specific topic of sex and in fact with the concept of sexuality itself.

Sexuality studies have become a genre in anthropology. Partly this is because more attention is being paid to ideas about sexual preferences and there is a corresponding growth of focus on homoerotic relations, signaled in gay and lesbian studies and the concept of queer theory (Herdt 1997, 1999). Partly, the efflorescence is also connected with the worldwide problems of sexually transmitted disease, primarily AIDS. These somewhat convergent trends have contributed to the funding of large-scale projects that have the category of sexuality as their focus. The creation of this genre owes a good deal to the work of Michel Foucault, as well as to Freud, Kinsey, and a host of subsequent sexologists. Foucault, in his *History of Sexuality*, (1990), pointed out that in a sense sexuality was created as a topic of discourse by the very act of making it a matter of secrecy, wrongdoing, and confession in the European Christian tradition. He argued that "by speaking about it so much, by discovering it multiplied, partitioned off, and specified precisely where one had placed it, what one was seeking essentially was simply to conceal sex" (Foucault 1990: 53). Here Foucault was investigating both the ways in which sexual expression was being suppressed by religious formulations and ironically how these formulations themselves sustained a heightened awareness of the topic and were also the genesis of a medicalized discourse on sex that was well suited, in some ways, to be adapted for further use in the study of AIDS. "Claiming to speak the truth, it stirred up people's fears; to the least oscillations of sexuality, it ascribed an imaginary dynasty of evils . . . strange pleasures, it warned, would eventually result in nothing short of death" (pp. 53–54). The biblical overtones of Sodom and Gomorrah are evident here, as is the complex of Victorian ideas about the deleterious consequences of masturbation. Foucault lays stress on the development of ideas of Christian confession as the forerunners of the Victorian "science" of sexuality. "Sex was a privileged theme of confession" (p. 61), and this constituted "the transformation of sex into discourse" (p. 61). Power became involved in the person of those judging, punishing, forgiving, consoling, or reconciling. Confession paved the way to purification, redemption through doing penance. At a later stage, confession was recodified as a part of medicalized therapeutic operations. "The sexual domain was no longer accounted for simply by the notions of error and sin, excess or transgression, but was placed under the rule of the normal and the pathological" (p. 67). Sex had to be inscribed "in an ordered system of knowledge" and also became "an object of great suspicion," and "a fragment of darkness, . . . a universal secret" (p. 69). Freud's psychology clearly fit in well with all this, simply by carrying the production of "truth" into the center of this "heart of darkness" and asserting that the secret was indeed a secret, the impulse to commit incest. This same *scientia sexualis* was then carried over by psychologists and anthropologists into the remote and hitherto "secret" corners of the world in order to unlock the mysteries of sexual behavior in these "other cultures." It reached New Guinea with the debates about the rein-terpretations by Ernest Jones of Malinowski's materials on the Trobrianders, which we have noted earlier, Malinowski's attempt to rebut these interpre-tations, and a cohort of latter-day discussants, notably Melford Spiro (Mal-inowski 1955; Jones 1925; Spiro 1982).

Pat Caplan, in *The Cultural Construction of Sexuality* (1995), notes that "various writers have suggested that we are only likely to find sexuality thought of as a 'thing in itself' when there is a severance of sex from re-production; others suggest that the division comes from the 'commoditi-zation' of sex under capitalism" (p. 2). She remarks that the term "sexuality" first seems to have appeared in 1800, "which suggests that the concept came into existence with modern society" (p. 2). She goes on to ask, "[W]hen we talk about sexuality, are we considering behaviour or a set of ideas, and if both what is the relationship between them?" (p. 2). It would seem that Foucault has traced in a profound way this coming into being of the concept of sexuality as an object of inquiry and a "problem of truth" in modern society. It would also appear that if we wish to understand fully the rela-tionship between ideas and behavior regarding sex, it is necessary to step outside of this domain of sexuality as a framework of inquiry and take up the framework of sex and sensibility that we are proposing here. At the same time, for the Victorian era itself, we have to stay inside of the domain in order to understand the curious propositions made within it, such as the notion that women were without physical sexual passion, or that loss of semen was debilitating for men, and the struggles for social purity and parity that revolved around the issue of female prostitution (Caplan 1995: 7). Caplan cites Foucault's work here, including his studies of confession and how psychiatry took over the roles of the priest in regard to it (p. 8), along with the claim that "sex has become the explanation for everything" (p. 8).

In the latter part of her introduction to this set of collected papers, Caplan reviews the contributions made by anthropologists to the broadening of debates about sexual practices. She nods to the findings of cultural relativ-ism; points out that Malinowski, while opposing Freud's theory of incest, subscribed to a simplistic overview of the functions of marriage in human society; notes the protracted disputes over Samoan sexual practices involving Margaret Mead, Derek Freeman, and many others who followed, including some who, like Allan Abramson, suggest that both Mead and Freeman were right in different ways; and remarks on the development of relevant trends in anthropology, such as studies of the body, discussions of honor and shame, and analyses of gender relations that take as their focus the relation-ship between sexuality and gender. The various contributions to the volume abundantly demonstrate the ability of anthropologists to explicate sets of ideas and practices that are quite different from those of the twentieth-century West, even if they are all influenced by global history. However, Caplan does not return to her initial question of "what is sexuality?" Taking Foucault's insights seriously, we would say that sexuality is an object of study by a *scientia sexualis*, evolved from its Victorian prototype. On the other hand, the complexities of conduct in modern times (the era of contraception, medicalizations of the body, technologies of the self, and commodifications of the person all notwithstanding) correspond much more closely to a holistic model of sexuality. A glance at the topics of novels, plays, films, poetry, biographies, and the like from the contexts immediately around us tell us this. Should we ignore this in favor of a "scientific" approach, or should our science in fact take notice of what is around us in social contexts but is not a regular part of the gaze of sexuality studies? We must remember that good science always involves keen observation, noting all levels of variance and considering which particular variables to include or exclude in a model-testing scenario. It is important to pose this issue because if we allow into our discussion forms of data that relate to vernacular or popular forms of consciousness itself, we are better able to humanize the subjects of any study and to grant them the same kinds of agency and feelings that all human beings deserve to have attributed to them (see Cohen 1994 on this point). For anthropology, this humanistic aim is an important one that must constantly be set alongside the scientific aims that we may also have. This "humanizing effect" has not formed a prominent part of the writings on Highlands New Guinea societies, although it is found in works of biography (e.g., Stewart and Strathern 2000a with references therein); it especially tends to be missing in the often linked domains of sex and violence, where the exotic, surprising, and "different" have been stressed in accounts of male initiation, fighting, and sexual taboos. But all anthropologists should look at their own home societies, wherever they may be, and they will honestly find sex and violence scenarios of comparable, albeit different, levels.

We suggest, overall, that there is a place for both narrowly focused and broader approaches and that both have validity. "Sexuality" tends to be a focus for "modern" studies concerned with issues of gender construction, prostitution, and AIDS in cities (see Parker and Gagnon 1995). Bristow (1997) reviews the ongoing repercussions of Victorian sexology and argues that Foucault's own work in the history of sexuality "paved the way for queer theory in the 1990s" (from the summary of his book in the front matter, no page number). He also "looks at the decisive postmodern emphasis on erotic diversity" (Bristow 1997: front matter). These emphases reflect interests similar to those in Parker and Gagnon's book, extended into the realm of bisexual eroticism. All of these studies remain within the realm of sexuality as an object of analysis. Because they deal with contexts in which sexual behavior appears to be separated from other aspects of behavior, sexuality becomes in a curious way the successor to "kinship" in earlier anthropology. The richly textured expressions of all peoples, in all sorts of sexual contexts, need to be looked at in addition to the analysis of the sexual acts themselves—only in this way can a fuller appreciation of sexuality and sexual diversity be gained. As in Foucault's prediction, where kinship was once invoked to "explain everything," now sex itself is called on to do this in some instances. Yet clearly sex must also be situated back into kinship and the relationships of formed communities.

As anthropologists we should be concerned with contextualizing phenomena as broadly and deeply as possible. Abstractions for analytical purposes are valid in their own right but need to be placed alongside more integrative analyses. There are two other ways, not yet discussed, in which we plan to do this here. Both have to do with favored topics that have in some sense replaced kinship as a focus of analysis in contemporary anthropology: rather paradoxically so, since both turn out also to have a great deal to do with kinship. One is the sphere of arguments about personhood in general, the other has to do with the emotions and the ways that emotional expressiveness encompasses and defines sexual identities.

Persons in New Guinea societies, as elsewhere, are partly a product of kin relations, ones in which sex, marriage, and procreation play a significant part. The idea of the relational person, which has been stressed in many New Guinea ethnographies, is essentially based on this point and on the ideologies of kinship relations found in various Highlands societies. The same ethnographic picture was given, often with more detail, in older ethnographies, in fact. We have coined the term "relational-individual" (Stewart and Strathern 2000b) to refer to this relationality while also giving recognition to the individuality of New Guineans, which even in the earliest ethnographic works is as clearly present as it is today. By looking closely at the language of the New Guinea cultures being studied, their metaphoric expressions, songs, balladic epic tales, myths, folk tales, and so forth, the nuanced expressions of people can be clearly presented. More and more we find ethnographic accounts from Papua New Guinea that have been completely gathered not in the local language of the people but in *Tok Pisin* (one of the linguae francae of Papua New Guinea) and sometimes in English. These ethnographic materials are valid, of course, but they miss out on the richness of expression that local language maintains and the meanings that do not translate well or at all into the imported vocabularies of *Tok Pisin* or English. Sometimes translations of materials from local languages are available for ethnographers to use to enrich their analysis but these are not always taken into full consideration.

The approach that some have taken of presenting the person as being devoid of individually defining features is truly a matter of semantics, since all individuals are composites of their experiences, which, of course, include their relationships with their kin and others. This is "true" for a New Yorker, a Castilian, or a New Guinean. The social structures in these places, including kinship ties, differ and thus the development of relationships is not the same but no individual anywhere is formed as an "untouched" person (i.e., without relationships). The exploration of the human conscious mind and the emotions clearly demonstrates this point (Cohen 1994). Our position on this debate is that its validity depends partly on the domain or aspect one is considering: ideas of the substances in persons do tend to stress relationality (or kinship, as it used to be called in the discipline), while cultural ideas of agency may equally stress autonomy or individual capabilities, whether seen in a "Western" model or not. Furthermore, in all societies the person tends to be composed of relational and individual elements, as we stated above. It is not, therefore, with this debate that we are concerned here (see Lambek and Strathern 1998 for a set of papers looking at these ideas critically in cross-cultural contexts; Strathern and Stewart 2000a for further reflections on the issues, seen ethnographically; A. Strathern 1996: 107–108 on substance and agency). Rather we want to point out a corollary of the acceptance of the idea that personhood in general contains relationality. This is that we cannot simply suppose that gender relations are founded on a global form of domination or antagonism, since they also are set into matrices of kin ties between people. For the New Guinea Highlands we are generally dealing with clan groups of variable size within which marriage (and normatively also sexual relations) is not permitted, so therefore they intermarry with people from other clans. Marriage thus links relatively discrete sets of people together. Moreover it creates individual kin relationships across such groups. All this is quite elementary. If, however, cross-gender relations were simply marked by antagonism or "separation of the sexes," it would be doubtful if these societies could continue to operate at all. As it turns out, exchange relations between intermarrying groups are in one way or another (with important variations) significant. Indeed for those of the Chimbu, Western Highlands, large parts of the Southern Highlands, and Enga Provinces, affinal and intergroup exchanges have long been seen as absolutely central to social processes. Although uncertain whether these societies should be seen as practicing unilineal descent, anthropologists have almost unanimously agreed that they all lay stress on exchanges of wealth and that either the affinal tie or ties of bilateral kinship springing from affinity form a significant axis for these exchanges and the patterns of leadership associated with them. These societies therefore all stress ideas of alliance based on marriage. It would be surprising if their ideas about sex and the ties between women and men were entirely negative, although we can understand that relations traced through women do not necessarily involve women's active agency or fully recognize their part in creating and maintaining links between people. In fact women's agency is everywhere recognized in one way or another, and expressions of alliance often turn on ideas of sexual relations. We have therefore proposed that a model of collaborative relations between men and women at least needs to be set alongside other models anthropologists have used, one of which we have termed the Male Exclusivity Model (ME), in contrast with our Collaborative Model (CM) (Stewart and Strathern 1999a). We will return to this theme when we consider "spirits as spouses" later in this book. Of course, proposing that there is an overall element of collaboration between the sexes, and that this is recognized to one degree or another in ritual cult activities, does not mean that relations are simply egalitarian or that there is no conflict, as we have already noted. All forms of description and analysis have their own perspectives built into them. We simply wish by introducing this model to stress an element of collaboration, recognized to be empirically present to varying extents by other writers, but often overshadowed by a stress on separation and antagonism.

If there is an element of collaboration in gender relations, what is it about? First, it is about interdependence in the domains of production and reproduction. Second, it has to do with the establishment of co-operative ties across group boundaries through the use of cross-sex relations of marriage and kinship. Third, it is concerned with the representation of these relations at the level of the cosmos. And fourth, it reflects the attraction between men and women that induces them to enter into courtship and sexual relations with each other. It is these experiences that we find mirrored in the expressive genres of songs and narratives, while the cosmic element is portrayed in cults. Further, attraction and collaboration must be accompanied by the expression of emotions. In the domain of sex, if certain sensibilities are in play these must be emotionally marked. This brings us to the question of the emotions in general as they have been theorized in anthropology.

The development of an interest in embodiment has led to the analysis of emotions as they are expressed cross-culturally. The topic brings us to the intersections among mind, body, and society that continually turn up in this arena of discourse. The idea of emotions refers in part to physiological, "visceral" processes, and in part to verbal constructions and representations. The idea that emotions are "culturally constructed" derives from the latter point, since emotion terms vary from one cultural context to another and within cultural contexts if described in different languages (see above on local language versus *Tok Pisin*), while the idea that, at base, various forms of human emotion are universal usually appeals to the level of physiology. The reason this topic is relevant here is clear: sex refers to certain embodied physiological processes, and sensibility to their representation and the forms of ethos that bring them into social being. And it is just these sensibilities that are culturally and linguistically structured.

Numerous studies exist that pursue either the theme of universality in emotions or the theme of cross-cultural variability in their construction or expression. A biological/natural science versus a cultural/humanistic divide understandably appears in these studies. Paul Ekman has been prominent among those who advocate the idea that there is a pan-human set of basic emotions. Like many of those working with a natural science approach,

Ekman tends to base his argument on ideas of adaptation and evolution. He suggests that emotional appraisals of situations emerge out of a long prehistory of attempts to read the meanings of events and so make adaptive response to them. These appraisals are built into the human organism, so they occur swiftly and may appear to be involuntary. Connected with this is the fact, Ekman says, that there is evidence "for distinctive patterns of autonomic nervous system (ANS) activity for anger, fear, and disgust and it appears that there may also be a distinctive pattern for sadness" (Ekman 1994: 17). He associates a range of positive emotions including sensory pleasure and excitement, for example, with a particular kind of smile. Ekman also distinguishes moods from emotions, arguing that moods last longer (p. 56). Presumably, moods may also be greatly influenced by communicational contexts and histories of relationships. Emotions, for Ekman, are all basic, since they all have biological foundations. But, of course, biological foundations give rise to greater or lesser forms of expression, depending on cultural and situational contexts, and thus it would be a great oversimplification to assume a general and universal human response to stimuli. Responses to events are driven by emotions that are biologically linked but culturally tempered.

Ekman's ideas, as he himself notes, are contested by others. Richard Shweder, for example, takes issue with the deceptive simplicity of the question of whether there are basic emotions. He takes a symbolic and interpretive approach, asking "whether people everywhere in the world give meaning and shape to their somatic and affective experiences as emotions," and also whether people who do use emotion concepts "use the same emotions to give meaning and shape to their experiences" (Shweder 1994: 32). The questions thus become more complex and explicitly raise the issue of cross-cultural variability. Shweder himself cautions that the answers are not reliably known. Shweder essentially accepts that there may be uniformity or comparability in somatic and affective states but relates the term "emotion" to the domain of culturally objectified expressions, which can be quite variable. He cites the warning that it is all too easy "to unwittingly assimilate other people's linguistic meanings to an ethnocentric set of analytic categories—the abstract 'emotional states' favored by the English-speaking world" (p. 33, quoting the work of Anna Wierzbicka, a comparative linguist); and he adds that the cross-cultural lexical mapping of "emotion" terms is bound to be controversial.

The problem that Shweder raises is classic, in fact endemic, to cross-cultural analysis generally, as arguments about the concept of kinship, or concepts of the person, abundantly indicate (e.g., Schneider 1984; Shweder and Bourne 1984; Strathern and Stewart 2000b). But such analysis cannot proceed at all without some idea of comparability if not commonality, any more than it can proceed by simply assuming a set of a priori constants. The analyst must in fact keep moving backward and forward between interpretations that touch on the universal level and ones that expand particularity and difference. It is notable that Shweder does not contest a level of commonality by way of somatic and affective states of the body, and Ekman's own work belongs to traditions of observational and experimental inquiry set up by Silvan Tomkins, who investigated affect, imagery, and consciousness as universal phenomena. Tomkins's investigations were conducted entirely in the language of the biological and psychological sciences, and he also operated with the idea of evolutionary adaptation:

It is our belief that . . . natural selection has operated on man [in the generic sense] to heighten three distinct classes of affect—affect for the preservation of life, affect for people, and affect for novelty. . . . The human being is equipped with innate affective responses which bias him to want to remain alive and to resist death, to want sexual experiences, to want to experience novelty and to resist boredom, to want to communicate, to be close to and in contact with others of his species and to resist the experience of head and face lowered in shame. (Tomkins 1961: 27)

It is apparent from a list of this kind that Tomkins is laying down the preconditions for a supposed cross-cultural commonality in human affective behavior that might be seen as underlying the variations in emotional expressions that are found.

Other scientists agree. These researchers, working within a similar framework to that of Tomkins, liken the idea of affect and "affect programs" to the notion of "emotion families" that represent clusters of comparable, if varying, tendencies found in different cultural contexts (Lazarus 1991: 194–203). Lazarus recognizes that such programs may be largely fixed, while emotional responses contain "flexible patterns of reaction" (p. 198). For example, he writes that "there is a common core relational theme and appraisal pattern for the adaptational encounter. All instances of the emotion family of anger, for example, share a common apprehension of what is happening, with of course variations around this central theme" (p. 201). Again, this formulation asserts strong commonalities while allowing for variation. A cognate approach is taken by Victor Johnston in his *Why We Feel. The Science of Human Emotions* (1999). Johnston is a psychobiologist who espouses evolutionary functionalism and therefore explains beauty in terms of its biological value in fertility, in the context of natural selection (p. 145). But, of course, "beauty" is completely culturally defined. Thus, it becomes difficult to extend this argument cross-culturally. A broader view is taken by Antonio Damasio in his *The Feeling of What Happens: Body and Emotion in the Making of Consciousness* (1999), a sequel to his earlier book, *Descartes' Error* (1994). The central argument in his earlier book was that "mental activity, from its simplest aspects to its most sublime, requires both brain and body proper" (p. xvii). In line with this viewpoint, in the later book Damasio stresses the importance of emotions in cognitive processing and in social life generally, and distinguishes between "a state of emotion, which can be triggered and executed nonconsciously; a state of feeling, which can be represented nonconsciously; and a state of feeling made conscious, i.e. known to the organism having both emotion and feeling" (1999: 37). Consciousness is important, because it is linked to our condition as humans. It also represents the means whereby feelings become expressed and thereby objectified, and so enter into and contribute to the realm of culture. It is in consciousness also that our own concept of sensibility is located. Sexual activity is a concomitant of emotions and feelings; its expression and meaning to those who engage in it feed back into and reshape the feelings themselves. Culture enters into and defines life experiences, and vice versa.

The emotions that we have been discussing as being expressed through fear, anger, arousal, and the like are bodily responses involving physiological reactions mediated in part by neurological stimuli. The complex neurochemistry involved in the release of neurotransmitters is the subject of much research that clearly implicates the brain in the body's emotional reactions. Sexuality encompasses the body's pulsations of emotional responses to the stimuli of arousal. Music, massage, taste, imagination, and visual stimuli can all produce an aroused state—be it weak or strong. The conscious mind may be involved in promoting or repressing emotional responses, but the unconscious mind may struggle for expression through the release of targeted neurotransmitters that support or oppose the body's response to the directives of the conscious mind, which also operates via neurotransmitters. Candace Pert's work (1997) has pointed to the significant role of the mind and its neurochemistry in the functioning of the body's emotions. She explains that

all sensory information undergoes a filtering process as it travels across one or more synapses [the junction points across which neuronal impulses travel], eventually (but not always) reaching the areas of higher processes, like the frontal lobes [of the brain]. There the sensory input—concerning the view, the odor, the caress—enters our conscious awareness. The efficiency of the filtering process, which chooses what stimuli we pay attention to at any given moment is determined by the quantity and quality of the reception [the physical responders to the chemical stimuli] at these nodal points. The relative quantities and qualities of these receptors are determined by many things, among them your experiences yesterday and as a child, even by what you ate for lunch today. . . . Using neuropeptides [chemical neurotransmitters] as the cue, our bodymind retrieves or represses emotions or behaviors. (pp. 142–43, quoted with permission)

Thus, emotions, as described by Pert, can be seen as the product of the chemical transmitters the brain transmits, which are received by receptors whose receptiveness is defined by the experiential existence of the person.

Philosophers also have entered into this arena of discussion. William Lyons (1985) sets out "three classical theories of emotions: the feeling, behaviorist and psychoanalytic theories" (p. 1). The feeling theory derives, he says, from Descartes. For Descartes the soul contained thoughts and desires but also the emotions or passions, which are stimulated by bodily perceptions and in turn prepare the body for appropriate forms of action. Emotion is therefore, by this account, a "feeling or sensation in the soul." Lyons thinks that this theory is inadequate, because of the problem of the linkage between body and soul (or mind) that Descartes's general philosophy faces. According to the behaviorist theory of J. B. Watson, emotions were seen as hereditary patterns of reaction involving profound bodily changes, especially in the visceral and glandular systems (Lyons, 1985: 18). But Watson thought that these patterns of reaction were to be found in their pure form only in newborn children and that they became profoundly modified in adults. For B. F. Skinner, the internal pattern-relation became instead the "operant behavior" patterns exhibited. For example, anger became for him the act of pounding a table, slamming a door, or picking a fight (Lyons, 1985: 21). Lyons objects that many different behavior patterns may be involved. How then shall we know when to call them anger? As anthropologists we may comment that both Skinner's scheme and Lyons's objection to it in fact broach the question of culture. On psychoanalytic theory, Lyons says that Freud did not in fact develop a systematic theory of emotion or affect as he called it, "but tended to restrict himself to giving accounts of the workings of particular emotions, particularly anxiety" (p. 25), partly because of his primary concern with therapy. Freud's explanations of anxiety appealed to the notion of unconscious and unfulfilled wishes, impulses, and drives—desires we may say—and these, rather than emotions in general, were his focus. He tended to locate these drives in the early history of the individual or even of the human species as a whole. In general, his interest lay in the pathological, and Lyons comments that this was probably not a good way to develop a general theory that would encompass the nonpathological.

Lyons also examines another theory, the cognitive theory, derived from Aristotle, which traces emotions back to states of mind affected by perceptions of situations as well as to desires. The cognitive aspect here is again an element that is represented by our notion of sensibility. Sensibility includes perceptions shaped by both culture and personal experience in life. Lyons calls his own extrapolations from this cognitive theory his "causal-evaluative theory" (p. 53). The theory is intended to apply to emotions as occurrent states, involving physiological changes and desires but also an evaluative aspect that enables us to differentiate the emotions from one another. Evaluation here, like cognition, depends on an implicitly present cultural element, we would argue. Lyons's theory appears to be consistent with the ideas enunciated later by two writers, Michael Stocker and Elizabeth Hegeman (1996), whose book was published in the same Cambridge Series of Studies in Philosophy to which Lyons's text belongs, although they do not list him in their index. Stocker and Hegeman's chief argument is that emotions reveal and depend upon values. Clearly, values are socially inculcated. For these philosophers, therefore, whether they phrase the matter in this way or not, emotions involve culture. The same is true for the biologists who give importance to consciousness, since consciousness is related to knowledge of others as well as of oneself, an argument that has also been made by the anthropologist Anthony Cohen in his exploration of the concept of self consciousness (Cohen 1994).

Sensibilities, as we define them, are the properties of individuals that they display in their interactions with others. The concept of sensibility, however, belongs to the domain of the socially defined, just as we have found the concept of emotion does. Sensibility and emotion overlap as concepts, sensibility referring more to the cognitive-evaluative context of emotion itself as defined by Lyons and emotion signaling the domain of the biological and the physiological. How, then, does this all square with anthropological treatments of the emotions, including those of the people of the New Guinea Highlands, but also those living in other areas of the world?

A recent collection of studies from Amazonia bears on this issue (Overing and Passes 2000). Amazonian societies stress the ethos of interpersonal ties, and the contributors to this collection all start with the significance of this "affective emphasis" and with the notion that the idea of "conviviality" underlies it. Community is seen as defined by conviviality (compare Knauft 1985 on "good company" among the Gebusi of Papua New Guinea; there is a close parallel in the materials here but Overing and Passes do not cite Knauft's work in their Introduction).

Overing and Passes explicitly use the term "sensibility." They argue that indigenous sensibilities have in fact often run counter to Western sociological thought. For example, there is the Amazonian idea that the self is autonomous and that the creation of a collective domain depends on the efforts of such selves; that the self is nevertheless other-directed; that there is an antipathy to formal rules, so instead there is a stress on how to create productive emotions, to be compassionate, or to avoid dangerous anger (Overing and Passes 2000: 2). These observations are highly pertinent also to New Guinea, where we find that discussions of emotions refer to the tonality or ethos of social relations. We might say therefore that the idea of the social is embedded in such categories, and that the body becomes the prime locus of social values; while at the same time social relations are seen as being produced by persons who have, or do not have, a correct orientation toward such emotional complexes.

By the same token, if emotions as they are culturally constituted are signposts to conduct, the modes of their expression are also significant, and so "we must familiarize ourselves with indigenous poetics, and their aesthetics of living a human sort of life" (p. 12). At the same time, also, this does not mean that we are prioritizing emotions over other forms of action stimuli

(p. 19). In our own discussion of the work of philosophers of emotion, we have seen that they accept a cognitive-evaluative aspect as a part of emotion itself. Overing and Passes, in similar vein, if not employing this specific insight, argue that for Amazonians both "cognitive and affective capacities are embodied" and social living requires a harmony of thoughts and feelings, mind and body (p. 19). Exactly the same can be said for the Hagen people of Papua New Guinea, as expressed in their concept of the *noman* or mind-substance and its place in the body as a whole (see Stewart and Strathern 2001a). The *noman* is a locus of both thought and feeling, just as Londono-Sulkin tells us is the case for the Muinane people in Colombia, whose "social sensibilities" he explores in the Overing and Passes volume (Londono-Sulkin 2000: 172). The Hageners' concept of *noman* is also closely paralleled by the Enxet people of Paraguay with their idea of the *waxok*, the "cognitive and affective centre of the person" (Kidd 2000: 114; see also Gregor and Tuzin 2001 and Descola 2001 on Melanesia-Amazonia comparisons). It is in the *noman*, for example, that desire is said to arise, just as "true" thoughts or predispositions to proper conduct do. Bodily emotions and social dispositions are said to have the same point of origin.

From the point of view of this book, what these observations about the emotions mean is that studies of "sexuality" must be set within the study of "sensibilities" if they are to be relevant to the social contexts from which they are drawn, and if they are to be true to the persons who engage in them. Sensibilities are informed both by people's bodily experiences and by the social contexts into which these experiences are set. Of course, there is the problem of where to draw the line in our descriptions once it is accepted that sexuality is to be understood in a broad rather than a narrow sense. We will treat that problem flexibly and pragmatically. Where we see relevant connections we will point to them. At the same time we will handle our materials with a view to illuminating the overall context of sexual behavior and the emotions that it generates. As the contributors to the Amerindian studies remarked on above recognize, the scope includes elements such as anger and jealousy leading to violence as well as ones of sympathy or love.

The expressive contexts in which we will be looking for the display of emotions will include myth, ritual, and song. While myth and ritual are often treated as frameworks for social organization and structure, we will here regard them also as repositories of experience that feed on and into everyday experience. Myths and folk tales are, or were traditionally, recited in the course of the flow of life; and rituals of courting, marriage, and mourning for the loss of kin or spouses are also a part of that flow. We are particularly interested in songs, for several reasons. First, quite often their inventors may be known; second, they are recognized in terms of individual performances and creations but are also entextualized through repetition and offer us a glimpse of how personal creations enter into the realm of the social; and third, their specific form is designed to facilitate this translation of the per-

sonal into the social and vice versa. They are thus crucial elements of study
for any consideration of sensibilities. To illustrate this point briefly here we
cite a courting song from the northern part of the Hagen area, collected in
the 1960s (A. Strathern 1974). The singer as a young man has traveled
north from his home in order to court a girl in whose place the White Bird
of Paradise (*köi kuri*) is found.

> Köi kuri eklka-maklka elna
> Ambokla manem ndip kaklnga
> Na kond enem a kaemb enem a
> Kona röngin kona ilya pöt röngan ka
> Nanga kopa kong ilya mbi ond a
> Lkömb kong ilya mbi ond a

> White bird of paradise plume, you sway back and forth.
> Girl, as your mother keeps the fire burning,
> I feel sorry, I feel sad.
> Dawn, come quickly in the place where you rise.
> I am going off to my place of mists,
> To the ridges where the light rain falls down.

The images created here all belong to the context of courting as it was
practiced in Hagen in the past. Girls received men as their courting partners
in carefully choreographed settings in which the men took turns to "turn
head" with the girls, making contact on the forehead and the nose, while
the others sang songs expressive of the occasion and the mother of one of
the girls typically watched over the event. The performance took place at
night, in a senior woman's house (men and women had separate houses that
they partially shared). The mother kept the fire burning so that she could
better see what those taking part were doing. After an event of this kind a
girl might choose to follow a man to his house as a mark of her preference
for him. The men were postulants, under the eyes of a chaperone. By magical means both women and men might try to engage each other's wishes
or desires. Often men, primarily unmarried youths, would come from fairly
distant places, some hours' walk away, having heard that a girl or several
girls were going to collect in the girls' courting house (*amb kenan manga*)
and were ready to receive suitors. Both girls and men decorated themselves
informally for the occasion. Girls might wear stripes of red face paint across
their foreheads in an area where these would make contact with a partner's
skin. The face paint might be mixed with magical substances. Men wore
bird plumes that moved to and fro rhythmically as they made the head-
turning movements.

All this the song deftly depicts. The singer expresses his *kond*, his *kaemb*
(two terms for sympathy), for the girl, because her mother is watching over
her and he cannot proffer any particular intimate gestures to her. In this

context these two emotion terms stand for the fact that he is attracted to the girl and therefore wants to stay with her, but his impulse to stay is counterposed to the fact that by etiquette he must leave, since he cannot remain in the sponsoring woman's house beyond the customary night period of the courting itself. His own place is distant. He needs to get up early to walk back to it during the day. The girl comes from a low-lying place where the White Bird of Paradise is found, the Jimi Valley north of Hagen. His own place is a cold one, a high mountain ridge covered with mists and rain. When the image of mist appears in these songs it marks distance as separation from one who is desired. The warmth of the fire contrasts with this image of a cold climate and of separation. Still, the singer realizes his courting has not worked, so the sooner he is off the better. He expresses determination to leave. At least he will be going back home. A song like this might be sung as a test, to see if the girl would indicate a wish for the singer in fact to stay longer. By referring to his own place, the singer also alludes to the possibility that the girl could follow him for at least a temporary stay (*keka-nga*) at his place, should she so wish. The occasion expresses desire, anticipated separation, constraint, the need to depart, the possibility of renewal, and circumstances of distance and how these mirror the state of the singer's feelings. The male is active in his singing, but he is dependent on the choices of the girl's own *noman* (mind), and he is also under the surveillance of the mother, who monitors the girl's wishes and who would have to receive an important gift as part of any brideprice to be raised later. The sensibilities involved here clearly involve desire as well as an anticipation of loss. They also reflect important aspects of social structure. The song itself is highly balanced and poised in its expression. The first three lines set the scene of action and express the central emotion. The final three lines depict the singer's intended response and provide an image of his own place. Warmth is poised against cold, linked by the potentialities of *kond* and *kaemb*, terms that apply equally to sexual relations and to sentiments among kin, into which sexual relations must be set. The song's structure has a dynamic that reflects the dignity and restraint of the courting scene itself. The mother's fire represents both her watchful surveillance and, on the other hand, the sexual feelings that potentially are forming in the courting house itself (*muntmong wonak wonak nitim,* "the heart lights up, lights up," is one expression for desire). The mother stirs up the fire to watch over the two participants in the courting; but the fire is also the desire these two feel for each other.

Courting practices of one kind or another have been found by ethnographers working in a number of the Highlands societies of Papua New Guinea, from Chimbu (Simbu) in the east through the Wahgi, Hagen, and Enga areas, to parts of the Southern Highlands Province including Pangia, Kagua, the Huli, and the Duna. We will discuss some of these later in this book. In the meantime the example given may help to indicate the kind of

ethos of expression that surrounded these events in Hagen: spirited, evocative, humorous, deftly poignant. Many of these societies are the same ones
that have been portrayed in quite a different way in ethnographies that have
focused on gender relations via notions about menstruation, usually by
stressing concepts of "pollution" and an ethos of male denigration of
women. Such portrayals are quite distinct from the image we have just
shown here.

Of course, we do not deny that contradictory concepts, situationally separated or not, can coexist, perhaps uneasily, in a single social milieu. Here
it might be argued that these concepts belong to different contexts. But we
would argue that negative ideas about menstruation have been allowed to
overshadow other aspects of gender relations, largely because of the ethnographers' own preoccupations with portraying gender relations as marked
by antagonism and male domination or exploitation. In this regard, essentializing Marxist analyses, while making many positive contributions, have
tended to tip the balance toward this kind of portrayal, while having no
particular analytical or theoretical use for other aspects of the ethnography
such as those represented by courting songs. We also argue, in a more holistic vein, that the place of menstrual blood itself in the universe of ideas
about "humors and substances" in these societies needs to be seen more
comprehensively, since it is a recognized marker of fertility, reproduction,
and power. To stress its so-called polluting aspects is to pick on one moment
in social process, view it in a particular way, label it in an essentializing mode,
and obliterate the other moments to which it equally belongs. It is also to
ignore or downplay the point that has emerged from this fundamental issue—that it is the moral handling of blood, or any other bodily fluid, that
determines its evaluation in the social scheme of things. The same sorts of
comments could be made about semen or other powerful bodily fluids. It
is not, then, so much that substances are seen as in themselves beneficial or
lethal, *tout court*, but that the way of using them determines whether they
are seen as dangerous, protective against danger, or life giving (see Stewart
and Strathern 2000c). This principle is reflected most clearly in the context
of various cults of fertility directed toward female sprits in some Highlands
societies of Papua New Guinea. Furthermore, there are empirical variations
in the ideas about the dangers of blood in general. In two cases (Pangia
and Wahgi) it appears that historically menstrual taboos marked by seclusion
huts were not found. In Pangia these taboos were in fact introduced at the
same time as the Female Spirit cult practices; while in parts of the Wahgi
area this cult was not practiced, and menstrual huts were not introduced at
all. Hagen women who married Wahgi men ceased to observe these taboos,
while Wahgi women who married Hagen men learned to do so.

The contexts we will be looking at are historical for the most part, going
back to the 1960s or earlier. We are not dealing with timeless instances.
Ethnographers have made their observations at different times in the course

of colonial and post-colonial history. We will try to take this fact into account. It is also quite clear that the societies we particularly focus on have been subject to numerous ongoing changes. In Hagen, the "girl's courting house" practices began to disappear in the 1970s, along with an increase in Christian church membership and preoccupations with other matters, although these events were sometimes held into the mid-1980s with dances for ceremonial exchange occasions. Menstrual seclusion huts and separate birth huts also have tended to fall into disrepair and have not been rebuilt. Clinical methods of contraception using Depoprovera or intra-uterine devices have been available since the 1980s as have clinics that advise couples on fertility problems. There is a growing awareness and indeed consternation regarding AIDS and other sexually transmitted diseases (STDs) throughout the whole Highlands region of Papua New Guinea. Previously established ideas, as well as contemporary twists and opportunistic inventions of "customary" notions, tend to re-cluster around new syndromes such as AIDS (Strathern and Stewart 1999a: 149–151). The attrition or disappearance of earlier aspects of the use of space and material culture, such as separate dwellings for menstruation and childbirth, does not by any means imply the disappearance of ideas surrounding these phases of life. For example, food taboos may continue to be observed. In Hagen, a menstruating woman may decline to shake hands with a male visitor on grounds that her hand is bad (*nanga ki kit*), just as a man who has been working in the gardens and whose hands have earth on them may do. Both practices continue today as before. It might also be argued that notions about the powers of menstrual blood, which were inculcated into young people in the past by their seniors, assisted in restraining certain aspects of sexual activity. But menstrual huts were themselves sometimes used as trysting places for clandestine sexual encounters between adulterous partners, occasioning the need for rituals to purge the potentially dangerous consequences of this action from men. Thus, the institutions of the past could be subverted by the idiosyncrasies of personal action. In the Duna area we found that while menstrual huts were no longer being built in the 1990s, each married man tended to build for himself a small "men's house" of his own, which he could use during his wife's menstrual period. Thus, the man went into a semi-seclusion hut rather than the woman. When a new collective men's house (*anda pirapea*) was built in one Duna settlement, Hagu, in the later 1990s, men used this collectively at the times of their wives' menstrual periods as well as for other occasions. Correspondingly, some of their individual semi-seclusion houses fell into disrepair. Subtle transformations and adaptations of this kind occur all the time and are largely unnoticed by outsiders.

Older Hagen leaders in the 1970s and 1990s, such as Ru-Kundil and Ongka-Kaepa, saw alterations in gendered practices and compared these situations nostalgically to earlier times (for further details from these two male leaders, see Strathern and Stewart 1999b, 2000c). Their observations indicated that the changes arose in part from urbanism and the tendency for village people to frequent the stores and open-air market of Hagen township. Prostitution and casual sex were practices often adopted by young male migrants from the Highlands who went to work in or near major coastal cities such as Lae and Port Moresby in Papua New Guinea (PNG) from the 1950s onward. These were mostly heterosexual practices, but sometimes there were sexual relations between males, especially with outsiders such as Australians living in Port Moresby. These young men therefore brought back a range of practices, experiences, and bodily conditions and predispositions when they returned home (see Jenkins et al. 1994 for a national study of this and many other contemporary themes). In local areas the Christian churches attempt to combat such influences with their own teachings, inculcating notions about pre-marital chastity, "the body as a temple of God," the desirability of marrying in church, and the need to have a "blood test" for AIDS before being permitted to marry. Paradoxically, Christian forms of disapproval of mentored courting practices, such as the "girls' courting house" customs in the past, have themselves led to the dissolution of methods of control over young people's sexual behavior; and there are also proverbial jokes regarding church services in which men and women mingle instead of worshiping at separate sides of the church, and these movements become contexts for surreptitious communications via eye contact and touching that may lead to sexual activities later.

These remarks indicate that there is a broad sphere of contemporary activity that needs to be canvassed when we seek to understand the transformational trajectories of sexual conduct today. They also suggest that such changes are only a part of a wide array of historical processes emanating from the development of state-based institutions and globalizing images from the outside world. Exploring the emergent and partial sensibilities associated with these changes would be a massive task in itself. We will provide some incidental observations in this book that are pertinent to such an exploration. But our main aim is to paint a portrait of expressive sensibilities as they were in the recent past, as a counterpoint to the predominant images created in some of the earlier anthropological writings. One of our goals is to bring song and the imagination into the study of gender and sexuality in the Highlands, a project that falls well into line with anthropological poetics in general (Brady 1991). This will allow us and perhaps others who may take this approach to show through ethnographic materials a side of the lives of Highlanders that is often not highlighted or fully appreciated.

Chapter 2

Courting Songs: I

Courting songs may also be referred to as love songs but the term "love songs" begs the question of the sense in which the word "love" is being used. The term can be applied to courting songs, such as the Melpa *amb kenan* from the Mount Hagen area of Papua New Guinea and elsewhere. Love is in any case a broad and diffuse category and our aim is to look for specific modalities of sensibility that appeal to a combination of values and senses. Such a combination may, for example, appeal to visual senses of landscape, making mountains and clouds stand for distance and separation. This is a theme frequently found in the *amb kenan* courting songs. In the Duna area of the Southern Highlands of Papua New Guinea *laingwa* songs sung by men to girls constantly referred to foods available in their areas, appealing to the girls' sense of taste (Stewart and Strathern 2000d). In Pangia, some courting songs took the form of chants whispered into the ear of a girl, *oi angale*, appealing to the coercive power of repeated words themselves, and to the importance of the sense of hearing. Seeing, tasting, and hearing all emerge as modalities of sensibility. Smell, however, is important in various ways in all of these cultural contexts. In Melpa sweet-smelling marsupials are often named in courting songs, for example, and all the plants used or cited in courting magic tend to be aromatic also. There is a connection made among health, wealth, beauty, bright color, and sweetness of taste associated with the perfume of flowers and herbs that runs through both coastal Austronesian and New Guinea Highlands materials. Appeals to the different senses set different modalities of relationship: for example, a visual stress indicates the power of space and time and the drive to overcome this power by means of exchange; a stress on taste implies ties to a locality and the enjoyment of residing there; a stress on listening suggests the coercive influence of the courter over the one courted; while the power of smell refers to the polyvalent domain of general attraction.[1]

When we look at a broad range of Highlands societies, we see the striking fact that throughout the region there were courting practices in which *singing* was a primary component. The singing formed part of the ritual sequences in which couples were permitted to get to know each other and to express their personal preferences for each other. These courting occasions were also invariably ones at which magic was expected to be used to attract or sway the inclinations of a desired partner. Both men and women were thought to use this sort of magic. Courting songs were, then, a vehicle for choice, inclination, and imaginative expression. They were also instruments of communication and influence. The poignancy of these songs is set into another major feature of these societies. Marriage took place through the payment of brideprice (or brideweatlth), seen primarily as a payment by the groom's kin to the kin of the bride (although in some areas such as Hagen it was, and remains today, obligatory to make substantial return gifts at the time the brideprice is paid and later). Two recurrent scenarios followed from this fact. First, a couple might wish to marry, but the young man could not raise the brideprice required, either because his kin were poor or because they opposed his choice. Second, the kin of another suitor might come with an offer of a larger brideprice for the young woman, and her kin might urge her to accept this marriage and so "get pigs and shells" for her parents. Dramas of resistance, frustration, and sometimes elopement could follow. The customary practices encompasssed a basic contradiction between sexual choice and family notions of what was appropriate: the same basic contradiction that is played out endlessly in other parts of the world, in terms of ethnicity, class, and nationality. In the Highlands the modality involved was interfamily alliances based on marriage exchanges; or simply the wish of a girl's kin to obtain a large bridewealth payment for her. The prime items involved in this payment, pigs, were also to a large extent the products of women's labor, so women had a considerable say in what marriages were arranged. This did not mean that the wishes of the girl to be married were necessarily given priority. In the Duna area a daughter's bridewealth was used in part by her father to repay those who had helped him a generation earlier make the payment for her mother (Stewart and Strathern 2002). This rule set up a particular constraint on choices. On the whole, however, since none of these societies were based on lines of clear class distinctions, most families had access to the means of producing the wealth needed to make a marriage payment or could expect to be helped by kinsfolk in this regard.

There were strong apparent differences between areas in terms of the interplay between choice and constraints on choice of partners for marriage, and also in terms of the possibilities for sexual relations prior to or outside of marriage. Looking back at the early ethnographies, we can see some major differences between the Eastern and Western Highlands societies of PNG, at least in part correlated with different patterns of intermarriage and political relations.

EASTERN HIGHLANDS

In the Eastern Highlands, local territorial groups, or districts, were often enemies of one another and frequently there was no enduring framework of political alliances between such groups. Sexual relations and marriage were therefore set into this context. These were also societies in which male initiation was practiced for boys. K. E. Read's (1965) account of the Gahuku-Gama people near Goroka set the tone for an ethnographic model of this kind of society. Read's interpretation of the ethnographic materials emphasized male domination, sexual separation, and sexual antagonism. A startling feature of this rendering of the society is the number of occasions when women of the community made ritual attacks on the men, including times when they ambushed men bringing pigs for a brideprice and tried to kill one or more of these pigs before they could be delivered. Read sees this as a kind of ritual rebellion, but one that could genuinely threaten men's control. It is hard to understand this phenomenon without knowing the bases of solidarity between women in the community. What the ethnography does reveal is that marriage could become a focus of behavioral conflict (as in most New Guinea societies), which surely had to do with the contradictions we have noted here.

Somewhat in contrast with this part of Read's account is the notice that he gives to courting activities. For example, he records the arrival at the village of Susuroka one day of a set of girls led by an old woman. The girls were displaying themselves. "The open boldness of their walk matched the extra care they had taken with their dress, the freshly oiled plaits and the jaunty bustles of colored leaves caught at the waist by clean string aprons" (Read 1965: 191). These girls and their leader sang songs to draw attention to themselves, and during the daytime visited neighboring villages, returning after dark to a vacant house that they used for courting. They also spent their days bathing themselves and resting in cool taro gardens. Read writes (p. 192) of the heat in the courting houses and the smell of aromatic oils that the participants wore as well as bodily odors. He describes the couples as lovers, singing and laughing—"a row of faces decorated with red and yellow pigments" (p. 193). "A couple faced each other lying on their sides, the girl's head pillowed on the boy's forearm while they rubbed their chin and lips together aggressively" (p. 193). The girls were supposed to reject having intercourse, but Read says, "[T]he boys hoped to prevail" (p. 193). There was no adult supervision (unlike the situation in Hagen). The courting with its constant rendering of songs went on for a week.

In another section of the book Read describes the life of boys or young men who were initiated together as age-mates. At initiation each boy was betrothed to a girl, with brideprice paid, but without cohabitation being allowed. At the same time it appears that these boys also took part in courting occasions. Senior men warned their juniors that women might entice "men to casual dalliance, initiating affairs to satisfy their own desires, or, perhaps, to accommodate a sorcerer who had designs on the life of their partners" (p. 153). Such a sorcerer might perhaps encourage the girl to obtain a piece of clothing or hair from the boy that contained his life-force, which the sorcerer could then manipulate to attack him. The context of political enmity between groups seems clear here. Yet novices were also instructed in men's houses on methods of magic to influence women's desires; and, Read says, men's dances with their "pendulous tossing plumes" as headdresses "had fairly obvious erotic implications" (p. 154). "Every youth went to courting parties armed with magically treated cigarettes and unguents that, hopefully, would break a girl's resistance as the couple lay together" (p. 154).

The contradictions involved here are apparent. Boys were betrothed to a particular girl, but were also encouraged to court others. They were warned that girls might seduce them, but enjoined to practice magic to seduce the girls themselves. They were betrothed to a particular girl but were free to break the betrothal. Yet, if the girl betrothed to a particular boy deserted him, the boy was subsequently shamed by his age-mates. Read also mentions that he was told that in the past if a boy began cohabiting with his betrothed before the others did, his age-mates might punish the girl by killing her; and that if a girl left her betrothed and went to another man, the betrothed might kill her later in revenge (p. 155). Such practices had been outlawed by the early 1950s when Read worked near Goroka under the aegis of the Australian administration. He implies, however, that the tensions that caused them still existed. We might suggest that they were in fact exacerbated by the new colonial situation in which the Gahuku "warriors" were "pacified" and forcibly made subordinate to outsiders.

Regardless of this possibility, our point here is that Gahuku practices set up a series of contradictions surrounding courtship and sexual behavior that resulted in difficult choices for both genders. Courting occasions recognized the agency and inclinations of girls as well as boys, but placed constraints on them. Read does not discuss the contradictions girls were faced with, other than the apparent plight of a girl sent into marriage when she was very young. But it is clear that courting was a "testing time" in some sense for both sexes. In general this was also true elsewhere, but Gahuku practices, as Read presents them, were conducive to conflict to a degree that was not found in the societies farther west that lacked the "age-mate structure" of the Gahuku. On the other hand, Gahuku practices also appear to have given a good deal of short-term license to young people trying to find their way into sexual maturity.

Not far from the Gahuku were the Fore, described in detail by Ronald Berndt (1962). Berndt's account of sexual practices and ideas among the Fore and their neighbors is challenging because of its portraits of people engaged in a great variety of activities. It is difficult to separate fact from fantasy in the accounts, although all of the case histories are presented with names and localities. Here we will discuss only some points regarding court-ship and betrothal, for comparison with the Gahuku. The work of Ronald Berndt and Catherine Berndt in New Guinea took place during the same time period as that of Read, the early 1950s (1951–53). The people they studied had recently been brought under colonial influence and were in a situation of confused change. The Fore practiced betrothal "with substan-tiating gifts" (Berndt 1962: 116), like the Gahuku. On one occasion re-ported to Berndt, a senior man, the bride's half-brother, intervened in a betrothal occasion, angrily declaring that the boy should not marry until he had killed a man. "It is not good that he look at a girl's vulva before shoot-ing a man," he declared. This admonition reflected the rule that a youth should have killed a man before marrying; this was a rule that was becoming hard to follow under colonial control. After a fracas, the brideprice was actually accepted. The boy was ashamed, and in revenge he and some of his friends all had intercourse with the girl and then sent her back to her own place, telling her not to come back. Later he shot a man, and his father then arranged for him to marry a girl he addressed as "half-sister" (p. 116), while the girl whom he rejected married someone else.

This incident shows several things. One is the immediate effect of "pac-ification" on practices of killing, which we also saw affected the Gahuku. But the Gahuku do not seem to have had a rule that a boy must establish himself as a warrior before marrying. Another point is the exercise of sexual violence inflicted on the girl brought into marriage. This too seems to find no Gahuku parallel. A third point is that the Fore, highly distrustful of outside sorcery, like the Gahuku, allowed marriage to a kinsperson ("half-sister") as a means of perhaps reducing the dangers of out-marriage.

Berndt recognizes two kinds of courtship practices. One was arranged by older men, who invited girls to visit their village; by contrast, in the other pattern, parties of girls went "from village to village to engage in love-making" (p. 117). There was some preference or bias toward marriage with a cross-cousin, *nenafu* (pp. 32–33), and immediate cross-cousins, in any case, had sexual access to each other. Berndt remarks that courting occa-sions, which could occur only when there were peaceful relations between villages, provided opportunities for seniors to point out to young people who were the *nenafu* they were eligible to marry. The male youths involved had all passed their final initiation, and had begun entering the sweat houses where their bodies were expected to produce a kind of flowing substance known as *avagli*, indicative of their manhood (pp. 75–76). Berndt says that these flows were marked on the bodies of the men with a sharpened cassowary bone, and the designs were said to make them attractive to women. When the youths were ready for a courting party, they were decorated with body designs (p. 188), also said to be attractive to the opposite sex. We may suggest that these designs highlighted the *avagli* incisions. Women, who assisted in the ritual with foodstuffs and decorations, called the initiates "red parakeets" (p. 77). The youths lined up near the men's house of their village or in a specially constructed shelter (perhaps like the Duna *yekeanda*, see chapter 3), each one facing a girl who called him *nenafu*. They began to rub chins. The young men's parents prepared an earth oven of steamed food to share later. If a girl liked a boy she rested her hands on his shoulders. The girls' brothers also supervised these proceedings, which happened in daytime and were followed by feasting at night. The participants were permitted to hit each other with sweet potato vines. On the third day the youths presented the girls with "plaited rope, arrows, shell, salt, and so on" (p. 118). Later an exchange visit to the girls' place might occur. Berndt's informant told him that participants might slip away at night into the darkness to have intercourse, or the males might draw the females onto their thighs as part of the chin rubbing ceremony and also have intercourse, if the rituals continued into the night.

In a variant practice in Kogu the brothers of a group of girls would make magical preparations, building a mound with an aperture into which they put salt and chewed leaves (p. 119). The brothers made their own noses bleed, in order to induce the girls to lose their shyness and join in the activities. The blood fell into the aperture of the mound and was covered up. The brothers gave the girls the food they had prepared. Then they all visited a neighboring village where the girls entered a house and took all the possessions of the boys huddled there: "shells, arrows, drums, salt, and so on. They take off, too, the youths' decorations and waistbands, leaving them naked" (p. 119). The boys then emerged from the house, singing and prepared for the chin rubbing, which ensued. During this phase, the girls' brothers danced down the rows of couples, pushing their buttocks into view and singing, "I show you the girls' road [vagina]. Come, eat it!" (p. 120).

From another reference it appears that young men and women played tunes for each other "on the jew's harp, each with a different meaning and used as sign language between lovers" (p. 121). This feature was also prominent in an area far west of the Fore, among the Wiru people of Pangia.

Fore practices of courtship, if we follow Berndt's account, seem to have been fairly uninhibited, and this appears to be in keeping with the rest of what Berndt delineates regarding sexual practices in general. It is clear that there were multiple pathways to marriage, almost all involving choices on the part of the participants. The courting rituals represented a kind of ritual punctuation, or stamping of collective affect, on what also occurred in individually diverse ways. A predominant theme in the courting rituals is the reciprocity of visitation between communities and the significance of sister-brother ties on either side of such visiting arrangements. The narrative from Kogu suggests that the brothers, in fact, represented their sisters' vaginas with their own anuses, although Berndt does not discuss this symbolism further at this point in his text. In general, these courting rituals accommodated choice but also attempted to set it into a framework of intergroup reciprocity, a theme found also among the Siane, who lived west of the Fore.

"Siane" is a term for what W.E.H. Stanner in a foreword to R. F. Salisbury's book *From Stone to Steel* (1962) calls a "vague congeries of native people" (p. v) in the Eastern Highlands of what is now PNG. Salisbury's fieldwork there took place in 1952, around the same time as Read's among the Gahuku and Ronald Berndt and Catherine Berndt's work among the Fore and other groups. Salisbury applies the word "Siane" to some 15,000 people so labeled by the Australian Administration. They comprised sixteen tribes or small political units of between 400 and 2,000 persons (Salisbury 1962: 7). The term did not imply any common consciousness of unity or a bounded society or cultural unit. Nevertheless, owing to the "entification" process that sets in with ethnography, they have acquired some distinctness in the literature. With this proviso we will also use the term "Siane" here, referring to the area where Salisbury did his work.

Salisbury's account of courting ceremonies among the Siane is interesting to us here for two reasons. First, it shows the familiar shifting patterns of comparable customs across landscapes, which holds throughout the whole Highlands region. Second, Salisbury's account situates these courting practices into the overall religious system of the people. Siane rituals were directed toward ancestral spirits, and included the First Fruits festival, in which the Yam-Taro ceremony was significant; the Pig Feasts; and individual rites of passage. The Yam-Taro ceremony was held by each clan group about once every three years, between Pig Feasts. Sacred flutes were carried in a procession around the clan lands, to show the gardens to the spirits (*korova*) (Salisbury, p. 33). "When the crops from a large garden, planted specifically for the ceremony, are ripe, the young girls of another clan come *en masse* to visit the host's clan for several days as 'temporary wives.' A ceremonial form of courtship dance and singing (*awoiro*) is performed every night by the girls and by the boys of the host clan" (p. 33). In the daytime comic pantomines are put on, simulating the actions of men and women in raising crops. Then the hosts take the produce from the garden, which they have prepared, and give it to the clan of the girls.

These details show a strong emphasis on the collective and religious background to courting visits. They also indicate a stress on food, the ability of the boys' clan to grow food and give it away to the girls' people, setting up a consubstantiality between them that provides a context for sexual relations and marriage. We will also see the theme of food intertwined with courting practices among the Duna, who live far west of the Siane (chapter 3). The Siane Pig Feast and initiation practices tie them in with the Fore and Gahuku. One example is the cane-swallowing complex of actions practiced by men to cleanse their stomachs by causing them to vomit. But the focus on food giving as a part of courting links them more widely to other Highlands cases.

Adolescent Siane boys visited other villages along with youths of their own place and engaged in *awoiro* singing at night. They learned of the dangers to themselves from sorcery and "designing women" (Salisbury, p. 36), even though they were being taught also to be "designing men," as we have seen for the Gahuku. Boys sought to lie close to the girls they favored, to defeat rivals in song, and to sing songs in triumph as they returned to their own villages "at first light" (p. 36). The visiting boys brought bangles and face paint as presents for girls on these *awoiro* visits (p. 195). The visits tended to be reciprocal, and Siane girls were unwilling to court boys who did not make their own sisters available for the girls' brothers: this is the same pattern we saw with the Fore, and one that demonstrates an attempt to create some closure or limitation in connubial circles between groups among whom enmity was always a possibility. The designation "temporary wives," which Salisbury uses for girls visiting a host clan, appears to refer to an institutionalized form akin to what in Hagen is called *amb keka*, the temporary visit of girls to a homestead in order to "turn head," or court with boys there. Such visits also had to be honored with small gifts when the girls departed. The girls might return later as actual brides, if they so wished and the boys' kin offered bridewealth for them. Here again, then, Siane practice shows affinities with customs found farther west.

CHIMBU

The Siane lived just east of Chuave Patrol Post, which marks a point of entry into the Chimbu area. From Chimbu westward through the Wahgi Valley courting practices were highly developed. The Lutheran missionary W. Bergmann, who was officially stationed in the Chimbu area between 1934 and 1968, gives a detailed account of courting activities among the Kamanuku (or Kamanegu in the transcription of Brown 1972), a tribe living in the eastern part of the area (Bergmann n.d.). (Bergmann wrote in German. We have translated his materials into English here.) Bergmann worked in Chimbu from the earliest times of "discovery" and colonial administration to the period of change marked by the introduction of Local Government Councils in the 1960s. He finished his manuscript in late 1969. Bergmann recognized three different contexts in which courting activities took place: in one, young men visited girls in a group; in the second, a particular youth visited a single young woman; and in the third, a group of young women went to visit a set of boys.

In preparing a boy for his first participation in a group visit, his elders would first find some field rats in the long grasses. They took a banana trunk and made a little imitation oven in it, lining it with leaves and sticks, and then cooked one of the rats in it (p. 148). Over the rats they placed *wamugl* grass leaves. They decorated the neophyte, rubbing his skin with grass and leaves and then with pig fat, cleaning his hair, and hanging decorations on him. When the food in the oven was cooked, they opened it and threw the *wamugl* grasses out to the winds, saying to the boy that he had lived so far with his mother and sisters but now he was to go out to visit girls in the same way as they threw these grasses from the oven. They took ginger and some small greens and poked at them with a little spear, murmuring a spell. The boy had to eat some of the ginger and his legs, arms, and shoulders were then rubbed with the greens. This was all done to protect him from harm.

Then they took him to the settlement where the boys were to meet the girls (the village was always one with which there were established ties of marriage). The girls were ready, sitting at either side of a selected men's house, facing inward. The boys, and also some young married men, entered, and each sat opposite one of the girls. They were supposed to take hold of the hands of their partners, but if shy or unfriendly they would not do so. The youths' leader, who sat at either the beginning or the end of the row, began a song. The youth next to him then began singing also, either the same song or a different one, and this continued along the line, each singing to the girl opposite him until the last in the line had done so. Then the leader began a new round of singing. The participants, male and female, waved their heads and upper bodies about as they came closer and closer to each other, sometimes touching the head or the face, and so it continued throughout the night (p. 150).

The girls had to tend the fires in the middle of the house and keep them burning brightly with logs. From time to time the participants would take a break and refresh themselves with sugar cane. In the morning the boys went home. Bergmann says that sexual intercourse rarely occurred on these occasions. If a pair wanted to have intercourse they could arrange to do so by meeting elsewhere on some other occasion. Fights and blows sometimes occurred as boys competed to sing with a particular girl, but boys also shifted places over time. Girls, too, fought over boys. In some localities there was a custom by which the boys did not just enter the courting house but had to linger outside and then crawl in on their knees (p. 150). This detail interestingly parallels the practice in some cults that are in the Hagen and Enga areas directed to Female Spirits by which the male participants had to crawl on their knees into the cult enclosure where the spirit's sacred stones were kept. The young men visited various places on these expeditions.

After a youth had been on these visits a number of times, he might call on a single girl by himself, one on whom his eye had fallen (p. 151). If he wished to make such a visit, his seniors would warn him that another suitor might be there who would beat him, or wait for him on the way, ambush him, and kill him. So he must be careful. But usually, he would make such a visit only if the girl had invited him by name. He would go, not to the men's house, but to the family house of the girl where she lived with her mother and sisters, and would be invited in. He would then sit side by side with the girl, facing the fire with her as they were holding hands, jesting, and laughing. They would sit together like this for some hours, enjoying the warmth of the fire, while the mother of the girl was always present, watching over them. Late at night or even in the gray of morning the boy left. If the girl liked him she would tell him to visit again and probably would set a time for him to do so. But girls invited more than one boy to come and see them in this way, and boys also visited several different girls. If a boy had switched his affections, he could expect that his former girl-friend might be angry and beat him or in her jealousy might stab him in the chest with a knife and cause him serious injury (p. 152). Bergmann says that sexual intercourse would not usually take place on these visits, but if a girl wanted to she would give the visitor a sign as they sat together and would then, on one pretext or another, follow him after he had left the house so that they could engage in it. If a girl became demanding and the boy was unwilling, he avoided her and sent others to her instead. A girl who did not like a demanding suitor would tell him not to come again.

If a girl did have intercourse with a boy she would usually soon follow him to his settlement and would live there with him, but if bridewealth was not paid she would leave again and go to another man. A girl might also choose to have sex with a married man, and neither of them would say anything about it.

Bergmann's third category entails the visit by girls to young men. The girls would prepare themselves in various ways, including the songs they would sing, would send notice, and would go to visit, accompanied by their own male kin. The party would set out one evening and might arrive in the middle of the night. As they came up to a men's house, they freed the entranceway to it quietly so that no one would hear. Once in the house they made a loud cry and trampled and stumbled on the legs of the sleeping occupants of the house. These young men sprang up and saw the house full of people but quickly understood and were happy to be visited (p. 153). Some of the girls might bring with them little bamboo tubes filled with "water," usually their own urine, and they shook the tubes over the sleepers before walking over them. Then they all sat down in the customary rows, opening up the thatch in the roof a bit if the house was too hot or smoky. If the girls were given sugar cane to eat, they would improvise a new song; if they were given ripe bananas, they would make up another one; if they received water, yet another song was sung. The young women would stay for several days and nights, perhaps a week, holding dances in a circle during the day, and singing at night. Small girls aged eight to ten would also take part in the daytime dances in which everyone held hands. The girls would have pork to eat and would rub fat on their skins. Dances of this sort were held after the pandanus harvest or after a large pig-killing festival (p. 155). Girls might have intercourse at these dances with married men, who would then boast of it. Young men generally gave pork to girls they hoped to marry before they departed and accompanied them part of the way home.

Bergmann gives some examples of courting songs, noting that their tunes are also very fine. The first example was of the kind of song sung when the men crawled into the house on a visit (p. 156):

> Brushed by dew,
> Wet with dew,
> Through dirt, through mire,
> I come, you girls, you grown-up girls,
> On your behalf, we come, and
> Here we are now.

Once in the house the boys would sing directly to the girls, beginning with the conventional phrases *wai i ye e e wai, wai ye i o wai*. (These words are very similar to those commonly used in Hagen courting songs.)

> You grown-up girls,
> You girls,
> We youths have come,
> Have come from up there,
> And now we're here.
> Our place up there, where is it?

> Over towards Bomai, over towards Taupa
> It lies there, in an open space,
> It lies there.

> You grown-up girls
> You two girls [are]
> Like the *bekiri* bird
> With the white fleck on its breast,
> Like the *wauka* bird.

> You two are like the feathers of the bird,
> Soft as the plumage of the *towa* bird,
> Beautiful like two equal lengths of cane
> Made ready to encircle a fine belt.

Fine like the dark-colored *ombo* leaves
Like the *daga* croton,
Splendid like the *moglki* shrub,
Fine like the *kaglki* shrub.

Another example follows:

You girls, you girls,
All of you, all of you
Here we are now
Here we are at your sides
Here at the edge we are,
Here at your side.

That you kill us,
That you bring war to us,
When we knew it,
When we saw it,
We knew the answer.

On a narrow path,
On a tight pathway
Perhaps you have laid an ambush,
A little ambush, perhaps
You have laid one there.

We hold you.
We hold you by the hand,
We hold you by the foot,
We hold you.

Your heart shudders,
Your spirit is aroused,
You shake and cry out "u a,"
You call out loudly "u a"!

I am a boy,
I am a man,
I sing a song to you.
I want to drown in water,
I want to hang myself,
I want to die.

Bergmann also gives an example of a song sung by girls when they went
to visit boys:

You boys sing,
You men sing.
We want to stand up and stretch
And go outside a little.

To which the boys reply:

Don't say the boys should sing
Don't say the men should sing,
Girls, the time is here now.
Let's go into the house again,
And sing again.

The first theme that these songs reveal is that of place and distance. The males sing of their own places, saying they have come through areas wet with dew and mud to reach the girls. Perhaps the girls have laid a little ambush for them on the pathway. This could mean that the girls have captured their affections. There is also an obvious reference to danger. The second theme is the praise sequence. The males compare the girls to the soft feathers of birds and to the glossy leaves of aromatic shrubs, crotons whose leaves were also actually used in body decoration and as adornments on the borders of garden areas, as well as to pieces of cane that will be used to decorate a belt. Persons, birds, shrubs, and canes are thus all brought into the same spectrum of the senses. The sensibility involved fits perfectly with the emphasis on bodily decoration in the Chimbu area. The third and final theme is the theme of passion. The males sing that the girls have killed them; that the girls' hearts are moved and shaken by the singing; and that if the girls do not accept them but go off and marry someone else, then they wish to die by hanging or drowning themselves. This elaborate protestation has to be set in counterpoint with the fact that both men and women might entertain a number of suitors. On the other hand, there was in fact much jealousy and conflict, a sign that feelings of pride, possessiveness, and attraction were all at work.

Bergmann's materials are particularly valuable because they relate to the earliest times after outsiders entered the Highlands in the 1930s, and because he gives us both his observations of practices and at least some examples of courting songs that expressed the people's imaginative ways of conveying their feelings. He follows this section with an equally striking discussion of how rapidly all the delicate balances within these practices were upset by the arrival of the colonial administration, with its indigenous workers from the coast and elsewhere. These workers cashed into the courting practice, giving valuables in return for sex with both unmarried girls and younger married women. When administration and church control were more established after the disruptions of World War II, these activities were in turn proscribed. He points out that as a result of this period of turbulence courting practices of the kind he has described were given a bad name. In other words, outsiders who came later misrecognized the effects of change, and dubbed local practices as "bad," not seeing that their current form was itself a product of colonial interactions. By the time Bergmann left Chimbu, he says, smaller courting parties had been reestablished on a more orderly basis (p. 161), with a greater emphasis on individual visits, presumably in family contexts. His account gives us a glimpse of the kinds of radical, often extreme, dislocations that were rapidly caused by the arrival of Australian patrols throughout the Highlands region. These dislocations often involved the transformation of the historical sexual practices of the Kamanuku people as they came into contact with the shell wealth the newcomers brought with them. These same patterns were found from Chimbu through the Hagen area. (See also Read 1980: 190 on changes among the Gahuku, which are typical for the Highlands as a whole.)

The Chimbu writer Ignatius Kilage, in his fictional account, which nevertheless appears to contain a good deal of ethnography, also comments on these changes, in the persona of Yaltep, who tells his life story in the first person. Yaltep is portrayed as having been born during the decade of 1930–1940 when the Australian colonial presence was first felt. Yaltep observes that the courting ceremonies were first changed by aspirant "bosboi," locals who had been appointed as community officials by patrolling "kiaps" or government officers. The bosbois arranged *kuanandi*, or courting sessions, in special houses built near the kiaps' rest houses where they slept while on patrols, and there they made girls available to the kiaps' entourage. The bosbois did this to secure the favor of the police and other workers, and would beat anyone who opposed them with the cane that was a mark of their office. People who wanted to protect their girls from this influence moved to the high mountains and threatened to shoot anyone who came there with intent to lure the girls away. Yaltep also comments on the *ambu inju belkua* custom in which girls visited the men's houses of other groups for courting, as described by Bergmann. The girls' male kin, according to this account, picked up booty and left, while the girls were entertained in *kuanandi* style, but with "accompanying moral depravity" (Kilage n.d.: 12–13). Kilage, through Yaltep, is clearly describing what Bergmann called *yagl yunggu beglkwa*. Bergmann's account does not mention "picking up booty," however. Presumably this was part of the "modern transformations" of Chimbu life, which both Bergmann and Kilage point out. Kilage was himself an ordained Catholic priest. Later he became Papua New Guinea's chief ombudsman and seems to have left the priesthood. His portrait of sexual practices has a strong moral content.

The Chimbu writer Toby Waim Kagl gives an account of Chimbu life that perhaps dates to the 1970s (Kagl 1984). He describes how Kallan, the male protagonist of his novel, went to dance at a *bugla gende* pig festival, and there a girl, Meyoki, noticed him and sent him an invitation to come and court her at her house. His two kinsmen were asked to come and court two other girls. Once they were gathered there, the girl began the first *gilang* song, in a high-pitched voice. "Kallan tried to catch the note. He failed. On the second attempt, Kallan caught the note the girl was singing and followed leisurely. Together they came to a stop. They laughed again and enjoyed each other's laugh. Their voices echoed like one" (p. 111). They held hands. Next morning the girl decorated herself and chose to return to Kallan's house with him. The elders of Kallan's group, the Kombri, congratulated Kallan for attracting "one of the most beautiful girls for kilometres around" (p. 111), and so bringing honor to their group. Meyoki was dressed "in her best finery" with a long front apron and a headdress of the brightest bird of paradise plumes. The women watched Meyoki with admiration also, as she came to Barengigl, Kallan's place, for a *yagl kiake* (this is the same term as the Hagen *amb keka*, "woman visit"). Kallan's old mother Druakindal in her excitement "ran rings around the dancers and the girl" and prepared in her mind to accept Meyoki as "part of the family" (p. 113). Kagl intersperses these passages with contrary ones about men in Chimbu society and the duty of a woman to work for her husband's family. His own account, however, seems accurately to reflect certain aspects of male/female relationships and emotions: the respect given to the choice-making agency of the girl, and also the boy's mother's feeling that the family is hers, one she has brought into being by her fertility and her work.

WAHGI

Kagl's description also points to another element, one that is brought to the fore in ethnographies of the Wahgi Valley just to the west of Chimbu: the theme of "the success of men belonging to a prosperous clan in achieving sexual attractiveness" (Reay 1959: 94). This notion projects the model of the interclan courting party onto the ideological plane of political relations generally. This, in turn, reveals the fact that sexual attractiveness itself is seen as part of a kind of magical, cosmic competition for health, prosperity, and successful reproduction over time. This social value is ramified through a number of domains of action. Marie Reay, whose first fieldwork was conducted from 1953 to 1955, writes that Kuma youths would boast of the number of girls who had sent for them, that is, invited them to come and court them; and also of the number of married women who had "tried to seduce them" (p. 169), that is, offered them intercourse. Brothers were delegated to watch the fire at courting occasions and to take messages on behalf of their sisters to youths of other clans (p. 169) They thus learned that, later, their own prestige would depend on the choices made by girls (in spite of the fact, Reay says, that women in general were considered by some men to be "nothing"). Mothers taught daughters to look forward to growing up and taking part in the courting ceremonies. They sang courting songs nostalgically and spoke of the life a girl would later lead.

Reay says (p. 175) that there were no special rituals connected with a girl's first menses or first attendance at a courting ceremony. This was quite unlike the situations in Chimbu and the Eastern Highlands societies. A girl joined the ceremonies when her breasts began to develop, it seems, and was coached on how to behave at them by her elder brothers and sisters in her sub-clan. During this time she was free to go around and seek the company of other young people. A couple would sit together, holding hands, with the girl's legs placed inside those of her male partner (p. 176, illustration 17). After a year or so of courting, her kin accepted a betrothal payment of pork for her, after which she would continue to meet other men but would avoid her betrothed. Her bethrothed was supposed to be her own choice, as girls were said to be free to choose whom they would marry. But after this period of sexual freedom, girls were often in fact sent to a bridegroom chosen by their kin. Mediating this situation, a mock fight was sometimes staged in which the groom's relatives came to capture the girl against the "resistance" of her kin (p. 178). The girl might later try to run away or drown herself. Reay identifies this contrast between the freedom of her pre-marital sexual life and the hard constraints of marriage as a fundamental contradiction in a woman's existence (p. 180). (Compare this with the con-tradictions that males experienced in societies where initiation ceremonies abruptly altered the ways that boys could behave and interact with the op-posite sex.) Some women cut themselves off from their kin and became wanderers, going from place to place, *waburamp*. The Wahgi term here is the same as the one used in Hagen for the introduced category of the pros-titute, *amb wapra*. In Wahgi, Reay says, wandering women were passed around from one man to another (p. 185). Given the kinds of changes Berg-mann remarked on from Chimbu, we suggest that the "wandering woman" may have been a new colonial category or a transformation of the older category of "runaway" from an unwanted marriage. Reay points out that the treatment men gave to such women was intended to be a warning to their own wives and a demand upon their own loyalty (p. 186). If so, it could certainly be that the warnings had recently become more dramatic because of the greater possibilities of choice afforded to women by pacifi-cation and road transport through the Highlands from the 1950s onward. One term for prostitute in Highlands *Tok Pisin* is *pasindia*, which literally means "passenger."

Michael O'Hanlon (1989) sets these Wahgi materials into a more recent context, with his fieldwork in a different part of the area, carried out from 1979 to 1981, more than twenty years after Reay's initial work on which her 1959 book was based. Although O'Hanlon's fieldwork was much later than Reay's, it is evident from his account that many Wahgi institutions had continued to exist. He distinguishes two forms of courting, *man ngo* and *kanand*: "In both, and in courting more generally, the initiative is thought to lie with the girls" (p. 40). Men considered ugly found it very hard to persuade women to marry them. *Man ngo* involved a couple holding hands and singing to each other; or several couples doing this together when a new house was built or beside the ceremonial ground when a pig festival or food exchange was taking place. Men would vie for these favors and at massed dance occasions "men of the participating clans compete to attract each other's unmarried girls, and extensive ritual preparations to this end precede such displays" (p. 40). This quotation reinforces Reay's earlier interpretation of these events. In *kanand* girls collectively invited men of another tribe to visit them. The visitors came in the early evening, led by a ritual expert whose job it was to remove bespelled objects local suitors had put down to obstruct the guests (a point that resonates with the themes of Hagen ballads, see chapter 5). The visiting men paired up with girls, and as they sang together "the couples so formed sway towards each other, rolling foreheads and nose together, before moving on to a new partner" (p. 41). Girls showed their preferences by "turning head" more enthusiastically with a given partner. Girls also often fought over a particular youth (p. 41). O'Hanlon notes that by the time of his fieldwork both practices, *man ngo* and *kanand*, were less popular. Older men declared that the young no longer decorated themselves as finely as they had done in the past, and that today youths and girls simply *pasingia* in coffee groves. (*Pasingia* = *pasindia*; the implication is that sexual behavior has become looser; yet Reay's account certainly suggests that girls in the past were free to have intercourse with any man they chose, until marriage.)

O'Hanlon worked with a "North Wall" Wahgi people, the Komblo, whereas Reay's work was with the people she called the Kuma (or Konumbuga) of the Kugika clan in the "Middle Wahgi" or Nangamp area, living near the government station at Minj. In her classification, the Komblo would be Danga, not Kuma (Reay 1959: 1, 4; O'Hanlon 1989: 10–12, 25). The Komblo show some traits apparently linking them more closely to the Hageners than is the case for the "Kuma." Geographically, they do live closer to the Hagen area. O'Hanlon points out that North Wall Wahgi (i.e., Komblo) men expressed attitudes of disapproval over premarital intercourse, as well as concerns about the dangers of their skin becoming ashy and unpleasing if they had too much sexual contact, owing to the loss of "grease" (i.e., sexual fluid). Komblo wives also protected their husbands against "debilitating colds" by not giving them food while they themselves were menstruating (p. 42). All of these features are reminiscent of ones found in the Hagen area in the 1960s. There is even the reference to "turning head" rather than "carrying leg," which O'Hanlon remarks duplicates Hagen custom. That being so, there are still many features that clearly link the Komblo to the other Wahgi groups. Girls might be sent in marriage against their will, and would be "oiled and decorated" before this was done—although a girl might also *choose* to decorate before going willingly. An initial payment of bridewealth was referred to as for "cutting off the bride's armlets and hair" in preparation for the work she would do as a married woman (O'Hanlon 1989: 44). Married women, in retaliation, might make spells to prevent their husbands' decorations from making them attractive to unmarried girls, who could become their rivals (p. 86). This was done by bespelling the husbands' food and thus making their skin bad (p. 91). The clear correlative of sexual prestige was, then, sexual jealousy, and women were as intimately engaged in struggles over these issues as were men. O'Hanlon notes that Wahgi men would try to counteract the effects of their wives' spells by performing rituals of their own. In one ritual they retired to a stream in the forest and rubbed their skin with slippery leaves that were supposed to remove the spells and make their skin as clean as the stream's edge (p. 91). This was called "removing the wives' sweet potato," the major food women gave to their husbands. (In Hagen this act of giving sweet potato is also synonymous with sexual relations.) In a second ritual men sacrificed a small pig to the *kilyaki* spirit, which was associated with streams and uncultivated places, and was thought to bestow a fine appearance. In their songs for *gol* dances men called on waterfalls and the faces of marsupials, which the *kilyaki* spirit was thought to "look after." *Kilyaki* was in turn linked to a spirit female (*golyomba ambel*), who was said to be heard singing and laughing at the head of waterfalls. Finally, men might also secretly bury shells packed with "exuviae" from girls, obtained covertly while courting them, and other substances found on pathways, in the ceremonial ground. These packages, along with the sounds of men's drumming, were said to excite women who came to watch the dance (p. 91). *Gol* songs themselves often referred to birds, which were said to "call out" (*wi to*, compare to Hagen *wi roromen*), and they played on notions of pathos, with visions of ceremonial grounds becoming deserted of men, in counterpoint to the actual displays of wealth and power seen at these dance occasions (p. 96). The political context of competitions to attract girls, and therefore the political power to reproduce, into the group is shown pervasively. In one example given by O'Hanlon, dancers from a visiting group, the Omngar, were determined to attract Komblo girls as compensation for the death of one of their kinsmen who had been taken in by the Komblo and apparently "killed by a policeman for pig stealing" (p. 133). The Omngar men appealed to the dead man's spirit to help make them attractive, telling him that "they never paid compensation for you!" (p. 133); and they tried to bind the spirit to their drums along with the sticky pellets used to tune them. This last detail gives further meaning to the idea that girls are attracted by the sounds of drumming. Spirit presence arises from the mingled music, decorations, bodily movements, and odors that pervade the ceremonial ground. It is also explicitly drawn in by actions such as adjusting the pellets on drums. These pellets are made from an insect wax known as *pönd* in Hagen (a term that also means "dark brown," which is the color of the wax itself); and men constantly adjust the pellets to make their drums beat more deeply, loudly, and clearly.

O'Hanlon's ethnography resonates clearly with materials from the Hagen area. Hageners, however, explicitly distinguish themselves from the Wahgi people with remarks such as these: "They do not use menstruation huts," or "Their young people lead freer sexual lives than ours do." Or they cite the various dances that are special to the Wahgi such as the *gol* dances, which O'Hanlon vividly describes. At the same time we have seen, at least for the Komblo, many overlapping themes in basic ideas about intergroup relations. The same general sense of competition between individuals and groups for the preferences of unmarried women at dances is seen in both the Hagen and Wahgi people. But the emphasis in Wahgi appears to have been greater. In Hagen direct sexual competition was partly displaced by competition over wealth giving itself, in the exchange sequences known as the *moka* (see Strathern and Stewart 2000b).

HAGEN

Courting ceremonies in Hagen commonly took place during 1964–1965, in an area where many *moka* events were held in an enchained sequence between groups (A. Strathern 1971). As was the case with the Chimbu and Wahgi peoples, courting occasions were synchronized with these major events. At times when people were gathering together for the amassing and distribution of pigs at a *moka*, young people took the opportunity to decorate, visit, and hold a "turning head," or *amb kenan*, occasion. The structure of these occasions paralleled those in Chimbu and Wahgi. News would go out that a number of girls would be gathered in a particular women's house (not a men's house as in Chimbu). Some, or one, of these girls would be a novice, who had signaled that she wished to begin "turning head" with men. *Amb kenan* always took place at night, and was always closely supervised by at least one senior woman, who would nevertheless enjoy the spectacle and the singing (remembering her own participation as a girl in the way Reay also mentions for the Kuma). A fire always had to be kept brightly lit in the middle of the house, its smoke escaping slowly through the thatch. The visiting youths would enter carefully from the dark outside, holding up their netted aprons so as to avoid soiling them as they bent to come through the low door. They would sit down carefully on one side of the fire where the senior woman or women were, and would collectively begin a song. Their singing was explicitly designed to encourage the girls, who were said to be shy (*pipil*, a term also meaning shame, in relation to the gaze of others), to come out from the sleeping compartments at the back of the house. These were separated from the main living room by woven cane walls, with small entranceways. Eventually one girl would come out, then the others, and they would kneel with their legs and body covered with a piece of red or blue or multicolored tradestore cloth. In precolonial times they would have worn a netbag as hair covering and a long string apron, along with arm ornaments. By the 1960s the availability of cloth and mission teachings about clothing the body had influenced ideas about decorative styles. The girls continued to cover themselves with the cloth while using it also as a form of decorative enhancement. They might also sprinkle their fronts liberally with talcum powder as a kind of perfume, and apply perfumed oils rather than the traditional pig fat to their skins. They had rows of tradestore beads around their necks, but might also wear a pearlshell suspended at their breast. The visiting males were decorated in a kind of "second-best" costume, different from the full dance regalia, but with a fresh head net, some charcoaling of the face perhaps, and leaves, grasses, ferns, and oil to adorn their heads, as well as bird plumes, which would sway in time with their body movements. The males sat to the side of the females, legs crossed, and bent their heads gently forward to meet the sideways waving of the girls' heads, until they joined on the nose and forehead. They then turned this way and that three times and together twice ducked their heads down to the floor until picking up the initial rhythm again.

Doing this successfully required coordination. It also brought the pair very close together physically, but in a controlled movement, and in view of the specators who were also assessing the performance. Both men and women might rub their foreheads and skin with magical substances to draw out the desire of the other. There was much camaraderie as well as competition all around. The girls were in competition to see which of them was the most popular, and who liked them the best. The visitors might be unknown to the girls in advance. But they were more probably invited to come, either on hearsay, or because they had been seen in public (as in the Chimbu example of Kallan in Toby Kagl's novel). The ability to turn head well together was taken as a sign that a couple might be suited for each other. If one of a pair caught sight of the other on some occasion and "their eyes fought" (*mong rakl el etingil*), this was a sign of desire or interest. Another expression was *mundi kong ronom*, "the heart's ridge is struck." If a pair discovered they liked each other, this was described as *kandek titingil*, "they saw and caught hold of each other," an expression that could also refer to a sexual tryst. The ability to sing well was admired in either sex—as we have also seen for Wahgi and Chimbu—and a lighter rather than a darker hue of skin was most admired among the Hageners. Light-skinned women were said to be more passionate than dark-skinned ones, and a man with a light-skinned wife was said to be happy. However, light skin was also a mark in mythology of cannibal beings known as *Kewa wamb nui wamb*, "foreign, people-eaters." These were to be distinguished from other light-skinned spirit beings of the sky who were beneficent and creative, among whom was the powerful Female Spirit, Amb Kor herself. In some respects these Sky

Beings, the Tei Wamb or Tae Wamb, were also seen as akin to the cannibal spirits. These contradictory images reveal the ambivalent evaluation of beauty and attraction, connecting these qualities in certain regards with danger, in others with transcendent values. Such contradictions resonate well with the atmosphere of excitement and potential danger that surrounded courting expeditions, for which youths might have to go through hostile areas and might court girls whose kin had a history of at least minor enmities with their own, although they would try to avoid this circumstance.

Hagen courting songs were highly expressive and were composed skillfully by both men and women. Vicedom and Tischner in their early ethnography on the Hagen area, compiled largely from the Central Melpa people in the 1930s, have some perceptive things to say about these songs and about the history of courting generally in Hagen. They report, for example, that the practice of holding the *amb kenan* courting occasions had historical antecedents and that senior informants, such as the man Yamka Ko, knew of earlier traditions by which young people would take woven pandanus mats and sit together on these in daytime beside a river and sing to each other. A girl might tell her suitor that he buzzes around her as busily and noisily as a scarab beetle; that he should wind his arm around her as tightly as a snake; that he must protect her as bravely as though she were being swept away in a flood and he must save her. The youth would reply with similar hyperbole, praising the girl and saying that she has swept him away as a flood carries away a stone; or that she has fine pig's tails hanging from her temples (a decorative practice) and that she should bend over to let him see the other side of her face. In the evening they would go to the girl's mother's house, where they would be fed and would sleep embracing each other. Vicedom and Tischner comment that these scenes from the past convey a sense of romantic love and courtly love (*ein Stück Liebesromantik und Minnedienst* [Vicedom and Tischner 1943–48: vol. 2, 190–91]). They mention that such daytime meetings still occur in the Chimbu area, so perhaps the older Hagen practices were related to those from Chimbu (which are discussed above).

Vicedom and Tischner go on to remark that courting dances were mostly held among the "poorer people," since the "rich" simply sent their daughters in marriage without further ado (p. 191). Rephrasing this observation slightly, we can see how in the case of families with high status in the exchange system, marriage was a pivotal way of making new alliances, so that daughters, and sons also, would probably be directed to marry as their parents wished. At this time also, in the 1930s, new supplies of valuable shells were flooding into the area, brought by traders and government officials (Strathern and Stewart 1999c), so that established patterns of hegemony were being transformed. By the 1960s the clear distinction between the behavioral patterns of "rich" and "poor," or "important" and "ordinary," people had been much weakened. This might help to explain the pervasive stress on choice, and the possibilities for conflict which this stress engendered, that held in the 1960s.

Vicedom and Tischner further point out that if in the course of the ceremony a youth wishes to indicate that he has won the affections of a girl he begins to improvise a new song, and the spectators will join in when they recognize it. For example, he may sing that the girl, whom he names, should eat the sugar cane that he grows, and that he will marry her and take her with him. If she replies that she has steamed or roasted some sweet potatoes for him, it means that she agrees to this. Later, the authors note, if a girl breaks such a promise, her disappointed suitor may start a fight by snatching her away from the man whom she has married (p. 195). If the girl's mother now sings that the youth can also eat the sweet potatoes she has cooked, this seals the agreement, although an actual marriage depends on the payment of wealth. These songs of "agreement" may also provoke disagreement and conflict between rival suitors. For example, if a girl elopes to the place of a man she likes after being pushed into an unwelcome marriage, the first husband must get his payments back and the new husband must pay at least as much. Courting therefore often leads to mistakes, and in the past could even lead to fighting in which the girl's parents were at risk of being killed (p. 194). This is a theme that we will see emerges in the Hagen ballads (*kang rom*) later in this book (chapter 5). Girls, too, might fight each other over a particular man. Sometimes a girl commits suicide by hanging if she is disappointed in love (*aus enttäuschter Liebe*) (p. 194).

Furthermore, Vicedom and Tischner write, love magic was used in the courting ritual. If a man wants to marry a girl, he rubs his skin with the bark of a particular tree, and when he turns head with a girl she smells the magic. Then she thinks about the man all the time and longs for him, and she says she wishes to marry him (p. 194). If the pair are thwarted and she is married to someone else, her lover will go to her house and take her with him into the bush and have intercourse with her, and then they will elope together. "The magic has such force that the woman is subsequently also bound to the man" (p. 194).

Finally, they supply a few more examples of actual songs. In one the suitor says he sits at a riverbank and calls to the girl and waits to hear her voice in reply. In another he offers her sugar cane, or if she is sick he offers to bring her water or to dig up sweet potatoes for her to eat (taking on the work of the woman in order to help her). Vicedom and Tischner recognize that girls also composed songs. In one the girl tells the youth he must decorate her with his own big baler shell. (Women wore these on their chests.) She says: "I am not happy to lie alone in the sun, my mat is so hot! Why must I go around in unfulfilled longing? I embrace you, Welyi Wakl, you must embrace me!" Vicedom and Tischner note that the girl's song expresses a more frankly erotic feeling, while the men's songs are more reticent. They point out that affections and gratitude in Hagen can be shown only by actions of giving, not by "empty concepts" (*leere Begriffe*) (p. 197). Actions speak louder than words. Yet the songs themselves also show the importance of words, as the markers of people's minds (*noman*). "Love" itself is expressed by *noman mondui*, "to make *noman* to be there" for some one (see Stewart and Strathern 2001a: 113–37). Vicedom and Tischner's examples of song themes are echoed vividly also in the texts given by Strauss and Tischner (1962: 323–24).

We will provide some further examples of these songs and will discuss them individually and synoptically. Many of these examples belong to the period 1968–1970, prior to the numerous social changes that accelerated after Papua New Guinea's independence in 1975, although in the 1990s we were still able to record versions that older people remembered. These examples also belong to the area of the Kawelka people among the Northern Melpa or Dei Council, part of the Hagen area, where *moka* exchange cycles were strong, although extensive cash cropping had permeated the council and the influence of the local Lutheran mission, based in Kotna, was considerable (see Strathern and Stewart 2000b, 2000c for reviews of these changes). The missionaries disapproved of "turning head" ceremonies, perhaps thinking of the transformations in these that had occurred earlier in the Chimbu area, but no such alterations had taken place in Dei. Courting parties there were sporadic, small in scale, and still focused on the earlier patterns of behavior. Some of the examples given below are from a collection published in 1974 (A. Strathern 1974). Others are from our collection of these materials.

Girls' or women's songs might be made up about a particular youth or youths, sometimes with the name disguised. They could be sung either in the context of an actual turning head event or outside of it among the girls themselves, in which case they could be seen as practice performances for a later occasion or simply as comments on their own feelings. Such commentaries were classified as *mörli* songs, not *amb kenan*. The songs reflect local personalities, places, and ideas about travel and change, mingling these themes in with expressive images, as in the following examples. (Songs 1–5 are all *mörli*.)

Hagen, Song 1

1. Kelua kona wi ile
   Mata baik ik e pilip
   Mata kar ik e pilip
   Wuö Mongakl Pim Madang
       nutn e mel noklna ka

5. Mongakl wak elna
   Nanga noman-e paul enem
   Int int pömbil
   Sikel manga wetim tömbil
   Yand yand wömbil

10.   Plang sikin manga ile peimbil.

> Up there at Kelua
> I hear the cry of a motor bike,
> I hear the cry of a motor car.
> Pim of the place Mongakl, you've gone to Madang,
>   to eat there as you ate before.
> You've left Mongakl
> And my mind is disturbed.
> Let's go away together,
> Let's go and wait in the store,
> Let's come back together
> And sleep in a house made of planks.

This song is particularly full of the marks of contemporary changes at the time. The Highlands Highway was being opened up, linking Hagen to coastal places such as Lae, and later Madang. Plane services carried people between coastal cities and Highlands townships. Young men went as migrant workers to the coast or to the Eastern Highlands. The horizons of consciousness of girls also were opened up by these events, and in rural areas such as Dei people wanted to travel in cars to Hagen town and buy trade-store goods. They had aspirations to live in new-style houses, built with pit-sawn planks rather than in the thatch and woven-cane houses that had themselves been novel in the 1950s (the weaving techniques had been introduced from outside via the Lutheran mission). The song begins (lines 1–3) with an image of a vehicle, its noise heard from a distance, echoing across valleys. These new noises always captured people's attentions at the time. They would be working in their gardens, hear the sound of a vehicle, guess whose it was, and rush to see it. A solitary country road made its way through the northern part of Dei, surrounded by homesteads, streams, and hills through which the sound of a vehicle can echo, arousing interest. Next (lines 4–5), the song invokes the object of the singer's attention. The name chosen is that of a relative, not the youth in whom she is actually interested. His place is marked by a large stand of bamboos and hence is called Mongakl ("bamboo place"). Then the singer, in a single line (line 6), announces her own feelings: her *noman* is "fouled," she is confused, disoriented, because Pim has gone away to Madang and is there "eating as he had eaten," that is, perhaps he is courting another girl (see Strathern and Stewart 1998a and Stewart and Strathern 2001a: 113–37 for more on the concept of *noman*). Now the singer expresses her own wish in another image: she and Pim should travel together, wait in line to buy something at a store in town, then come back and sleep together in a "modern" house on a plank bed. The unmarried singer of the song belonged to an area into which "development" was only just entering, bringing with it new aspirations, anxieties, and restlessness. The terms the girl uses for a motor bike and a car reflect the association of all these changes with the "whites": it is *mata*, meaning "master," which is a *Tok Pisin* term for Europeans, derived from colonial experiences. This is also a creative "mishearing" of the English word "motor."

The next song, by a different singer, also plays on the idea that a desired youth has gone away, and the singer seeks to evoke sympathy from the youth himself.

Hagen, Song 2

1. Mongakl okla moklp
    Okla pon ndip e kaklp
    Mana an ndip e kaklp
    Kaklp wurung wurung int ndop

5. Köni wamb nam kanem nda?
    Köi, ting e mbi ngoklmba ka
    Wete wöngi mbi ngoklmba
    Kondis mam mbukl ile monom
    Ka ent mona mon nda

10. Köi mana tek pilana
    Mana mana tek pilana.

    Up here at Mongakl
    I've cooked on the fire above,
    I've cooked on the fire below,
    I've cooked and pushed the food aside.
    Who is there to see this?
    Köi, I gave my cheek to him,
    I gave my side to him,
    But now he is gone on the back of a plane.
    Am I crying or not?
    Köi, ask me softly,
    Softly, softly, ask me.

The singer says she has cooked some food for the youth she likes, at her own place, Mongakl (a small settlement of Kawelka people living at the time among the neighboring Tipuka). The reference to cooking on the fire above and the fire below may also be a way of referring to her own bodily feelings. *Pon* and *an* may also be used in reference to love magic, which is seen as burning like fire. But the youth is not there, so she has set the sweet potatoes aside, and who is there to witness her sadness in doing so (lines 1–5)? She tells how she turned head with Köi (another sobriquet, with a relative's actual name). Her cheek and her side touched him: she "gave" these parts of herself to him (lines 6–7). But now he has gone away in a plane, which she refers to as a *Kondis*, the term Hageners used for the DC3 planes formerly used as passenger aircraft prior to the introduction of the Fokker F28 and jet services. As the plane flies away she mentally makes contact with Köi, as though she were still with him. "Am I crying or not? Ask me softly," she says as she cries. Youths tended to be more mobile than young women at this time. The girl tries to reach the boy she likes through her feelings for him.

A third song combines to some extent the sentiments of songs 1 and 2.

Hagen, Song 3

1.   Mongakl kan wailis
    Pokta kan wailis
    Tep salim etep telmba
    Mongakl kang Köi e

5.   Mong eting ting pinim
    Mön na ngotn e nda
    Pol na etn e nda
    Mön ngur kang e ya
    Tilika ngi ndopa

10.   Kondis mam mbukl ile tinim
    Wete gras kom tamb-a wan a

> At Mongakl I've sent out my radio message,
> At Pokta I've sent out my radio message.
> I've sent it out and
> The boy of Mongakl, Köi,
> The one whom they stared at, he feels it.
> Boy, you who sang to me,
> You who talked playfully to me,
> You, the one to whom I sang!
> That boy tightens his silk shirt
> And goes on the back of the Kondis plane.
> Come back and I'll comb your hair for you!

The singer here is the same as for song 2. She uses a "modern" image to convey the idea that her thoughts are going out in her song. Her thoughts and words are a "radio message" going to Köi. Radios were entering the Dei area at this time. From the Hagen radio station it was possible to send out *toksave*, informational items, to kin and neighbors; and the singer appropriates this idea. She thinks that Köi will receive her thoughts. Magical substances applied to the body in courting and passed onto the skin of the courting partner were also considered to have this effect—of making the partner think of the other in absence (lines 1–5). Köi is the boy with whom she has had contact in this way. They have given each other their *mön*, which refers here to the courting songs they have exchanged, but equally means "magic" (lines 6–8). The youth is wearing new store-bought clothes, finery that she calls "silk" (line 9). He has dressed himself up, fastened his shirt, and gone away on a big plane, the kind that flies to the coast, far away (line 10). But she adds a line, instead of ending with the departure and her sorrow as in song 2. She addresses the youth directly, again as though he were within earshot: "Come back and I'll comb your hair for you." Combing the hair was an unusual act, done for special occasions, and practiced only by those who no longer wore headnets or wigs for such occasions but teased out their own hair with plastic or bamboo combs. She offers to do this as an intimate act for Köi. The song therefore ends on an active note, with an assertion of agency and mutuality, as in song 1.

Song 4 combines these themes of agency and claims on a partner in a slightly different way.

Hagen, Song 4

1.   Na waia kopi tep salim etep telmba
     Ombil mam pol tinim
     Pol tep tem ila
     Na köu mbi nda
5.   Köi nim konta pömbil
     Wuö Mongakl Köi ye
     Wan tiling yarong ndan a
     Na mep pamb, mep Aken okla pamb
     Tilika kumba-kin wamb.

At Waia I have picked my coffee and set it out for sale.
It goes along the bridge of the Ombil River.
Along that way
Am I to go alone?
Köi, let's go together
Köi, man of Mongakl,
Give me a shilling.
I'll take it, I'll take it up to Hagen,
And come back with a silken cloth to wear.

Girls at this time often picked coffee cherries, which they pulped and dried. They then stood with the coffee that was in bags at the roadside waiting for a coffee buyer to drive up and buy their produce. The singer says she has sent out her coffee from Waia (Mongakl) and that it goes along the river Ombil that runs beside the road. Is she to follow her coffee alone? She wants to go along with Köi. And she wants him to give her some money so she can go to Hagen in a car (some thirty miles away) and buy a piece of silken clothing for herself. In her case it will be a cloth that she can wrap around herself and close in the front, in the style called *kumba* ("door").

In this image her body becomes a house, closed by her clothing as by a door. A small monetary element enters in here, playfully. A girl could not properly ask such a favor from a youth unless he were a relative. "Köi" in fact is the name of a relative, so she can ask for this favor, and the envisaged trip to town can be seen as a brother-sister expedition; except that girls did not in fact sing songs of this sort to their own kin. So the song plays on this ambiguity. The actual addressee of the song also lived nearby and his identity would be known to listeners.

Finally, in this set the same girl asks Köi to take her around, just as the singer of song 1 asked Pim to do:

Hagen, Song 5

1. Na Pokta ya moklp kant mel o e
    Met Aken pon ndip i lait enem
    Köi gras kom peng ile
    Na ya kunung e tamb wal e tamb
5. Köi na mekon Mint pan-a,
        Mbant pan-a
    Andep noman e weng ndamb-a
    Pokta wömbil.

    I am here at Pokta and I see
    Down at Hagen the lights are glowing.
    Köi, the boy who combs his hair,
    Let me take my sleeping mat, let me take
        my netbag.
    Take me to Minj, to Banz,
    Let me go around with you and lighten my mind,
    Then we'll come back to Pokta.

Pokta is a settlement near Mongakl, named after the *pokta* tree that grows (or grew) there. The singer imagines she can see the lights of Hagen town from her place (lines 1–2). (This would not in fact be possible at a distance of thirty miles with hills in between: her imagination takes a leap.) She uses the term *pon ndip* for these electric lights, an expression we saw used in song 2 for cooking food on "the fire above," so perhaps there is a further reference here. In any case the bright lights of the town beckon. She calls on her "modern" boy Köi, the one who combs his hair, to take her further afield, however, on a more exciting trip beyond their own language area, to Minj and Banz, two government stations in the Wahgi Valley where the young people were known for their "carrying leg" courting customs. This would be a trip of some forty miles. After this trip they would return safely home to Pokta and be together. The singer's imagination reaches out to other places and their connotations of urban luxuries or different courting customs. She will experience these things with Köi, but then they will always come back home: as in song 1, *yand yand wömbil*, "let's come back, come back, together." Images of home and images of travel and other places are blended together in this statement of her wishes.

The songs women and girls made commented on a wide range of matters besides courting, and the sensibilities expressed in courting imagery can appear in references to kin. For example, in one mourning song (*ka*) a woman sang of her brother as "the boy who combed his hair," echoing the courting song usages. We have also seen how girls used the names of brothers or nephews in their courting songs as a disguise for the youths whom they addressed. A young woman could make a song for a sister's son, away in a coastal city like Moresby, expressing sadness at his absence—just as girls in the songs given here did for those for whom they felt an attraction. A young married woman might sing to her husband, also away in a coastal city, typically Port Moresby, the capital of the country on its southern coast, saying that she cooks sweet potatoes but has no one to give them to. A young woman might sing to married men, offering to come from the back of the stream where she lives and be with them, if they are not satisfied with the food their first wives cook for them. Girls singing together might express impatience with men who just come to turn head with them and do not have enough wealth to pay the brideprice. They are not too sorry for such men. (This kind of a song is in response to songs men sang about not having the wealth needed to marry the young women they desired.) A widow might sing in praise of her dead husband, recalling that he wore a fine big ceremonial wig, but now he does not enter her house to see her. A girl might confess directly in a song her wish to marry a particular man, causing her listeners to laugh. One woman sang in mourning for her brother, relating that his wig has fallen down and she cannot find him (*lepa nggokla nilinga korop kelep nint*), echoing the phrasing of the widow's song. These examples make it clear that in terms of feelings of attachment there was a conflation of sensibilities toward kin and potential or actual sexual partners; while certain images belonged specifically to the sense of attraction in sexual terms.

These images of attraction often in turn dealt with ideas of magic, expressed in terms of cool grasses and mosses (*kengena pöu, yara pöu*), also worn as decorations; and in terms of *krai kiya*, the light of *krai*, a reference to kinds of "love magic" that would manifest themselves as forms of glowing light or fireflies. We may recall here the references to *pon an*, fires and lights, in the set of songs we have given above (Hagen, songs 1–5). Since courting parties often went out at night, they might take burning reed torches with them to see their way, so the image came from the activity of courting itself. A man's song expresses this notion. (Nowadays the same lights can be seen illuminating the paths as young people go to nightly prayer meetings where they also meet potential partners.)

Hagen, Song 6 (*Melpa Amb Kenan* 1974, no. 15)

1. Na Rut ken a mep oklmba
   Mökö mam kep ile
   Mana ponom o
   rol nde lo ndan wa ya

5. Amb wentep pren ya kiya kanda
   Kiya kanda
   Krai kiya palta
   Kiya kanda o
   rol nde lo ndan waya

   I bring my magic down from Rut
   Down to the edge of the big river Mökö
   It falls down.
   Young girl, my friend, light a torch for me,
   Split a torch for me,
   Light your magic torch for me.

The common type of movement from place to place informs this song, as it does so many others. "Rut" is a term used here as a synonym for Mbukl, an old Kawelka settlement high in the hills to the east beyond the Lutheran mission station Kotna, looking over both the Waghi and the Baiyer River Valleys. The name *Mbukl* means a "ridge" or "backbone," reflecting its geographical position in the landscape. The singer says he will bring his torch down as far as the big Mökö River, which runs eastward out to the Waghi. His friend must light a torch and come to meet him, or guide him with its light. The torch will be a *krai kiya*, a torch of magical attraction, like a firefly.

Krai kiya was associated with hillsides and streams. Youths attempted to find and catch pieces of magic particular to their own area and then to use these in their courting expeditions, as the next song shows.

Hagen, Song 7 (*Melpa Amb Kenan* 1974, no. 10)

1. Na Mina ken o e
   Nu Poklkane mam kep ile
   Pasim etep tep o e
   Rorlop amb o Mone tip ile
       wurlung pon nda

5. Nim kandep a
   Wör ile moklp pamb.

   I found the magic of Mina, a firefly
   At the edge of the Poklkane stream.
   I fastened it and kept it.
   Rorlop girl Mone, are you going
   To sit in the corner away from me?
   I'll watch you from the side, then, and go.

Mina is a place farther up the road from Mbukl, at an altitude of around 7,000 feet above sea level, a settlement area full of streams and cool wooded paths marked by abundant plants of the rain forest, a suitable environment in which to find the magic of attraction. It is the singer's own place (the place of the Kawelka Kundmbo clan). He takes some of this Mina magic to a courting ceremony where the younger sister of a woman already married into his group is turning head. But it seems she avoids him, and he has no chance to use his magic on her skin. He just looks at her and admires her from a distance, then leaves.

The next song follows from this one.

Hagen, Song 8 (*Melpa Amb Kenan* 1974, no. 8)

1.   Mina oa ile rona pön a
       Ndamb oa ile mana wön e
       Kona kit e we mat e
       Kepa kinim möra ronom o e
5.   Yerol ndan waya
       Rorlop amb Mone okl nde
       Nilna kandep kae pint e
       Kiki rokon o ruk ongon e
       Mbe ndokon mboi ndan e
10.   Yerol ndan waya

       Go up the slope of Mina,
       Come down the slope of Ndamb.
       It's a hard place, you'll say, and yet
       Its smell is sweet like the *kepa* marsupial.

       Rorlop Mone,
       I watch you turning head and admire you,
       Come back here, come close in and
       Turn your head down, down to the floor.

This time, the singer manages to obtain his turn to court Mone. Her place is some way off and as she walks up and down around Mina she might find his place hard to get to (lines 1–3). But it is a rain forest place and smells sweetly of the marsupials found in the forest (line 4). (The girl will smell these odors because he has put magic on her nostrils. The marsupial named here, the *kepa*, is the same one that appears in the origin story of one of the fertility cults, the Eimb: a man reached for a *kepa* marsupial, then fell into a pool and was carried underground.) He enjoys watching her turning head with others, but now he asks for his chance. He looks forward to the motion of nodding their heads together (*mbe*) and ducking them right down to the floor (*mboi*) in the climactic movement before the cycle begins again.

An older man, Ongka-Kaepa, commented that not only did each generation make up its own songs but also the styles varied over time (see Strathern and Stewart 1999b and 2000d for more on Ongka-Kaepa). He
described the movements of the head they used to make as *mint mint* and
mbe, referring to a more gentle kind of nodding, in comparison with the
orla-marla, wide swaying movements, "which they make now." Ongka gave
an example of one of these old songs, which shows that the stock of images
was similar to those of the 1960s (he was turning head in the 1930s, before
the time of colonial pacification).

Hagen, Song 9

1.   Pokal tit woit mana onom.
      Kwoinimb amb Kokla,
      Rut uin mona mon e?
      Pokal tit a mana onom o e

5.   Tit woit mana onom o e
      We rol nde
      Kwoinamb amb a Kokla
      Rut uin mona mon o e?

      At Pokal a little rain falls down,
            a little drizzle,
      Girl from Kwoinimb, Kokla,
      Will you come to Rut or not?
      (repeated)

The theme of rain falling down implies a possible dampening of hopes, a
setting in of distance between partners. The girl Kokla belongs to Kwoinimb
settlement, the singer is from Rut (Mbukl, see song 6). In between them,
at Pokal, rain falls. The effect of the song depends on the local knowledge
of where these places are. Perhaps the singer has turned head with Kokla
already and wonders if she will visit his place on a *keka*, an exploration, for
a while. In any case, he is not too sure what she will do. The song is designed
to attract her and appeal to her to come, in spite of the rain. The concern
over rain is shown in another song.

Hagen, Song 10

      Erol nde paya wayo e
      Mina kona onom e
      Ndamb kona mana nö ui e
      re rol nde parol nde
      Pren kona rokl amb e
      Kona prun nda?
      Ant e pendep mep a pamb a
      Erol nde nde

As in other songs, some of the vocables, such as *erol nde nde* above, do not have semantic meaning. They belong to the refrain.

> At Mina the rain falls down.
> Rain, do not fall at Ndamb.
> Friend, girl from a distant place,
> Did the rain make you wet?
> Let me take you off before it gets too late.

The "girl from a distant place" has come as far as Mina, and the singer asks the rain to stop before it gets to Ndamb, close by. He will offer to accompany her back to her own place in the daytime before the rain falls in the afternoon.

Rain is a dampener of spirits, but waterfalls, tinkling streams, and water splashing on rocks and in pools are all used as markers of attraction, so that mentioning them in songs is said to make the songs "sweet" (*tingen*). We may recall here the reference to the *golyomba ambel*, the spirit woman heard laughing at waterfalls among the Wahgi; and in general the fertility spirits were intimately associated with forest pools, springs, and streams.

Hagen, Song 11 (*Melpa Amb Kenan* 1974, no. 9)

1. Erol nde paya wayo e
   Mina ronom e
   Ndamb ronom e
   Ndep ndep nu e ninim erol

5. Erol e paya wayo e
   Wentep Mone a
   Mba mondopa onom a
   Mundi kong roklnga a ninim erol

> The Mina stream floods,
> The Ndamb stream floods,
> Water drops down, drops down on stone.
> That girl Mone
> Goes married but returns.
> Her heart's ridge is struck, she says.

The mention of water flowing strongly in streams and of it dripping and splashing on stone was said to sound "sweet" to possible partners and make them want to come (lines 1–5). The second half of the song announces just such an event. In this case it refers to a young woman who has gone, either in marriage or perhaps on a *keka* visit, but her feelings lie elsewhere and she returns. Water, therefore, has two meanings. As rainfall, it marks separation and is perhaps a bad omen. In ceremonial contexts, if rain falls or threatens to fall, this is a sign of ancestral disfavor and speakers at an event will call on the rain not to come, just as the singer does here in song 10. As a running, splashing, or gurgling (*ndil mbol ninim*) stream, water is a sign of attraction. And in a deeper sense, paralleling the sense of rainfall as bad omen, stream or spring water is a mark of spirit fertility, since cults directed to such fertility incorporated springs and the streams that sprang from them as one of their central symbols. The Eimb cult, for example, was held in areas where a spring source made the ground swampy. *Eimb*, used in a verb complex, can mean "to capture." *Eimbipi*, "going to Eimb," means to have intercourse. Such deeper mythological and ritual backgrounds lie behind the notion that mentioning stream water makes girls feel "sweet." Perhaps there is also an echo of the old practice recorded by Vicedom and Tischner in which courting took place in the open beside streams.

In a humorous expansion of ideas based on the same trope, singers conveyed a special message.

Hagen, Song 12

1.   Nde paya o wai a
     Nu komboklpa kelpa e
     Nu Mina ku mot e ndonom e rol
     Nde paya o paya waya

5.   Rimbri amb ye wentep ye
     Mbil ik e nan e.

     Oh, when the water dries up,
     The stone shows in the Mina stream.
     Young woman of Rimbri
     Say we can go together.

The "stone" here is a reference to the young woman's genital area, which the singers wished politely to tell her was showing while she was turning head. The image of the stone completes that of water here, since river stones were in fact the marks or "houses" of the fertility spirits such as the Eimb (and also the Wöp and Nganap, or "Male" and "Female" Spirits [see Stewart and Strathern 2001a: 99–112]). A light-hearted song therefore follows the lines of ritual notions, showing how such notions criss-cross with and interpenetrate the experiences of "everyday" life, or at least the context of courting occasions that stand in between everyday life and large collective ritual events.

An appeal to a girl through the pathos of a small mundane event appears in a song sung by a youth who says he has come down a long slope to court with a girl, wearing a fine Princess Stephanie plume. He is late in coming and as he arrives it is dawn and the turning head is over. Look, he says, I've still come to see you, and I've stubbed my toe along the way (*Melpa Amb Kenan* 1974, no. 3a). The note of pathos is echoed in another song (*Melpa*

Amb Kenan 1974, no. 13) in which the singer laments that a cloud is obscuring his view of the place of the girl of his affections. She has gone to turn head with the men of a big, neighboring group (*Minembi wuö num ile mba ponom a*, "she's gone to the lake of Minembi men"); but in spite of that, he won't let go of her in his mind (*nanom wak ri a na rop ond erol*, "I've not let her go, even though I'm back here"). Pathos, and the effort to raise wealth after one has succeeded in the courting, is found in another song (*Melpa Amb Kenan* 1974, no. 16) that also employs the image of obscuring cloud.

Hagen, Song 13

1. Konde moklp a kant mel a
   Wande kopa ropa wone ninim a
   Le pa win a pa wa ye
   Kng e korond a
5. Mel e korond a
   Pren nim kandepa kond enem a
   Le pa wina pa wa ye

   I am here at Konde and I see
   How mist covers over Wande

   I'm looking for pigs
   I'm looking for shells
   Friend, as I look at you,
   It makes me so sorry.

The sense of incompleteness, of lack, of longing, comes through gently in the song, as though it also were a figure emerging out of the mist. The emotion of *kond*, feeling "sorry," permeates these songs, beginning with the one we cited in the Introduction:

   Ambokla manem ndip kaklnga
   Na kond enem a kaemb enem a

   Girl, your mother stirs up the fire
   It makes me sorry, makes me sad.

The sensibilities expressed in courting all have to do with personal desires, and with a kind of tender regret at loss or parting. But the social system as such depended on the deployment of wealth and the creation of productive exchanges through it. Some marriages grew out of courting songs. Many did not, but depended simply on offers of bridewealth. Yet the choices of both men and women were considered important. The sensibility of *kond*,

which we find throughout these songs, defined the arena between choice
and constraint in which young people tried to negotiate their futures. Even
though a marriage might be arranged and not of a girl's choosing, she would
be able to hold onto in her *noman* (mind) the images of the courting times.

The modality of *kond*, however, was not the only one expressed in songs.
The genre of *mölya* songs, sung at collective public dance occasions or by
girls to express their individual feelings, was quite different in tone: more
exuberant, more direct, less nuanced and reflective. No specific emotion
term was offered in relation to this genre, but it can be characterized as
playful, outgoing, and declarative.

Hagen, Song 14

1.   I amb na ent
        Mund e kan, mund e kan
        I amb na ent
        Ruri kan ruri kan o

5.   Yalkau wi
        Wuö kwang Palyim wuö e
        Wuö kwang Rombukl wuö ent
        Nanga mbonong woint oa nt
        Palyim mundi weng ndoklmba

10.   Wuö rokl Pakla ye
        Kondis mbukl raun enem.

        I, this woman,
        Fasten my heart, fasten my heart
        I, this woman,
        Fasten my vagina, fasten my vagina.
        Palyim, the man like a beech tree,
        Rombukl, the man like a beech tree,
        [Both are courting me]
        My purple magic goes its way.
        I've made Palyim's heart feel relieved of its pain
        And the man as tall as the *Pakla* sugar cane
        Goes away in a plane.

The singer, a young woman, explains how she does not commit her affections entirely to one man, but has befriended three men, to whom she
gives fictional names. She uses her own magic on one of these men, and
she gives pleasure to one of the men, Palyim ("Cordyline Archway"), ne-
glecting Rombukl ("Struggler") and Pakla ("Tall Sugar Cane"). Pakla is
upset and migrates elsewhere on a plane to the coast. The song is an active,
almost defiant assertion of the singer's agency, which was expressed also in
her actual life.

Another example shows a similar exuberance.

Hagen, Song 15 (*Melpa Amb Kenan* 1974, no. 24)

1. Woipa ye
    Rona ndop kant mel e
    Ndakla ken a wi
    Nggröt im
5. Mana ndop kant mel e
    Ndakla Mek a wi
    Ulkup ronom e
    Roepa ronom e
    Yelkau wi a

I look up and I see
At Ndakla my magic fireflies
Glow red.
I look down and I see
At Ndakla the long black plumes
Wave
And bounce.

The song now continues, after some recorded laughter:

Ambokla Melpa
Arlang ambokla ent a
Waya Pet wuö ye
Ok ponom e
Kint ponom e

That girl from the Wahgi,
The girl from the east,
Takes the handsome man of Waya,
She supports him from underneath,
From above him she swoops down.

The girl is spoken of as from the Wahgi where it is said the sexual practices are more free than in Hagen. Waya (or Waia) is a place name, referring to tall bamboo stands, a synonym of Mongakl, the place named in earlier songs. *Waya Pet* is in fact a reference to the man's own genitals. The girl imagines herself as having intercourse with him in two different positions. *Waya Pet* also refers to the idea of the two sleeping on a modern bed with metal springs (a "wire bed").

On occasions of collective *mölya* dances, when men and women held hands and danced around in a ring after the more formal dancing (where the sexes performed separately for the most part), the songs could become quite ribald. Men might sing a verse including *kunduma oka kuk nonom o,* "the foreskin eats sweet potato flowers," an expression for intercourse; and the women would reply, *andekl kunung kaep kum ninim o*, "the vagina lies unfolded like a rain mat," so that *kunung mel pakeken pan o*, "you can wear it like a cape and go." *Mölya* occasions of this kind continued among the Kawelka people at Kuk up to 1986. Since that time church influence has become more marked and intensive, and there is less emphasis on dancing and *moka* occasions altogether. The examples given here are dated from much earlier, 1968–1970. Another category of song was sung, especially by men making a journey on foot or in colonial times when they were carrying out government work such as road building or dragging long tree trunks for bridge construction. This category was called *wi pakl*. An example was collected in 1969.

Hagen, Song 16

1. Mökö kep o
    Mana ndoklmba o
    Parpa oklka eya
    Monom o e
5. Waepa pa yo
    Waepa pa yo
    Na parp o
    We mbi no
    Ndakla wentep parp o
10. Waepa pa yo

    By the banks of the Mökö River
    I come down.
    Penis erect and testicles
    Come with me.
    My penis erect,
    I'll just go away.
    I wanted to have
    The girl of Ndakla.

Men might sing such a song, inviting women to respond if they wished. Indirect replies might be made in *mölya* songs made up for other occasions. In the 1960s songs began also to make reference to money transactions as part of the process of invitation and requests between young people. A girl might suggest to a youth that he should give her "one dollar" to befriend her. A youth might say to a girl, *paip dola wak ramba a kandekin pan o e a*, "let me give you a five dollar note, see it and go." This theme points to the entry of contemporary urban patterns of behavior, with their transformations of the custom of *keka* presents in the direction of commercialized casual sex and prostitution, and the emergence of narratives of violence against women involved in such activities. In Hagen prostitutes are known as *amb wapra*, the same term Marie Reay applies to the category of "wandering women," cut away from ties of kinship and marriage and open to abuse as they "passed from man to man." This term was also used in hostile verbal altercations between women in Hagen (A. Strathern 1993: 20). By the mid-1980s such altercations could contain assertions that one's opponent was a prostitute and suffered from gonorrhea. The entry of AIDS into Papua New Guinea and consciousness of it among rural populations during the 1990s has curbed the spread of prostitution somewhat owing to fears of the new disease. The Christian churches have weighed in heavily on the issue, urging chastity and HIV blood tests for young couples prior to marriage and trying hard to stop the practices of casual sex that go with peri-urban living. Senior people also comment unfavorably on young people running off to town and making eyes at one another in stores. Older women, however, recall with some pleasure and nostalgia the times when they took part in the courting ceremonies of the past, dating back to the 1960s and 1970s, the period when most of the songs we have given here date from. In 1998 we collected some songs from one such woman, living at Kuk.

Hagen, Song 17

1. Pongönt wi rona kana
    Klare wi rona kana
    Kopa mun e kandepa
    Erol nde pa
5. Ui amb Aklop
    Erol nde pa
    Kon-men ngolna
    Na mbi kond enem.

    Look up there to Pongönt,
    Look up there to Klare.
    See the top of the mist.
    Girl Aklop of the place Ui,
    You say maybe, maybe not.
    It makes me sad to go.

The story takes up the viewpoint of a young man who has been turning head.

We are back in the world of *kond*, the sentiment of being sorry. The geography here has shifted from Kawelka to Tipuka territory. (The two groups were neighbors and intermarried frequently.) Pongönt and Klare are two hilltops above the settlement area where the courting has taken place.

Perhaps it is the end of a long night of courting and the sun's first rays of dawn are touching the mountains and glinting through the mist that covers their summits. The girl he has been turning head with cannot make up her mind about him, or perhaps she is just being polite. He knows it is time to leave, but he is loath to do so. He feels *kond*.

Another song, provided by the same woman, refers to the fact that many Tipuka people were getting baptized into the Lutheran church.

Hagen, Song 18

1.   Pongönt ropa nde tinim
        Klare ropa ok ponom o e
        Erol nderol nde pa ya pa wa ya o e
        Ndembarui ni nu tilinga o e

5.   Nunga kang ye waka ile mor o e
        Erol nderol nde pa ya pa wa ya o e

        The Pongönt River floods and carries debris,
        The Klare River floods and carries sand.
        Ndembarui has become baptized,
        I, the boy of Nunga, am standing free.

Pongönt and Klare are streams that flow down from the hilltops of the same names. When rain falls and streams flood, you can see all kinds of things that are otherwise hidden, carried along in them. It is also like that when people turn head. You see what their feelings are. (The trope is widely used in other contexts, such as political speeches, to indicate how events reveal people's intentions and wishes.) One youth has become baptized (his name, Ndembarui, also indicates this). But the boy of Nunga is still available. Christians don't turn head, but those not yet baptized can do so. Since our female collaborator was remembering a song from her own early life, perhaps this was a boy with whom she turned head at the time. This woman herself now belonged to the local Pentecostal-style Assemblies of God church. She could be heard in the early morning near our fieldhouse loudly saying prayers and singing church hymns. In the morning children going to school also sing Christian songs nowadays. *Amb kenan* and *mölya* events are not heard or seen anymore. At night, instead, incessant drumming comes from meetings of charismatic Catholics, who adapted earlier tunes to their own needs, with unintelligible vocables, which some among them interpret in Pentecostal manner (Stewart and Strathern 1998, 2001b). Also, disco music could be heard in 1997 from a faraway settlement, where there was electricity. The music came from a "boom box," beer was on sale, and young people paid an entrance fee. These were the new "courting parties," equally frowned on by church authorities as was the old *amb kenan*. Marijuana smoking, introduced according to some from Chimbu, was also said to be a feature of these events: another replacement of the older forms of magic.

NOTE

1. Scoditti (1996: 125–300) gives a continuous series of "poetic formulae" for Kitawa (Nowau) in the Trobriands of Milne Bay Province, PNG, richly exemplifying the imaginative metaphors created to convey feelings and desires. As one might expect from a people living on a small island, windblown and surrounded by the sea, images of wind and water are liberally drawn on. In one song, the poet says that his thought "flows, like a stream's hidden current," like a gentle undercurrent below an apparently calm surface (pp. 126–27). Items of material culture, such as baskets, canoes, and women's skirts, also stand for parts of the human person, including the mind (*nano*). Fruits stand for sexual organs (pp. 135, 142). Plants are invoked for their aromatic powers: "I'll strip the leaves of young plants to make a wreath: the perfume of its crushed leaves will enfold for me the woman of Gawa" (p. 139). Songs themselves are said to give enchantment to garlands (p. 148). A lover's whole person is offered as a gift (*weimapu*) (p. 150). A woman comes lightly to a man, lapping over him like waves (p. 153). Girls going to a dance move softly like lines of waves, "like waves edged with foam they move to the dance" (p. 155). These few examples from an extensive corpus indicate a synaesthetic power similar to that found in Hagen songs, a power that is drawn from the layering of thoughts onto the life-world and the instant fabrication of multivocalic meanings expressed in visual terms.

Chapter 3

Courting Songs: II

PANGIA

In the Pangia area song composition by both women and men was as highly developed as in Hagen, with different categories of song for different contexts. There was no exact equivalent, however, of the Hagen *amb kenan*. The materials we have on Pangia mostly date from 1967, only seven years after Australian administrative control was established there. The Wiru speakers of Pangia are horticulturalists, planting sweet potatoes and other crops and rearing pigs for exchanges as the Hageners do (see Strathern and Stewart 1999d). Their language shows some vocabulary cognates with that of the Hageners, but belongs to a different language family within the Highlands as a whole. In 1967 they had recently been brought together into consolidated villages by the colonial officers in charge of census, health patrols, and local development. Previously they had lived in smaller hamlets, clustered in the vicinity of major ritual centers after which their political districts were named. In Pangia marriages were contracted within the district and between districts regardless of whether or not there were enmities between the intermarrying families. While there was a strong emphasis on life-cycle exchanges, particularly in terms of exchanges with maternal kinsfolk, there was also considerable ambivalence in these relationships because of the lines of political enmity across which they were contracted (Strathern and Stewart 2000e). Wiru society was greatly disturbed by the arrival of explorers, missionaries, and government officers from the 1930s onward, and there was a period of "madness" just after 1960, in which Wiru men were said to have rushed around causing mayhem. Narratives describe them raping women and destroying property (A. Strathern 1977; Clark 1999; Stewart and Strathern n.d.). In the 1960s issues revolving around the behavior of people in the domain of sexual relations were causing considerable concern, as government control had removed the possibilities of severe punishments for infractions. This was a situation commonly found in early years of administration activity throughout the PNG Highlands, for example among the Duna, with whom the problem continues to this day (Stewart and Strathern 2002).

Formal courting in Pangia consisted of a youth visiting an unmarried girl at her own place and sitting beside her in her mother's house, as was done among the Chimbu. Apart from talking and exchanging pleasantries generally, the youth might whisper a long series of statements into the girl's ear. The verbal performance was called *oi angale*, "whisper talk." The girl did not have to make any reply, but the words themselves were intended to influence her *wene* (mind, will, intention, mood). The performance can therefore also be seen as a form of magical incantation. Until the girl took notice of, or became aware of, the suitor's presence, his courting could not be successful. He had to get her attention. If he succeeded in this she would say that she understood him or became cognizant of him (*ne wene tokou*, "I made *wene* for you"). This could also happen when some kinds of magical substances were passed into food, such as pork, that she consumed. The whispered chants were secret, and knowledge of them was carefully guarded. *Oi angale* was the equivalent in Pangia of *rome* among the Kewa; Josephides (1982: 43) notes that knowledge of *rome* had to be purchased from senior men.

Oi angale, however, was only one of the means whereby courting was carried out and young people found self-expression. The general category of *loo*, songs, was a popular genre to which people were always adding, similar to the Hagen *mörli* or the general meaning of *kenan* in Hagen. Moreover, in the 1960s a favorite way of conveying messages was by playing tunes on a mouth-harp (*mōyo*), and incorporating the words of a song into the tune itself. The communication was oblique and coded. A girl could in this way send a message to a youth without everyone else understanding it fully, and the youth could reply similarly.

In this chapter we provide some examples of *loo* composed in this modality. The first is from a collection (Paia and Strathern 1977); the remaining are from our recordings. The images in these songs are local and indigenous, much less inflected by historical change than the *mörli* songs from Hagen that date from about the same time. This reflects the relative isolation of the Pangia area at the time, where people had less access to money and consumer goods.

Pangia, Song 1 (*Beneath the Andaiya Tree* 1977, no. 2)

1.   Awanipa yaika yai
     Pene ambela Yali parua
     Nekene mariyane
     Bukuke eweremoa piko pue

5.   Klosi pala tumberekene tumberandene
     Wakinakila-ye
     Ekai konio ini yopaikirame
     Likunu yakome kondekaloa
     Moroko yomo Leri pine

10. Peiraie okalepa tokouna kila ye
     Tokouna kila ye.

     Stranger, only yesterday you came down,
     The youth from Ialibu.
     A fine cloth is folded away in a box
     And kept there. Why could I
     Not be like that, so I would grow up later?
     Now, I'm like a fine bird,
     A flying fox that roams around at night
     At the foot of a Leri tree, stealing fruit.
     I, of the Peri group.

The singer addresses her song to a newcomer who has come down from Ialibu, a high-altitude area north of Pangia, which was pacified and brought under administrative control in the 1950s a few years before Pangia, and was therefore seen as a point of origin of introduced goods and "modern" life. Apparently, the singer was married earlier and now regrets this. If she wishes to befriend the newcomer she must do it by "stealing fruits," like a flying fox does at night as it roams around trees at the edge of a village.

Another song expresses a contrary opinion.

Pangia, Song 2

     Pene ambela Yali parua nekene mondo
     Konome kiripa nakuyake
     Tewilawene kunu Pure parukakome
     Nekene mondo mbaila
     Ondenepa ei wakilaye
     Wakilaye

     Only yesterday that sweet potato,
     The Konome, came down from Ialibu.
     I'm eating it, but
     The one that comes from behind the hill

Where Tewi lives at Pure, that's
The one I miss, those *mbaila* men.

Sweet potato here stands for "man." This singer says she has married a
Ialibu man, whom she calls Konome, after a type of sweet potato that spread
through the Highlands after the Administration came. However, she now
longs for someone from the old Wiru area to the south, where the *mbaila*
sweet potato is still planted.

In the next song, a girl threatens her boyfriend or suitor, saying she may
actually run away to Pure.

Pangia, Song 3

Pene ambela Yali parua nekene mariyane
Oko angale koa tuu Akipe tepe kou
Tokale pekene Tarumariane
Kunu Pure lekekome
Piko wendo naipalikirame
Kunu Paiya momoranepa
Kunuka poanda

You boy, who came down here from Ialibu,
you have spoken harsh words, and
My stomach is bitter, like the gall
In the Aki possum's stomach.
I will climb over Pure mountain
and stay down there in Paiya,
Where the mist covers up the trees.

Pure here represents a remote backwoods part of the area, far from the
government station. She will prefer to retreat there and distance herself from
him. The landscape here stands for a mood, just as it does in the Hagen
songs, where mist, *kopa*, stands for separation.

In this instance the girl simply expresses a wish to leave her boyfriend. In
other cases *loo* express a desire for a particular person.

Pangia, Song 4

Awanipa konio ini Dulukirame
Tukurukoa aru piriko
Tindu wane Peirango lawepa
Telo poime koloi wia pendanea
Piko wakilaye
Piko wakilaye-e-e.

That fine *dulu* bird
Folds his legs and sleeps

in his nest, a Peri man.
I swallowed hard as I saw him,
My heart was struck and bent.

Here the singer compares the man in whom she is interested to a bird that settles down quietly on its nest. Swallowing spittle is indicative of desire. It can be dangerous to the one who swallows, if the desire is not fulfilled.

Girls sang songs of this kind to express their agency and their will to make their own choices, as we have also seen in the other areas surveyed; although their wishes were thwarted in practice at least as much as they were fulfilled.

In another song a boy rebukes a girl who has changed her affections.

Pangia, Song 5

Awanipa konio yoroko
Pukanea yaketokono
Nekeraine tokomu tai ako tondo
Walia peke narepa
Owano pala ye.

Fine girl, you walk around,
In the shade of your father's sugar cane.
Bend over there and cry,
Cry a little there.

The singer says that the girl is proud to be in the shelter of her father's place and has forsaken him. Men of substance grew sugar cane in order to give it away as a mark of their wealth on pig-killing occasions, so the girl's father is probably a leader. But the singer predicts that from time to time she will think of him, and then she will cry quietly to herself.

These songs were an important part of assertions of agency on the part of young people, as we have repeatedly seen. The potential power of song, and of the imagination that informs it, is expressed in the following song.

Pangia, Song 6

1. Enipa tene kono teo kiri
   Oka parulawa ali pandame
   Akoma angopa morokale kiripa
   Weiriai yene werikandeme
5. Oro kerea kako yomo Andaiya pini
   Peiragopa ni endanea parulawa
   Kondolini buku yaku eweremoa
   Piko tue napi auapa
   Yawakilaye

10.   Yawakilaye

> If someone asks
> Whose daughter it is that sings this song,
> It is a girl who was married
> And could greet her husband nicely
> In the place shut off by the Andaiya tree.
> A girl whose talk is like
> A little knife, wrapped carefully in paper,
> The kind they sell in white men's stores.

Talk, then, can be as sharp as a concealed knife, when it is expressed in the idioms of song. But the overall sentiment of these songs is the expression of feelings themselves, and the *ela*, or emotion of being "sorry," which we also found in Hagen. These feeling are closely associated with notions of absence and of missing the presence of a partner. Some songs end simply with *ela tumbea toko ye*, "I am so full of sadness," a sadness that is simultaneously a feeling of sympathy and concern for the partner and a sense of loss as a result of the partner being away from home.

As we have also seen, the same expression for being "moved" emotionally also covers the sense of loss evoked in death. The temporary absence of a partner is imaged, then, as being like a death. Separation and distance are seen as social death, a sentiment that understandably emerges out of face-to-face relationships in small-scale situations where people are bound together by kinship and courtship and marriage. This pattern is found widely throughout New Guinea and elsewhere.

Mourning songs express the pathos of loss through vivid descriptions of the day-to-day existence of couples that is broken by death. Among the Kaluli of the Strickland-Bosavi area (Schieffelin 1976), a ceremony called "Gisaro" takes place, in which highly decorated male performers dance and sing to an assembled audience in a longhouse to mark special occasions in which transactions of social reciprocity are enacted. The Gisaro dancers sing of the landscape, the relations of the people with their land, and the relations between people themselves. "The deepest and most violent sorrow evoked by Gisaro song is that evoked over death" (Schieffelin: 182). In the following lines the singer is evoking the sorrow of a man who had only recently lost his wife:

> I have no brother. Where shall I go?
> I have no cross-cousin. Where shall I go?
> A *Kalo* bird calls [in] a leafless *haido* tree,
> Come see the Saeluwae stream.
> Come see the sago there.

(p. 183)

The pathos is expressed by verbalizing through song the deep fears and thoughts of the widower—who would work with the sago at Saeluwae?—who would share in its consumption? Being with people means making gardens, producing food, and sharing in its consumption, and death is the negation of this process. The Duna people have made this fact central to their courting songs.

DUNA

The Duna people live in the far western part of the Southern Highlands Province of Papua New Guinea. As with Pangia, their area was brought under administrative control later than most parts of the Eastern and Western Highlands of PNG, in the 1950s and 1960s. The Duna speakers we have studied inhabit the ridges, valleys, and streamsides in limestone forested country from Lake Kopiago station west to the Strickland River (Sillitoe, Stewart, and Strathern 2002). They are horticulturalists and pig rearers like the Wiru of Pangia. Their social structure differs from that found in Hagen and Pangia, however. In Hagen, there is a generalized stress on affinal alliances between in-laws; in Pangia these alliances are expressed primarily through exchanges between maternal kin and their sisters' children. Among the Duna there are no maternal payments as such, but each individual maintains close ties and obligations to both paternal and maternal kin, ordered through the cross-generation obligations that flow from brideprice payments. These variations in practices form a transformational set in which the importance of exchanges remains constant, but their locus shifts within the total nexus of kin and affinal ties. Duna courting songs centered to a good extent on attempts by youths to attract girls to come to their places, which after marriage would become their fixed homes. We have seen the same theme in Hagen songs, too; but for the Duna this aim was particularly vital, since a wife's main job was to stay at her husband's place and work there, seldom going back to her natal place to visit (Stewart and Strathern 2000d). In Hagen and Pangia such visits were often positively encouraged, for a wife would go to give some items of wealth to her kin and to solicit return gifts from them as part of a general cycle of exchange activities.

Yekea

The Duna say that their term *yekea* is the same as the Huli term *dawe*, one of the meanings of which is "courting dance." A special house would be built in which young men would "sit down on top of the laps of" the young women who had gathered therein. Songs of invitation to courtship and marriage were performed during these occasions. The boys would play tunes on their jew's harps (*luna*) and the girls would do likewise but use mouth-bows (*alima*) to make their music. As in the case of Pangia, words

were also conveyed through these instruments. Those gathered would express words and feelings that indicated their preferences and inclinations
toward one another. The boys who participated in the *yekea* had all "grad-
uated" from the *palena anda* (boy's growth ritual). Usually several years
might pass and participation in a number of *yekea* take place before a couple
would enter into marriage. These "courting" events were similar in some
ways to the *amb kenan* discussed earlier (chapter 2). They have not been
practiced in the area where we work since at least 1991 and probably much
earlier.

But *yekea* had more than one dimension since it was also one stage of
death rituals as well as rituals for the renewal of life. Similarly the Huli made
a spatial and temporal conjunction between courting rituals and death rituals
or ghost-propitiations (Glasse 1968: 53). The *yekea* house would be built
over a place where a person had died. This structure might enclose the
former residence of a dead person, or the building of the *yekea* house might
coincide with the removal of the bones of a dead person to a place of secondary burial. (For a further discussion of burial practices among the Duna,
see Stewart and Strathern 2001c, 2002.) This aspect of *yekea* was directed
at settling the *tini* (spirit) of a dead person into the place of the dead in the
high forest areas (Stewart and Strathern 2000d).

If a woman died in her husband's area, rather than her natal area, and
subsequently some of the husband's kin became ill, the sickness might be
attributed to the desire of her *tini* or spirit to be transported back to her
own place. Brothers of women who died in their husband's area often ask
for the bodies of their sisters to be returned to them so that they can be
buried in their natal area and thus their *tini* can be cared for directly. This
demonstrates a close cross-sex tie between siblings among the Duna. Sometimes the brothers may say, "I want my sister's body to be buried here rather
than elsewhere. If not, I will think she is still alive somewhere [thus causing
pain and confusion]." The *tini* of a woman who died in her husband's place
was transported back to her own place in the form of ashes and stones taken
from her cooking fire. Some of these ashes were placed into the ashes of
fires used for cooking pigs at the place of the *yekea*. Male dancers celebrated
the return of the woman's *tini*. One of the men dressed as a woman, wearing
the type of netbag that women wear when they leave their natal place to go
off in marriage. This special bag is called *ma nu*. The sequence of bringing
back the dead woman's spirit to her natal place was described as *heka yaru*
("bird pandanus sleeping mat"). The image is that of the woman's spirit,
flying like a bird that is covered with or is carrying a sleeping mat of the
sort that a girl might traditionally give to a boy who is courting her. The
bird is on its way up to a high rock shelter, where pandanus nut trees grow,
that will be its secondary burial place. For the event a young female pig that
had not borne piglets would be killed along with one male pig.

On the same occasion as this event, the courting dances were held inside the especially constructed *yekea* house. Here unmarried girls were attracted to come and stay with their suitors as their "wives," leaving their brothers and other kinsfolk behind. The courting phase of *yekea* took place before the other events, which included a number of different individual dances (e.g., *tawe, komea, heka kiliapa,* and *pilaku*). These dances had overlapping but distinctive purposes. *Tawe* dances and songs accompanied the return of the dead woman's *tini* to her natal place; *komea* dances were made to honor one of the environmental spirits known as *tsiri; heka kiliapa* ("parakeet bird") dances were for the Payame Ima (Female Spirit); and *pilaku* dances were said to have been borrowed from the neighboring Hewa people. This last dance was said to be imitative of the bodily actions first made by an originary *tama* (spirit being). *Pilaku* dancing was said to "make the earth warm" (*tindi rorowa*, Stewart and Strathern 2002: 85).

All of the dances assisted in curing sickness and they would be accompanied by sacrifices and divinations. The *tawe* dance was directed specifically at sickness caused by a dead sister. Clearly, then, the rituals of courting were very deeply implicated with these rituals of healing and mourning, and also with the translocations of sisters and wives in the processes of the life-cycle (for further details on Duna healing practices, see Strathern and Stewart 1999a).

The following is an example of a *tawe* song to demonstrate the genre:

Duna, Song 1

No ne harurunya kane kone ma
Liwa suwa-o
Limbiya suwa-o
Mbara suwa-o
Mayungu suwa-o
Epana suwa-o-no
Kulu kua koyana-o
Aku kua koyana-o
Ayuku kua koyana-o
Ayu ko tindi-no ngano-o
Ayu hatama
Puape apuape
Akomali nderepo nderepo

Go, my true sister, go along with me.
Take your things and come to Liwa,
Come to Limbiya,
Come to Mbara,
Come to Mayungu,
Come to Epana.
Put on your marriage netbag,
Put on the netbag of your marriage,

Put on your wedding netbag.
Now you are going to your own ground,
Go there now,
Go, go,
Waving your feather head-dress go, go with the dead.
Heka yaru is over.

                              (Stewart and Strathern 2002: 86)

The places named here include a number of well-known secondary burial locations up in the mountains that are seen as cared for by the local Female Spirit (Payame Ima). The Payame Ima is thus involved in welcoming the new spirit back to her own place. Since the Payame Ima was also thought traditionally to assist the male youths of the community to grow into adults and therefore be ready for *yekea* activity, it is clear that she had an integral part to play in the whole cycle of *yekea* practices, helping living young men and women and the spirits of the dead to achieve their place in the overall cycle of life.

Brothers would call a sister's spirit back to her own area and then send it on to the world of the dead, and at the same time youths would be enticing the spirits of unrelated young women who came as their courting partners into the *yekea* house, trying to make them want to re-settle in the youths' own place. They were implicitly assisted in this process by the *Payame Ima*, who was said to help make them handsome and attractive in the *palena* cult.[1]

This conjunction made between courting and the death rituals for a married sister appears to be particular to the Duna and perhaps the Huli (Glasse 1968: 53). In Hagen the holding of an *amb kenan* event was incompatible with rituals of mourning for a dead member of the group. On the other hand, such an event might explicitly be staged in order to exult over the death of an enemy and provoke resentment. This in turn was a form of logic that did not occur to the Duna. For them, the sending away of a dead sister's spirit had to be balanced by the attraction of new wives into the group. Putting on an *amb kenan* as a hostile act in Hagen was similarly an assertion of group strength, but it was expressed at the expense of enemy groups; whereas with the Duna such an expression was contained within the group itself.

One characteristic kind of song sung by young men for courting occasions was called *laingwa*. A few of the larger corpus of these songs, which we have recorded, are presented below.

Duna, Song 2

Nane wane Liya naiya
Ko tanda kone rakuku rapa
Limbiya naiya

Ko tanda rakuku rapa
Atara naiya
Ko tanda rakuku rapa
Liwale naiya
Ko tanda rakuku rapa

Girl at Liya, make your garden,
Drink water, come and sit near me.
At Limbi make your garden,
Drink water, come and sit down;
At Atara, make your garden,
Drink water, come and sit down;
At Liwale, make your garden,
Drink water, come and sit down . . .

(Stewart and Strathern 2000d: 95)

The singer continued to name other places that evoked the poetic presence of settlements surrounding his own natal home. The song is an invitation to girls to come and participate in a courting ceremony. The refrain "Drink water" indicates that the girls should relax and feel refreshed—water being a prime source of reinvigoration and regeneration in life. The song also refers to the girls making gardens and sitting down at (staying at) the place of their potential future husbands. This is a metaphor for the reality that the girls will be fertile and raise children at the place of their husbands. It also reflects the actual social pressures on a newly married wife to stay at her husband's place and not visit her own kinsfolk's area, where she might become disinclined to return to her husband.

Laingwa songs are generally addressed to sets of girls from neighboring places and present invitations, enticements, remonstrations, and offers.

Duna, Song 3

Ino ana etona narapela iri nariyanda
Wara kowaya kewe
Uli narapela iri nariyanda
Wara kowaya kewe
Apuli narapela iri nariyanda
Kawaya kewe
Alepa narapela iri nariyanda
Kowaya kewe.

Up here we have plenty of watercress.
Girls, the streams go down
Into the holes at Uli, at Alepa,
And at Apuli. We cannot just
Describe it for you.

> Come and look for yourselves,
> It grows well here.

The young men offer the girls an image of a lush environment with fresh running streams gushing into limestone sinkholes and plenty of watercress, an introduced plant that can be seen as a luxury food, growing in them. All of the place names in this song and in the ones that follow are "signature" names, marking ritual sites and secondary places of burial, sites of ancestral power, death, and regeneration within the territorial boundaries of the boys' parish area, Hagu. The names appear in pairs or in sets of three, and turn up as equally in songs of mourning as in these songs of courting, indicating once again the unity of life and death that *yekea* circumscribed.

Another song also offers access to resources, in a different part of the environment, the high forest, where men would go to harvest the rich, oily nuts of the pandanus tree.

Duna, Song 4

> Hara rumara kuruku lii keleta
> Rata nengele ndu raliya raya
> Yapi kuruku lii keleta rata
> Nengele ndu raliya raya
> Yawapi kuruku lii keleta rata
> Nengele ndu raliya raya.

> Up here in the forest plenty of pandanus nuts are growing,
> Not covered up by leaves.
> They are lined up
> At Yapi and at Yawapi.
> There is no woman here to eat these nuts.
> If you want to eat them, come and marry us.

Pandanus nuts are a delicacy. Traditionally only men harvested those that grew wild in the high forests and were considered to belong to the Payame Ima, the Female Spirit (Strathern and Stewart 2000a: chap. 6). But women certainly expected to eat them and to be given a good share of the harvest of them. The reference to the nuts being unbound means that they were plentiful and not concealed or protected from tree rats.

The next song refers to a further use of the pandanus nut tree.

Duna, Song 5

> Hara wara apuna paka rokota
> Irinia apunda wano
> Yawe apuna paka rokota
> Irinia apunda wano

Yapale apuna paka rokota
Iriania apunda wano

Here at this place there are plenty of pandanus leaves,
Which women use to make their sleeping mats.
Here at Yawe,
Here at Yapale, there are plenty
Mats made ready,
Come and sleep on them.

Sleeping mats are much appreciated both for providing comfort at night for sleepers and as a protection against rain. Women do the work of drying the leaves, then plaiting and sewing them together. Moreover, a young woman might make a gift of such a mat to a youth she was courting, while he would offer her a cassowary pinion as a nose ornament. Here it is the youths who offer mats, ready made by their sisters or mothers, to girls as visitors.

In the next song the youths offer their cassowary pinions to the girls.

Duna, Song 6

Wara ngelene apora apondu reita
Rawae kone, hora hondu reita
Soko reikundana sokosa wae
Ali soko reikundana sokosa wae
Alima soko reikundana sokosa wae.

The girls sit down, sit down over there,
They're sitting by themselves.
Let's send them a cassowary pinion as a bridge,
To encourage them to shift and come to us.

The gift of a pinion is intended as a "bridge," across which the girls can "walk" and come to be close to their suitors.

A further song again pleads with girls to come and enjoy surplus pandanus supplies.

Duna, Song 7

Hora wara siawa likiloko
Ngata heka leika seya
Yawe siawa likiloko
Ngarata heka leika seya.
Yapale siawa likiloko
Ngarata heka leika seya
Yakoma siawa likiloko
Ngarata heka leika seya.

> Here there are plenty *siawa* pandanus nuts,
> They fall down ripe and lie there on the ground
> No woman to eat them, and the wild
> Cassowary comes and eats them instead.
> Whoever wants to come and enjoy these nuts, let them come.

Images of forest abundance are projected, fruits and nuts that do not require the arduous labor needed to make gardens and houses and tend pigs. The women are appealed to—to come and eat up the free surpluses that otherwise will go to wild cassowaries. For a people who suffer periodic droughts and food shortages, these images of plenty obviously conjure up good feelings, conducive to hospitality, courting, feasting, and marriage.

In another song the youths offer their little bamboo flutes to girls, suggesting they should come and play them, a shift in modality from food to entertainment, possibly with some further meanings.

A further modality of these songs has to do with the youths' feelings about the girls not coming quickly to court them. Their responses range from quiet acceptance to an assertion of forceful protest. These compositions underline the point that it is the youths who are on offer and the girls who are the choosers, as we have found to be very common in the region as a whole.

Duna, Song 8

> Kulale ramene huta rupu
> Parata honia seriandapa
> Yapi rupu parata honia seriandapa
> Yapale rupu parata honia seriandapa

> We boys have come to sing the *tsole tse.*
> We have come like parrots,
> Looking for fruits to eat, we've come
> To Yapi and to Yapale, we've come
> Just to look around, so now we'll go back home.

This was called a *tsole tse* or *yake* song, not a *laingwa*. It would be sung in the *yekea* courting also. Here it is the youths who say that they have come looking for something to eat as parrots look for berries. If there's nothing for them, they can just fly back home.

In this song the image of mist, familiar from the Hagen songs, appears, with a similar meaning. Mist and rain mean a lack of success in courting. Things lie concealed. The sun does not shine. It's time to leave. But there is no expression of *kond*, or being "sorry," as in the Hagen texts.

Duna, Song 9

Hara rumara popo kariata
Irinia raluanania
Yapi popo kariata
Irinia raluanania
Yawepi popo kariata
Irinia raluanania.

Up there the mist comes down on the mountain,
Up there at Yapi
Mist covers over the mountain.
Up there at Yawepi
Mist covers over the mountain
Soon it will rain and so
Let's go back home.

The girls are tardy in coming to court the youths. The boys are impatient. They offer their cassowary pinions again.

Duna, Song 10

Soko sukisia roaepa sokosa wae
Ali soko sukisia roaepa sokosa wae
Alima soko sukisia roaepa sokosa wae

You girls are taking too long to come.
At Ali we'll put a bridge,
At Alima we'll put a bridge,
We'll put a bridge made from a cassowary's pinion.

The youths challenge the girls—are they ready to be married and so are they prepared to put into their netbags the soft leaves in which a baby can nestle? Or are they thinking of going to school and following a different path?

Duna, Song 11

Kili kipe kawali kipe
Ruku nane pepa kili kipe kawali kipe
Rukupe nane pepa kili kipe kawali kipe

What do you have in your netbag?
Have you put in it the leaves
Used to cradle a baby
Or is it a bit of the white man's writing paper?

The threat to chase the girls is probably empty (song 12), but expresses the deep frustration of the boys who are yearning for the girls to come.

Duna, Song 12

Walesia hilawano ponape heyanao
Limbiyasia hilawano ponape heyanao
Arapiasia hilawano ponape heyano
Eya ae ae

We are rough boys.
If you girls don't come to sing
At Limbiya, at Arapia,
We will come kicking up dust and chase you.

The *tsiri* bush spirit, as seen in song 13, was in fact considered to be cosmologically important (see Stewart and Strathern 2002: 54–57). But in this context reference to it indicates that the boys feel they are being treated as something other than human men. Men and women get married. Bush spirits do not. Which are they? Only the girls can make them sure they are men, by coming to court them. (Girls who do not develop properly into adult, marriageable women can be described as *tsiri*.)

Duna, Song 13

Warali gelene aposia tsiri kuru
Rane rembo reipe
Apia siri kuru rane rembo reipe
Arapia siri kuru rane rembo reipe

Girls, we've sung until we are tired.
You're looking down at us
At Apia, at Arapia.
Do you think it's bush spirits who are singing?

Overall, the sensibility revealed in these songs is playful and lighthearted. The singers are more inclined to chide the girls collectively than to declare their individual affections. They are waiting for the girls to come to the *yekea* house, and if they don't come they will just have to depart. Like parrots roaming around for berries, they can always look elsewhere. But there is always the underlying anxiety. To be adult men they have to prove themselves attractive to women. Ensuring that this would be so was one of the main purposes of the rituals that used to be followed in the bachelor's cult, the *palena anda* (see Stewart and Strathern 1997a).

By comparison with the Hagen songs, the Duna songs show a more overt offering of the virtues of place and food, and less concern with the nuances of individual desires. By comparison with Pangia, they also show less expression of intense personal feelings and a more conventional show of male collectivity. These are just tendencies. They correspond to nuanced cultural differences and the differences in patterns of colonial contact in these areas.

Duna wives married into strongly autonomous and virilocal territorial groups, and they did not become a focus of exchange relations between these groups until much later in their life cycle when their children grew up and married. By contrast, in both Hagen and Pangia, women's agency as both sisters and wives was important for "horizontal" exchange relations between in-laws, as well as for matrilateral payments to mothers' kin. The important thing was to convert Duna wives from outsiders to insiders. Duna myths warn men not to discriminate against their wives in distributions of pork and not to call them "wild" creatures, anything other than humans. Since women should not be called "wild," neither then should the youths who came to court girls be looked on as wild *tsiri* spirits. Humanity was something everyone had to achieve, and men and women needed each other's help to do so.

Our argument throughout this and the preceding chapter has been that courting occasions and songs provide an important ethnographic site for examining the play of imagination and sensibility in gender relations throughout the Highlands, at least in certain stages of the life-cycle. We will conclude with a brief look at other areas, in order to show arenas of further comparability.

FURTHER AREAS

The Strickland-Bosavi area south of the PNG Highlands is particularly rich in poetic traditions that encapsulate emotions and representations regarding sexual relations. Bruce Knauft (1985: 273–94, 295–318) has given a perceptive account of these genres for the Gebusi people, especially as they relate to spirit seances in which "the primary spirits who sing are young spirit women, whose corporeal form is usually the red bird of paradise (*Paradisaea raggiana*) or another brightly colored bird" (p. 295). These events were, however, in fact conducted by men. In about a third of the sixty-one seances Knauft observed the men involved also drank kava, a drink capable of producing intoxication. These occasions were marked by ribaldry and joking, with frequent references to sexual activity between men and the spirit women, and with humorous plays on the symbolic equivalence between noseplugs and penises. Knauft interprets these events in part as a means of discharging tensions that develop over the constraints of sister exchange marriage, turning hostility over heterosexual contexts into forms of male camaraderie, by means of "a fantasy of unlimited free love and sex that all men can share" (p. 299). (In sister exchange marriage, there is a reciprocity between sets of kin, and its constraints can lead to tensions and hostility over unpaid "debts.") The spirit medium who led these seances, which were actually inquests into deaths thought to have been caused by sorcery, was supposed to establish "a sexual liaison with a spirit woman and then marry her" (p. 306). Knauft provides an example of spirit songs, which he describes as mostly consisting of "a string of verbs, place names and raw percepts," for which the audience supplies the interpretation from their own knowledge (p. 300). This characterization might perhaps be applied also to the Highlands courting songs. However, the appearance of "bareness" in these texts is an artifact of their "embeddedness" in the local environment. To their indigenous listeners and participants they were instantly and highly evocative, although they could also encode private or restricted meanings.

The theme of loss and abandonment as expressed in the songs of the Kaluli people of the Strickland-Bosavi area is explored by Schieffelin (1976) and Feld (1982). Feld builds his discussion around the story of a boy who was out fishing for shrimps with his older sister. He begged her for the crayfish she had caught but she said they were for his mother and elder brother, not for him. Finally he caught a tiny shrimp and, putting its red shell over his nose, he turned into a *muni* bird, the fruit dove, whose mournful cry is heard in the forest. His sister now cried for him but he was gone (Feld 1982: 20). The theme of reciprocity or nurturance denied between kin or spouses is common also in the Highlands. Sympathy denied may turn into the sorrow of loss. We see from this example the power of the concepts of *kaemb* and *ela* in the Hagen and Pangia areas, and why there is a connection between contexts involving kin and those involving sexual relationships.

The associations of pathos with place are also delineated by J. Weiner for the Foi people who live in the Lake Kutubu area east of Strickland-Bosavi. Foi men's performances of *sorohabora* songs resemble the Kaluli *gisaro/ gisalo* performances in which highly decorated men sing songs at night that move their listeners to weep, through mentioning places once frequented by persons now dead. Weiner refers to a tableau in which young women hand bamboo tubes of drinking water to young men performing *sorohabora*, giving them a break from their singing (Weiner 1991: 151). Women do this to mark their attraction to the men, following such men with flaring bamboo torches. Weiner comments: "[A]round their most profound experiences of alienation, sorrow and abandonment, the Foi have constructed the life-affirming conventions of sexual attractiveness and enticement" (p. 151). We find here exactly the same emotive conjunction as exists in the Duna *yekea* performances, although the institutional setting is different. The loss of a sister is transformed into an act of bringing her spirit back to its own place and then sending it to the spirit world. In turn, this loss is balanced by "pulling in" young women as wives. Just as shell wealth was held to be pulled in by means of magic spells, so wives were pulled in by song. The kind of logic involved here also appears among the Foi. A newly married

Foi couple was supposed to have intercourse in the bush and make portions of their sexual discharges, mixed with special leaves, red ocher, red *Bixa orellana* seeds, scrapings from a pearl shell, pig-wallow dirt, and pieces of white limestone scrapings, into packages to plant at the fireplaces in their house. The packages would then draw in wealth to the house (Weiner 1995: 67). Loss of substance is converted into cosmic magic to draw in wealth.

Love songs from elsewhere in Papua New Guinea also play on the dialectic between loss and gain. We have seen in the Highlands songs how much agency is expressed in contexts of loss, anxiety, or frustration, the chafings of choice against the walls of constraint. Simon Harrison's study of "laments for foiled marriages" among the Avatip people in the East Sepik Province of PNG shows this theme very clearly, against the backdrop of the specifics of Avatip sociality. These laments were composed and sung by men, and were maintained for many years, commemorating former courtships with women who married other men, perhaps at the insistence of their kin. Although the songs were composed by men they sometimes adopted in them the persona of their female lover. All the characters in the songs were given totemic appellations, and their identities might be clear only to the singer and those he intended to understand the song. Sometimes the songs were not laments but simply proposals for, or concealed reports of, covert trysts. In one lament the composer speaks of the dry season when there is a thick heat-haze lying over the land of his lover. "He refers to the heat-haze as her 'sister' and says that he will weep for her, but she, living in a distant ward of the village, will not hear him" (Harrison 1982: 50). Harrison comments further that in these songs people were able to pass secret messages and to express themselves personally while adopting a language of concealment based on an elaborate set of totemic names for places and people. The songs mark important aspects of Avatip society. One is the basic dialectic between "a ritual system pervaded by notions of ascribed inequality, and an everyday world of relatively unrestricted and egalitarian competition between groups for important positions within that system" (Harrison 1990: 191). The songs pay lip service to a hierarchical totemic system while bearing witness to people's agency in subverting, or trying to subvert, it. Another feature is that of secrecy, which "to Avatip people . . . is an essential device for preserving personal autonomy. To them, the less a person is known to others, the greater his freedom of action" (1982: 26). Harrison quotes with approval from Simmel the idea that the secret is a first-rate element of individuation (1982: 26). Precisely the same impulse lies behind the allusive creations of Highlands songs.

We can, indeed, rephrase this point and make it even more general. All of these songs reveal what A. P. Cohen has called the "reflexive self" (Cohen 1994). Cohen also uses the terms "authorial" and "creative" in this regard, and by this cluster of terms he means to point out the significance of persons thinking and acting in full consciousness of themselves rather than automatically following sets of rules or performing acts of sociality because that is what is required of them. Cohen's basic idea of self-consciousness is well exemplified in the genre of songs we have been examining here. Equally we will find it in the realms of ballads and myths, which we will consider in the next chapter.

NOTE

1. The Payame Ima in this regard resembles the Female Spirit in the Enga area who was said to ensure that youths in the Enga bachelors' cults would look strong and handsome, with good skin. These cults were known as the *sandalu* or *sangai* cults and were similar to the Ipili (Paiela) *omatitsia* discussed by Aletta Biersack (1982). The Duna *palena* plants were the same as the Enga *lepe*. Wiessner and Tumu (1998: 215–44) give a detailed survey of Enga bachelors' cults, indicating that the sacred fluid kept in bamboo containers used in these cults was said to have been derived from the blood of the spirit woman who appeared in the cults' origin myths (pp. 218, 221). In these myths a "bachelor encounters a beautiful woman" whom he later betrays or harms, and her blood turns into the *sangai* fluids, while the *lepe* plants grow on her grave. These fluids and the plant can transform unattractive youths into handsome men (p. 225). One name of the spirit woman in Laiagam (Western Enga) was Mambeamo (p. 229). Bodies of poetry and spells, including the lengthy *sangai titi pingi*, marked out the origins and powers encapsulated in these cults. The Spirit Woman is always a *yalyakali*, "Sky Being." *Sangai* and *Sandalu* cults do not seem to have been followed by courting parties of the Hagen or Duna type, although girls would individually attach themselves to youths they liked when they emerged in full decorations at the end of a period of isolation, ready to marry (p. 238). Wiessner and Tumu also report that from the early twentieth century these occasions of emergence could precipitate fights between young women over a particular youth, and these fights became institutionalized under the name of *enda akoko nyingo* (p. 241). They suggest that as human women took a more prominent part in this stage of the festival, ideas about the spirit women became attenuated (p. 242); but other historical factors were probably also at work here.

Kundapen Talyaga (1975) includes a number of Enga courting songs in his collection of "modern" Enga songs in general. The songs he quotes tend to be in the same modality of personal statements, often tinged by a sense of grievance, that are found in Pangia songs, but without the emphasis on "being sorry" (*kond, ela*) that appears in both the Hagen and Pangia traditions and is particularly strongly developed in Pangia where some songs simply end with a reduplicated *ela tumbea toko ye*, "it makes me so sorry." See also, for their emotional tenor of expression, the courting songs and love songs from the Kewa area recorded by Josephides in 1982. A part of one *rome* courting song is translated as:

> I look at your face
> and it is as if I am looking
> at a parrot or *yariti* bird.
> The stars shake my ground at Yone.
> I must go, farewell. (p. 50)

The term *rome* here is perhaps cognate with Melpa *rom*, in the sense of "praise."

Chapter 4

Folk Tales and Oral Narratives

Songs, as we have seen, express a blend of personal, cultural, and historical experience. Such experience is also linked, even if indirectly, to the realm of the imagination. The imagination, in turn, often plays on the issues of court-ship, the ideal image of the spouse, and relations between cross-sex siblings and their spouses. The themes of folk tales are therefore linked to the themes we find in courting songs. In this chapter we discuss oral narratives that are explicitly seen by their narrators as products of the imagination. Into this category fall stories often labeled as myths, folk tales, or legends. To speak of these stories as being related to the imagination does not mean that their tellers and listeners think of them simply as "untrue." The question of whether or not they literally happened is not one that people raise. They are "stories," blending many themes from everyday and customary experi-ence with elements of a magical kind connected to the spirit world.

This spirit world, however, is also felt to impinge on, and to be the hidden background to, people's everyday lives, so there is no distinct boundary between the everyday world and the spirit world. Some kind of distinction is nevertheless made between stories that present themselves primarily as imaginative creations and stories that are seen as anecdotes of personal ex-perience or histories of events (see LeRoy 1985a: xi–xii). In the Hagen area, for example, stories of the first kind are called *kang* or *kanga*, while those of the second kind are termed *ik teman*, "accounts." Often the narrator of a *teman* will say that he or she saw some of the events or heard about them from someone who did. *Kang*, however, are described as passed on endlessly by word of mouth, with no particular stress on authentification. They draw, all the same, on customary patterns of life, and often dramatize these in ways that reveal their underlying dynamics, which emerge also in people's biographical experience. Ongoing experience and word of mouth tradition are implicated together in *kang* narratives, which also, for the ethnographer, provide glimpses into earlier historical periods of behavior. Some *kang* are also classified as "origin stories" in Hagen. These, however, tend to have a separate term, such as *kaklpa titim ik-e*, "the story of how things were straightened and laid down." Such stories we call myths. *Kang* in general may be regarded as "folk tales." *Ik teman* can be glossed as "accounts of" events set in the near or distant past. Such accounts may also include references to spirits. All three of these categories are, of course, narratives. We will be concentrating here on myths and folk tales from Hagen and on parallel categories of narrative from elsewhere.

Ideas about major spirit figures who were central to cults of fertility blend into the fabric of what we call folk tales here. We will be paying particular attention to figures from Hagen such as the Female and Male Spirits and their cults. Of particular interest is the fact that narratives about these spirits are tied in with folk tale genres that center on spousal and cross-sex sibling ties. Marriage emerges here as a major locus for sentiments and sensibilities but it is always in counterpoint to siblingship ties. The Hagen figure of the Amb Kor or Female Spirit combines elements of siblingship and spousal status in a kind of ideal amalgam of both: once again as an image of an idea that is not attained in practice but infuses practice with meaning. Similar notions emerge from a corpus of stories presented and analyzed by John LeRoy on the Kewa people of the Southern Highlands Province (LeRoy 1985a, 1985b; see also Josephides 1982). These stories also overlap in their themes with the stories regarding the Female Spirit as a Sky Woman in Hagen myths. Indeed we suggest that this particular theme and its connection with ideas of wealth, fertility, and spousal ties is widespread in the Highlands as a whole, although it is particularly marked in the language areas to which the Hagen and Enga peoples belong, including the Duna people and also the Wiru speakers of the Pangia area. We will make some allusion to materials from the Duna in support of this view, because the Duna figure of the Payame Ima or Female Spirit is directly comparable to the Amb Kor in Hagen. In Pangia the Female Spirit cult was diffused southward from Ialibu via the Kewa people and therefore also reflects the same mythological background as is found in Hagen. The correspondences with the Duna materials are in a way even more striking because of the geographical separation between the Duna and the Hageners; but given the possibility of a historical diffusion of ideas among the Hageners, the Enga (Wiessner and Tumu 1998), the Mendi and Wola people (Sillitoe 1996), the Huli (Frankel 1986), and the Duna (Stewart 1998; Stewart and Strathern 2000d, 2002), these correspondences of ideas need not be seen as independent "inventions" but as products of historical processes of transmission of ideas in "circulating cult" contexts (Strathern and Stewart 1999e).

CREATIVE SPIRITS IN THE EASTERN HIGHLANDS OF PAPUA NEW GUINEA

Before discussing these spirits, we will provide an example of comparable notions about creative beings found far to the east of Hagen, among the four peoples studied by Ronald Berndt and Catherine Berndt in the Eastern Highlands Province of Papua New Guinea in the 1950s, shortly after the beginnings of Australian administrative control there. Ronald Berndt (1962: 41–68) described parts of stories, mostly told to male novices in age-grading rituals of initiation, but also known by and large to women, "although some features are conventionally kept secret from them" (p. 41).

According to these myth fragments, there were two creative beings, Jugumishanta, who was female, and Morofonu, who was male. They were both said to have emerged from the ground at a cult site where a type of cane used in cane-swallowing rituals grew. In these rituals boys learned to put pieces of flexible cane down their throats to induce vomiting and purge their stomachs of food containing female blood from menstruation. The ground was actually a swamp, a detail reminiscent of the concept of the Eimb or fertility cult sites in Hagen that were established in places where there were swamps and springs of water (the same is true for the related *Wöp* or Male Spirit cult) (see Strathern and Stewart 1999f; Stewart and Strathern 2001a: 99–112). Jugumishanta was sometimes thought of as the earth itself and was the more prominent of the two beings. She (like the Female Spirits in Hagen and Duna) had different manifestations, for example, as a swamp, a type of red cordyline, a salt derived from red cordylines soaked in swamps, a species of grass used to induce nosebleeds in rituals to expel blood, or a stone barrier at a waterfall. Morofonu could similarly be a hornbill, a kind of taro, a waterfall, or a red parakeet (clearly comparable to the Nikint figure in Hagen, see below, this chapter).

In one narrative the two creative beings first lived under a black-palm tree that grew from an arrow they carried (Berndt 1962: 42). Jugumishanta made her own skin and body and cut her own vulva, then she made Morofonu into a human shape, pulling out his penis from his stomach and showing him how to copulate with her until she became pregnant. In another version, with a more competitive edge to it, the two sharpen their respective genitals on hard stones and Jugumishanta cuts Morofonu's elongated penis to a normal size so that they can copulate comfortably. The wind blew up the skin of the female and male child that Jugumishanta subsequently bore, making them like humans (Berndt: 42–43). Jugumishanta showed Morofonu how to use his bow and arrow properly, so he could shoot marauding sorcerers and kill them.

The two spirits caused water to come from certain holes, and they played the first bamboo flutes, used later in male initiation rites, carrying these in their netbags and giving them to people. They also put shell valuables into a cave in stone cliffs (after removing them from the origin-swamp because a bird called out that it had seen them do this). And they made a men's house, and many kinds of leaves and foods, wild creatures, and people, telling them to "look after" the ground (Berndt 1962: 44). They finally passed into the Land of the Dead at a place called Anabaga, where they became light-colored spirits and were said to have created "Europeans" and put them in "other places" (p. 46). (This detail indicates how myth is "porous" to history, since Europeans were not known to the Eastern Highlanders before the 1930s.) When the dead entered their domain in Anabaga, they were supposed to suck at the genitalia of the two spirits, acknowledging their kinship with them.

Another cycle of narratives explains how Morofonu stole the original magic flutes from Jugumishanta and claimed them for himself (see Knight 1991: 46 and Gewertz 1988 for parallels). He also planted the flute he stole in Jugumishanta's wild ginger patch, and there it grew into a clump of bamboo. Morofonu further planted his own vomiting cane and it grew into a large bush. In spite of the theft of the flutes, men are presented as still dependent on women for growing into men and becoming attractive to females (p. 53). In one story a woman actually warns men not to show their cane-swallowing acts to other women because if they do so they will turn into red parakeets (i.e., transforms of Morofonu). The "woman" here is clearly a manifestation of Jugumishanta herself. Male secrecy is thus actually enjoined by the female creative being, rather than simply being imposed by men themselves.

Berndt points out finally that narratives of this sort inform action. "They influence opinion, attitudes, judgements, and action of all kinds; and choices in specific situations are made against this framework" (Berndt 1962: 58). He is pointing out, as we do, that the mythological and everyday domains are not sealed off from each other. One does not refute or contradict the other. They do not have to be perfect replicas of each other. Rather mythology acts as a kind of background or "landscape" of thought, experience, and sensation, against which everyday action takes place. This kind of point is familiar to students of, for example, religious ideas in European history. It applies equally well to the present context.

The specifics of the notions Berndt brings out are different from those we meet when we turn to the Hagen and Enga regions. But they are similar in terms of the kind of "universe" they envisage and in their imaginative form. The primacy of a Female Spirit is particularly interesting here. We turn now to traditions in the Western Highlands and beyond.

DUNA

We have discussed Duna ideas about the Payame Ima at length elsewhere (Strathern and Stewart 1998b, 1999e, 2000a; Stewart and Strathern 2001a, 2001c, 2002). Here we wish to pick up on only a few points for comparison with the surrounding materials. First, in the Duna scheme there is no primeval couple such as Berndt found in the Eastern Highlands. The Payame Ima resembles Jugumishanta without Morofonu. On the other hand, she was said in some traditions to have a brother and/or a sister. She did not give birth to humans, however. Instead, she made alliances with human bachelors to help initiates grow in the *palena* ("ginger"/magical plant) cult. The myths of this region (which we signal as Hagen and Enga but include the Huli and Duna), then, do not stress sexuality, but rather its absence or sublimation in the case of the Sky Beings and their alliance with humans. Jugumishanta and Morofunu in turn have no connections with the sky. The Sky Being complex of ideas does not seem to be present in Berndt's materials, but is found universally in the Western and Southern Highlands (Strathern and Stewart 2000a: 59–77). The Female Spirit gives fertility to the land and all that lives on it. The land and its living beings are her "domain": especially the game in the high forests, which protrude into the sky itself. Forest game animals are her "pigs": an idea found very widely in the region. Duna stories (*hapiapo*, a category that corresponds to the Hagen *kang*, folk tales) reflect this environmental worldview. The *pikono* ballads portray these relations with the forest very dramatically as we will see in the next chapter. In a range of folk tales, men are said to have captured sky women and married them, only to lose them when they failed to keep a promise to them: a theme that records a sense of primordial loss and links this to the importance of keeping promises, especially between men and women in collaborative partnerships such as marriage. (Biersack 2001: 80, 90 interprets the spirit wife theme among the Paiela as ultimately reflecting "patriarchal power," but the theme certainly also emphasizes female power and inter-sexual collaboration. See further chapter 7.)

KEWA

The Kewa people are neighbors of the Wiru speakers of Pangia in the Southern Highlands Province. Their language belongs to a wider grouping of languages related to Enga. Borrowing of terms and mutual social influence have taken place between the Kewa and Wiru areas over time, and their customs of killing pigs at periodic festivals are highly similar (Strathern and Stewart 1999d). Kewa ritual experts first introduced the Female Spirit cult complex in Pangia, perhaps in the 1920s (Strathern and Stewart 1999e). The Kewa make a distinction between *lidi*, which LeRoy (1985a: ix) glosses as "tales" and the Kewa say contain elements of fiction; and *ramani*, which LeRoy calls "legends," and are said by the Kewa to include elements of historical truth. The distinction is by no means absolute. It corresponds to the Hageners' distinction between *kang* and *teman*. *Ramani* is clearly cognate linguistically with Hagen *teman*. The stories LeRoy presents and analyzes are all examples of *lidi* (pronounced *lindi*) and are comparable to the Hagen *kang*. Like the Hagen tales they abound with concerns for the morality of kin relations and they especially play on cross-sex sibling and spousal relations, which are tied in with ideas about jealousy, substitutability, betrayal, and sources of wealth and well-being. The first story we take from LeRoy displays these themes outside of the context of the Sky Wife motif. They are set instead into a picture of interethnic relations, in which Wiru women appear as overly self-assertive, violent, and vindictive. This is perhaps in line with the fact that the Wiru were historically less favored in terms of trading routes than their neighbors, and Wiru women were seen as rather grasping.

"Sister and Wife" and Other Stories

"Sister and Wife" is a Kewa tale filled with pathos. It expresses the close ties between cross-sex siblings and the tensions that arise between co-wives (LeRoy 1985a: 41–46). It also highlights the point that when girls marry they bring in wealth items to the family that make it possible for their brothers to pay bridewealth for wives of their own. In this story a man named Limu and his sister lived together and shared the work of keeping food gardens. Men would come to make bridewealth offers for the sister, who had come to be of a marriageable age. Each time Limu would tell his sister, "Now that men are coming, go to the garden and fetch some sweet potatoes and *padi* greens." But each time this happened the sister always returned without her pubic covering, shaming her suitors who would leave without pursuing the bridewealth negotiations any further. This continued to happen until one day men from Erave came with many wealth items to make a bridewealth offer. But again when the girl displayed herself naked in front of these men they took their objects and left, as all the other suitors had done. "Limu, both ashamed and angry, struck his sister on the head and went into the house to sit by the fire."

The sister left. At first Limu was so angry he thought he did not care but eventually he became sorry for his sister and went to look for her. "First he went to the forest of Apirawalu and hunted possums. From there he went to Karanda, over to Mount Kata, then to the forest at Alamu" (1985a: 42). It was here in the forest that he saw food crops growing and a young woman with long hair, wearing a white skirt made from dried reeds and planting sweet potato runners. The woman heard a noise and asked who was there. Limu recognized the voice as that of his sister, and when he replied she recognized his voice. The two shared in the cooking and eating of the possums. Before Limu left, the sister asked him to continue to kill and cook possums and pigs for her. She also gave him a couple of large pigs, two netbags filled with pearlshells, a bushknife, and an axe. She said, "All these things I have given you. In return you must come back with more pork for me . . . when you come here, do not do so along the main paths; but take the path I took when I fled from your house after you struck me. Near the edge of your house stands a tall *waria* tree with a mounded base, there you will see my footprints still. Now I am giving you this payment (*pe*). Use these things to marry. Take two wives. One must be from Ialibu land, and one from Erave. Do not take a Palea (Wiru) wife" (p. 43).

Limu took these items and agreed to follow his sister's instructions. He married a Ialibu woman, but then a Palea woman came and stayed with him even though he had not paid bridewealth for her. Limu was asked by other men in his clan why he did not marry an Erave woman as his sister had told him to do.

Every time Limu went to visit his sister in the forest he took pork for her. The Palea woman became jealous because he gave her only pieces of fat. She decided to follow the pathway from Limu's house into the forest. Along the way she saw an *opo* tree whose wood was strong and was used to make digging sticks. She took some wood and crafted a dagger with which she stabbed Limu's sister. After stabbing her she went back to Limu's house. Limu arrived at his sister's house before his sister died from the wound. She asked him, "Did you wish I should die, that you broke your word and married her?" (p. 45). She died and he buried her. Later Limu took the Palea woman to the burial site and tricked her into digging up the decaying body. He forced her to eat from the body until her stomach could not distend any further, then he killed her with an arrow. He broke his bow into two pieces and stuck these into his rear and flew off as a lorikeet.

Commentary: The story has a retributive structure. Limu kills his Palea wife in revenge for her killing of his sister. Jealousy between co-wives is proverbial, but here it is shown between sisters-in-law. The hidden sister, however, stands in the story like a Sky Wife figure, benevolent and nurturant but vulnerable to human attack. Her white reed skirt and her long hair are also imaginative features that otherwise are attached to the Female Spirit. Her long hair is in ringlets. These were a favorite fashion for women in precolonial times. Christian missionaries discouraged the style and supplanted it with shorter cuts of hair, as they also did for men. Her brother, in becoming a lorikeet, joins her in the realm of the spirits.

In another Kewa story a woman is also implicitly presented as a spirit, who was able to provide pearlshells magically for a poor-man and raise him to "big-man" status. It is clear that this woman is a Sky Woman because the poor-man hears women descending on a vine from a tree, laughing. He catches a good-looking one of them. The woman caused mist, rain, and wind to come and made him feel like the sky and earth were turning over, but he hung on to her and so she married him and he made a special seclusion house for her to live in, decorated with sweet-smelling ferns called *kapipi* (the same term appears in Duna, as *kapiruku*, which is also used in cult contexts). The Sky Wife gave him shells and told him to distribute them to everyone. But he skipped one poor-man, who became jealous and broke into the Sky Wife's house. She gave him shells also, but then he struck her on the head before he left with them. Dying, the woman reproached her husband and told him to make a shrine for her near the black-palm tree where he first saw her. He did so. He also took revenge on her murderer by killing him. People said, "If the poor-man had not killed this wealth-woman we would have plenty of valuables. Now we have only a few shells and they come from far away" (LeRoy 1985a: 84).

The details of the man catching the Sky Woman and her transforming herself into mist, rain, and other shapes exactly parallel Duna stories centering on local versions of the Payame Ima (Strathern and Stewart 2000a). Also, a transgression born of jealousy violates the spirit's secrecy (as though her cult center were broken into by an unauthorized male) and the source of wealth is withdrawn. The spirit woman does not command her husband to kill her murderer. Rather, she lays the blame at his own door. He, as a human man, takes a violent revenge, however, on her killer.

Further Kewa stories elaborate similar themes. In story 21, "The Jealous Sister," a man gives good marsupials to his spirit wife, "a young woman with long tresses." His two human sisters are suspicious and jealous, and they find the wife and stab her with a cassowary bone dagger. Retribution follows. The man kills one sister after showing her where he had buried the wife. The other sister commits suicide. Both sisters come back as ghosts and kill their brother (LeRoy 1985a: 73–75). In story 22, a man sees some young women climbing down from the sky on a vine and captures one, making a secret house for her. His sister finds out and is jealous because she thinks he is not bringing game back for her. She finds the Sky Wife and asks her for some of the fine red ocher paint she has over her whole body. The spirit woman gives it to her and falls sick as a result. The man kills the sister in revenge and throws a sprig of red cordyline to his wife, telling her she too can now die. "Because the sister stole the ocher from that woman, others no longer come down from the sky" (LeRoy 1985a: 77).

The red ocher motif here is widely shared. Red ocher is a mark of health and wealth. It was spread on pearlshells to display them. It was highly valued as a trading commodity. It gave the skin a glowing, light appearance. This theme appears strongly also in Duna tales (Stewart and Strathern 2002: 40). Red ocher is a mark of the Sky Beings in general.

Story 23 also turns on the sister/Sky Wife opposition.

"The Sister, the Sky Wife, and the Snake" (Tale 23, LeRoy 1985a: 77–80)

A brother and a sister lived together after their parents died and planted gardens. "One day the brother cut a shoot from a *konda* banana plant and planted it near the house. The following day, when he was alone in the garden, a heavy rain fell, accompanied by loud thunder. Afterwards the sun came out again, and it was then that the brother saw four young women come down from the sky" (p. 77). The man decided to take one of these females for a wife. This Sky Being had skin and hair that was colored red with earth paint. She instructed the husband to build her a house—near the garden.

The brother told his sister that he had sent all four of the sky women away and he forbade the sister to go to the garden area where he had built the house for his sky-being wife. The wife gave her husband red earth paint and ornaments to decorate himself for a pig kill.

The sister decided to disobey her brother and entered the garden where she found the sky-being wife of her brother. She asked the wife for some of the red earth paint and was given it. After she left, the Sky-Being woman died and a large python followed the sister back to her house. The snake forced himself on the woman, entering her mouth and disappearing into her stomach. When the brother returned he found his sister in her swollen condition and she confessed to having disobeyed him. He went to his wife and indeed found that she was dead. Upon his return, he began to cook pig fat, which the python could smell. "Gradually the brother enticed the snake out, using the piece of pork, retreating slowly into a corner as the snake came further and further out. Finally the tail of the snake whipped out. It struck the woman in the head, killing her" (p. 79).

The man took his axe and chopped off the head of the snake and cut its body into many pieces. Some he gave to Mt. Murray, Mt. Giluwe, and Mt. Ialibu, and they became the long curved ridges of these mountains. The python's head and tail turned into various small snakes.

This story also contains a motif that links notably with the Duna: the idea that mountaintops are the abode of the literally transformed shapes of giant pythons, which are also connected with the Sky Beings (Strathern and Stewart 2000a).

"The Sky Woman and the Broken Promise" (Tale 74, LeRoy 1985a: 225–27)

"A man lived alone. One fine day he went into the forest at Kolo Mountain. As he walked through the trees he saw some pieces of earth and ocher lying on some leaves. He thought about this. Had some men from around there left it, or had women from the sky (*yaa sone winya*) dropped it?"

(p. 225). He looked around and observed that the bark of a *walu* tree had been worn off and footprints could be seen by the tree. The man made himself a small hut to hide in and watch the tree. Soon he heard women laughing and he saw several young girls descend from the tree in order to collect earth paint.

The females went back up the tree one at a time, but before the last one could get away the man grabbed her and took her back to his house. She told him, "[W]herever you make a garden, there you must make a garden house for me. Others up there (in the sky) will look down at me, keeping watch. I cannot be seen outside the house by myself, so you must always accompany me. You must not leave me alone while you go somewhere on a journey. Now we must first make a hut and then the garden" (p. 226).

So he made a hut for her in each of his gardens. Next he collected a bridewealth payment of shells and pigs. The Sky Woman transported them and the objects into the sky where he gave his payment and then they came back to earth. Then he told her that he was going to a dance but she was not allowed to come. She thought to herself, "Why did he disregard what he had promised earlier?" (p. 227). She left the human man and went back to her own place in the sky. These Kewa stories strikingly set out the motif of the Sky Wife and imply an opposition between her and human women, exemplified by the men's sisters in these narratives.

HAGEN

The theme of the broken promise and its consequences runs strongly through from the Kewa and Duna to Hagen stories. It is always a human husband who is unable to keep a promise to his Sky Wife. Often, as we have seen, he is betrayed by a sister or a poor-man, both jealous and resentful that his attentions are diverted away from them. He may also have disobeyed his spirit wife's instructions. Hagen stories that appear in Vicedom and Tischner's early collection also reverberate with this kind of theme, offering explanations as to why an original sky-earth connection was broken (Strathern and Stewart 2000a). Hagen tales link the spirit world notably to the forest and its combination of abundance and concealment, a pattern encoded also in the Kewa stories we have cited.

Hagen oral narratives are rich in themes that speak eloquently to perceptions of the environment, the imaginary projection of social relationships into geographical spaces, and the workings out of the morality of social relationships. As is common in narratives throughout New Guinea, an overall retributive structure tends to show through the story sequences (see above and Trompf 1991, 1994, for a detailed exposition of the broad regional significance of this theme). The specific setting of many, if not most, of these stories is the forest; or at least this is so of the corpus used herein. These are mostly from the Kawelka and Tipuka people, who were living in the 1960s near to the forests of the Sepik-Wahgi Divide. The forest itself is the major or dominant symbol in the stories. It is an "other" place, opposed to the safety of the settlement and home. Yet it is also a place intimately known, into which people go to hunt for marsupials, cassowaries, and wild pig, or to clear areas of fertile land to plant new crops. It is a place of spirits, benevolent ones who can magically produce gardens or induce pregnancy, or malevolent ones depicted most often as cannibals who wish to kill and eat humans. These cannibals are described as *Tei wamb nui wamb*, "the Tei people who eat people," the antithesis of humans. They are the "bad" or dangerous, desirous, predatory, and consuming version of the "good" Tei people of the high forests or sky, who are the sources of fertility, wealth, and reproductive powers for humans (see Strathern and Stewart 2000a). Sometimes the cannibals are simply called "Kewa," meaning foreigners, from other places. The forest is a place of transformations and reversals. Protagonists in stories may meet an "old man" (*wuö anda*), a "short man" (*wuö etamb*), or a "woman with many netbags on her head" (*peng paka amb*). These are all images of senior people in the experience of the narrators, parental or grandparental in character, and they tend to represent the threatening as opposed to the nurturant or indulgent features of such senior kin: parental figures may become ogres when met in the forest. At the same time they are like strangers, enemies from groups hostile to one's own. The stories do not often name groups; but they sometimes give the names of living, local people to the actors in the events portrayed, indicating that these adventures are experienced by one's "own group" in relation to "the outside." The forest blends the outside and inside together.

The spirits met in the forest may want to kill and eat the humans; sometimes, however, they want to marry them (thereby consuming their substance in a different way). A "short man" is the prototype of the unmarried senior bachelor who would formerly have worked as a "servant" (*kintmant*) in the household of a leading man ("big-man," *wuö nuim*). Such bachelors were expected to want to find ways of marrying. A light-skinned Tei woman in these stories often wishes to marry a human man and supplant or drive away his existing human wife. Her light skin reveals her magical powers, her potentially cannibal nature, and her attachment to the spirit world. She may lead humans back to the place of her own kin, where they are imprisoned and then killed and eaten. But humans may follow and rescue their own, and they may be able to kill the Tei spirit and her cannibal kin. The Tei woman who appears in this guise is thus, as we have noted, a female spirit, but one who seeks to harm humans. She is very different from the Female Spirit who comes to bring fertility to humans and help them.

A brideprice is in a sense given for the Female Spirit (Amb Kor) when payment is made to the ritual experts who establish her cult. The Amb Kor is powerful and uses her power to confer fertility and health. Her abode is the high forests of Tambul to the southwest of Hagen, while the Tei people (both men and women) who are cannibals are pictured as belonging to the Jimi Valley, a low-lying area to the north of the Hagen area, a place of sorcery and witchcraft (see Strathern and Stewart 1999b; Stewart and Strathern 1999b). In myth, as humans draw near to the home of the cannibals, they see a river of blood, the blood of human victims, and a bridge of bones, the bones of people that have been eaten. In one Hagen story a man shoots a White Bird of Paradise (a bird whose habitat is in the Jimi). It flies off with his arrow in it. He tells his wife to follow the bird, and get the arrow back. This is a mistake and disruption follows. The wife follows the bird and it leads her across the river of blood and the bridge of bones. The cannibals capture her and the next day they eat her. The husband in distress follows, and when he gets there the cannibals tell him, "Here is your arrow which you came for, and there are the bones of your wife." He gets his arrow but it is of little use to him. He takes his wife's bones back and holds a funeral for her. The bird in the story is a transform of a cannibal woman, who on return to the cannibals' own place in the Jimi dies, and they are holding the funeral for her when the human man and woman come in search of the lethal arrow. A funeral among the cannibals is matched by a funeral among the humans and the retributive sequence is completed.

The theme of shooting the bird, which flies off and is followed by the hunter or the hunter's associates, is found in the Female Spirit origin story in Hagen, in which a man shoots a *Nikint* bird, a red parrot, which turns out to be a spirit woman. It is clear that the "cannibal" stories are thematically parallel to the "Female Spirit" stories, but are inverted versions of them, in which the spirits, both male and female, are hostile and destructive, as opposed to benevolent and productive. Thus, the spirit world like the human world has the two sides of interaction: destructive and constructive. It is also essentially a world of superior power. Christopher Healey (1990: 90) records that among the Maring people north of Hagen a Female Spirit of the forest controls access to game animals, which are her "pigs." She is basically benevolent, but may also make fun of hunters, laughing when they try to catch marsupials but fail because she is withholding them. This illustrates another modality of spirit-human relationships: humans cannot succeed without the goodwill of spirits.

Certain animals in these stories act as allies and friends of humans. Notable among these animals is the quoll or marsupial cat (*kui watinga* in the Melpa language, *yanai* in Wiru). The quoll is a small but wild and fierce creature, and appears in these contexts as a powerful being who can match its powers to those of the spirits themselves and is not afraid of them. It knows how to access other worlds or places beyond the immediate "other world" of the forest: ways into hillsides where spirits live or ways to go underneath the surface of pools and find replications of the world above such as beautifully laid out settlements, again the magical homes of spirits. Even more benevolent than the quoll is the domestic dog, itself a creature that knows the forest well. The dog is portrayed in some stories as bringing a wife to a man. In others a dog and a marsupial work together in providing a house, gardens, and a wife for a man. The magical or spirit character of the dog's and the quoll's actions is shown by the expression that sometimes appears in these stories: where they "played together" (*kintmal-mal etingil*) garden plants grew up. (The term for play here, *kintmal*, is curiously similar to the term for work done on behalf of another, *kintmant*.)

Each of these narratives tends to have a clear set of protagonists and to highlight these at its beginning: a cross-sex sibling pair, spouses, a set of brothers or companions, age-mates, a set of sisters or young unmarried women who go around together. "Horizontal" or same-generational ties tend to be stressed here, and inter-generational links may appear in disguised form, as we have noted, with a stress on ambiguity and hostility. A major theme underlying the activities of the protagonists in many stories is either their explicit search for a marriage partner or else their marriage as an unintended result of other actions. These narratives thus fit into both the major stories about spirits to whom cults were dedicated and into the theme of courtship and marriage and the sensibilities that surround this theme.

Another significant topic in the narratives is the power of talk, or gossip and rumor, usually presented as negative in its immediate effects, particularly *ik möra*, "cross-talk," directed at kin. Such cross-talk causes people to take impulsive actions, which then lead to good or ill for themselves or others. Talk is powerful and dangerous: this is a moral lesson that the stories convey clearly (see Brenneis and Myers 1991).

Below we will provide some examples of stories showing these themes. They were originally written down in 1964 and were translated and analyzed in 2001. Additional versions of these stories were also recorded in the 1990s. These may be readily compared with the corpus published earlier by Georg Vicedom (Vicedom and Tischner 1943–48, vol. 2, some of which was translated from German into English in 1977 by A. Strathern). The stories given by Vicedom were narrated to him in the 1930s before the outbreak of World War II and his departure for Germany from the Central Hagen mission site of Ogelbeng where he worked with informants of the Ndika and Yamka tribes, especially a man called Yamka Ko. In these stories the theme of obtaining a marital partner is also prominent. As depicted in Vicedom's stories, either the man or the woman may take the initiative in selecting a marital partner. If the meeting is at a dance it is customary for a girl to choose a man she wants and to follow him back to his home. In Vicedom's catalog of stories, number 47 tells of girls at a dance who fight over a handsome young man until their brothers settle the affair. While a girl can follow a man to his place, it is not regarded as proper for a man to invite himself into the parental house of the girl he is pursuing. The girl herself must conduct him in and present him to the parents.

We begin our selection here with two stories of how spouses were obtained.

1. The Story of Mara-Pil

A man had a young dog. When it grew big the two made a large sweet potato garden together, and when the food was ready in this garden, the man said, "Now that there is food in the garden we should raise a pig so that it can eat the good food." The dog went off and brought a male pig and a female pig back, and these they looked after until the female pig was big. Then they put it with the boar and it carried a large litter, so they had plenty of pigs. "Now we should find some gold-lip shells," the man said, and the dog went off and, breaking into a house, brought a large load of shells back. When these had been put away, he said, "Now we need some *kokla ranggel* (cowrie shells)," and so the dog went away and brought some back. Then he said, "I would like some *pela ei* (nassa shell mats)," and the dog went away and brought some back and the man put them into his netbag. "I would like to hold some money and look at it," he said, and the dog ran off and brought some for him. "Now I need a bush knife and an axe to cut trees, fence, and make a garden," he said, and the dog ran off and fetched these for him.

One day the man said, "I do not like digging up my own sweet potato, there should be a wife here to do it for me, then I could just prepare the garden and be able to go off." The dog then took some ripe *konda* bananas, and saying, "give me a piece of money, a single piece," he took this also and went off south toward Hagen. Arriving there he found a large number of young girls digging up sweet potato in an extensive garden. There was one good girl who watched while the other bad ones took sticks and beat the dog, and she told them not to beat it like that. The dog then ran up to the good girl and darted all around her digging stick. Next it jumped up and snatched her pandanus rain cape away from her and ran off with it. She followed after it, saying, "It has taken my pandanus away." Another girl came with her to help chase after the dog. On the way the dog doled out the bananas he had brought, and so they traveled on and on until they arrived home. The dog's owner thought, "So the dog has gone off," and he steam-cooked sweet potato, cut sugar cane, and bananas, and had these all ready for the arrival of the two girls. When they came he greeted them and said, "Did you see the smoke or hear the squeal of the pigs or did the dog 'grease' [divert, seduce] the two of you and bring you here?" They slept and the next day the dog and his owner said, "Let us take the pigs and shells off now." So they put on their grease and hair coverings, ate their food, and the dog went off first while the people followed. They walked on and on until they reached the girl's home. They paid five sets of pearlshells and ten sets of cowrie shells and nassa mats and twenty-five pounds in money to the parents. The next day they cooked a pig too and took it over, and received the return gifts for some of the items in the brideprice, which they brought back. Later, at the *kng mangal* ("house pigs") event some more pigs were cooked, and the dog and a young marsupial the man had caught and kept were looking after the meat. The two had just said, "Now let's take the pig off," when they began to rough and tumble about during which time some sugar cane rubbish went into the fire, and it blazed up and set the house on fire. The man's bow and arrow, baler shells, nassa mats, pearlshells, and pigs were all destroyed in the fire. Through a gap in the smoke the dog saw that the man's bamboo flute must still be in the house, as it was not among the items he had salvaged from the fire. He rushed in to fetch it but the fire burnt him up. The man and his wife came back and saw how the fire had burned the dog up and they cried. Then they lived on until they died.

Commentary: Here the dog obtains everything for the man, starting with the essentials of a food garden, and continuing with sources of wealth, which the dog simply obtains from others by stealing them, without further social relations. Money enters into the list of wealth items, signaling the 1960s perspective of the narrator, who was a young man at the time. When it comes to obtaining a wife, the man makes a very mundane remark, geared into the conventional division of labor. The sweet potato, however, is in fact a sign of home and the nurturant qualities of women as wives and mothers. It can also signify sexual relations. To get another human being for the man, the dog needs artifice, and a little bit of luxury food and monetary wealth. It goes south, in the direction of the town, into the populous Wahgi Valley area, and proceeds to steal things, at which it is adept, this time the sleeping mat of a girl who has been kind to it. It feeds ripe *konda* bananas to the girls who chase it, although the narrator does not mention how the piece of money was used. Perhaps it was held in reserve and was not needed. By the time they arrive at the man's place, the event is a *fait accompli*. He has prepared food for them as guests. Next day they set out to pay the brideprice wealth to the girl's kin. Processes that are often quite lengthy are speeded up and compressed in the narrative into their elementary sequential forms. The dog also stands in for the man's parents. The man is like an orphan without father or mother to help him. The dog is like an age-mate of his. Insofar as the dog also brings a wife to the man, it is like the man's brother-in-law. The term of address for a wife's brother in the Hagen language is *pöi*, and the dog in stories of this kind is described as an *owa pöi*, a *pöi* dog. *Amb kenan*, or courting occasions, do not figure into this narrative. The dog uses its magical powers to get a wife directly for the man.

The narrator does not explain the title he gives to the story. Possibly Mara-Pil is the name of the man in the story. Unexplained also, other than as an unfortunate contingency, is the death of the dog following the fire in which the man's wealth is lost. In this case, the play of the dog and the marsupial produces not a beneficial result but a disaster. The dog shows its loyalty to the man by rescuing, or trying to rescue, his bamboo flute, an instrument played for amusement but one that may have had an important role in ritual activities in the past, as is seen in other parts of New Guinea. This sequence may encapsulate a historical memory of the importance of flutes in initiation ceremonies. The story was quite a favorite in the 1960s and a number of people gave versions of it. (The *konda* banana was special to the Female Spirit in Hagen, so the mention of it in this story is perhaps not by chance.)

2. The Story of the Hole in the Cedar Tree

Some fifteen young boys all lived together. One day they were practicing spear throwing at the ceremonial ground near their house when an old man (a Tei man) came up. He had covered up his long fangs and came up to see them, and said, "Grandchildren, you are here." "Yes we are here, practicing our spear throwing," they said. "Where do you live?" he said. "Later on at night I will come back and sleep with you." "We live inside a hole in that tree," they said. "Goodbye then," he said and went off. At nightfall the children were not sleeping there. "Oh, where have those rubbish men gone to?" he said, and went away. The next day the children returned to their previous place, and the old man arrived again. He found the children by themselves and said to them, "Where did you go to sleep yesterday?" "Oh, we went to sleep in an old tree-trunk," they replied. The next night he came up to the old trunk and smashed it. The children scattered in different directions. Two of them went and settled in a place by themselves, where they made their own gardens and raised their own pigs.

One day they lit a fire and the light of the fire shone over to the mountain Mböngi where it was seen by a young girl who lived there along with her mother. She watched it and called out to her mother: "Mother, yesterday and the day before there was a fire up on the mountain over to the west and now it's there again. I'm going to see what it's about!" The mother replied, "Have you been to the place before? You can go tomorrow, today we'll prepare some food." She went to dig up red yams and red taro, and she brought vegetable greens and cut bunches of bananas. They cut wood and the next day they killed a big pig, singed it and cut it, peeled the taro and yams, and cooked everything. They slept and the following day washed the young girl's skin, opened up the oven, and took out the pig. The girl was given some of the taro and yams, pig backbone, head, lungs, tail meat, and liver, and she took it with her. She walked on until she came to the place where the fire was burning and then came in close to the boys' place. The two boys lived by themselves and when the girl came into their company they asked her "Where have you come from?" She said, "I live to the east of here. I saw your fire burning all the time and wanted to find out why, so I came." "Excellent," the two said, and took her into their house. "Stay here," they said, and one of them went outside and cut some *pakla* sugar cane and brought it back inside for her to eat. He broke it and gave it to her and said, "We will eat this and sleep and tomorrow you can go." So they slept. The next morning they got up and said, "Let's take the girl back to her home now," so the two bold boys gathered vegetable greens for eating with pig, picked banana leaves, split wood and made it ready, and then the following day at dawn they killed a big pig and cooked it and said to the girl, "Tomorrow you can go back to your place." The next day they took out the pig, laid out its two hind legs, its head, its backbone, its tail bone, its stomach, and its liver. They divided out all the other goods, and the next day they set out very early. They walked on and on and came up to the girl's home where the mother saw them arriving and said, "My daughter, you went away and now you have brought two strange young men back." The girl replied, "Mother, I went away and found these two men and have brought them back." "Good," the mother said. She ate the pig they had brought and gave her daughter to one of the men. They brought her back and one of them married her. The two lived together until they died. The end.

Commentary: The story falls into two parts. In the first an old cannibal man of the woods tries to kill a set of boys, but they outwit him by hiding in different places and deceiving him. In the second part they scatter and the narrative follows two of them, showing how the boys go away to live by themselves. A girl is curious about the fire from their settlement, whose glow she sees to the west of her house, and she goes off in a brave act to see what it is. Seeing a fire glowing in the distance is often cited as a reason for a girl to be attracted to a place: the fire is like the love magic called *krai* (see chapter 3). This theme of a boy or a girl going off to seek a marriage partner is a common one. This story was also very popular and several versions were collected. In most of these it was called "the story of *möre kopanda*," or "the story of the spear practice," because it begins as this version did with boys getting together to practice throwing sharpened sticks like spears with trees as the targets—a kind of training for warfare when they would grow up. In some versions of this story the boys deceive the old cannibal by hiding in different tree trunks, until a girl picks up one of the logs in which they are secreted and takes it home, placing it on the trestle above her fireplace. Then she hears the sounds of mouth-harps and bamboo flutes being played by the boys in the log. They come out and she marries one of them and her friends marry the others, so that everyone is paired off. Here the musical instruments appear as adjuncts to courting songs; or as an analog of instruments played in cult contexts of secrecy, which is followed by the emergence of the boys as marriageable men: another theme of initiation.

In this version, however, the narrator follows just two of the boys. The motif of the girl seeing a fire burning is classic. It appears in balladic sequences and also in origin stories. The image is one of distance, curiosity, "frontier" conditions of sparse population, and an urge to make new social alliances. The cooking of food—and especially pork—to be carried in net-bags signifies the potentiality of marriage and the sequences of eating and sleeping stand in for the idea of a sexual liaison. Hospitality, politeness, reticence, and implicit understandings come to the fore. The girl washes herself before taking away her pork, to make herself attractive. Her mother is supportive. The girl's father is conspicuously absent: the mother-daughter couple and their agency is foregrounded. There is no conflict in this case and the marriage takes place.

3. The Ringlet of Hair

Another popular Hagen story turns on a ringlet of hair belonging to a girl that a man finds in water, either in a river or in a funnel trap he has set to catch fish (sometimes a woman who has fallen into a pool is found in such a trap). He carries the ringlet off in a particular geographical direction (place after place is specified, giving the quest the character of a heroic journey) and compares it to those of girls he meets until he finds the one it fits. Then he asks the father of the girl if he can marry her. The father at first offers wealth items or other young women instead, but the man steadfastly refuses until at last the girl he wants is given. Personal agency is clearly emphasized here, in this case the agency of the man. Just as often, however, it is a girl in these stories who refuses to marry a man chosen for her and insists on marrying the man she wants. Dances are the occasions when a girl's desires may be aroused, by the appearance of a male dancer and his fine decorations and expressive body movements. We give an elaborate example of the use of this theme in the chapter on decorations (chapter 6).

4a. The Forest Parrot Man

One of the male characters who is portrayed as sometimes causing a stir of interest at a dance is Ndepana Nikint, Nikint of the forest, who is part man and part spirit. He inhabits a portion of the forest and its streams. A recurrent motif in these stories is the warning a brother gives to his sister not to drink from places in the forest where sweet, cool water flows but to stick to muddy areas trampled by pigs. Invariably the sister disobeys her brother, and he says that she has now chosen a life of work rather than the life of leisure she had while living with him. He means that his sister has become pregnant with the water and will bear a child and will have to work to look after it.

In one story Nikint himself has a sister, and they are both in search of spouses. In yet another the bird after which Nikint is named, the red forest parrot, appears in a beneficent role. A man chases after a white cockatoo that has seized the digging stick of his brother after the brother has tried to kill the bird with it. He comes to a pool and an old woman there gives him two fruits to throw into the water and tells him to dive into the water after them. He does so and two young women arrive (transformed from the fruits) and offer to marry him, so they go off together to his home. His brother is jealous and tries to repeat the exercise, but he gets two old women instead of young ones. To gain his revenge, he tricks his brother into going into the forest to shoot birds and leaves him perched up a tree, unable to get down. The man's two wives are upset and after a while go in search of him. Near where he is hanging helplessly, growing thinner every day, there is a nest with two young Nikint birds in it. The women take these and rear them. When the birds are big they fly off and find the man, rescue him, and carry him with magical strength back to his home, reuniting him safely with his wives. The birds represent the beneficent powers of the forest spirit. Later in the story the saved man takes revenge on his brother, killing him with a blow from a stone after inviting him to go on a fishing trip: an ending that completes the story's retributive structure.

The theme of the young woman becoming pregnant by the sweet, cool water directly relates to the traditions of the Male Spirit, Kor Wöp in Hagen, the central focus of which is spring water that is held to induce fertility in women (Stewart and Strathern 2001a: 99–112). The child of the woman who drinks from the sweet water in the stories is a boy who grows up quickly, because of the magical powers of his unseen father, Nikint. Nikint is thus akin to the Male Spirit, and in some ways is like a brother of the Female Spirit. The Nikint bird, as well as the White Bird of Paradise, can also be a direct marker of the Female Spirit herself.

In the following story Nikint himself figures in the "brother" role and is in search of a wife.

4b. A Story of the Forest Man Nikint

The man Ndepana Nikint and his sister lived by themselves. Ndepana Nikint said he would go into the forest and clear a space for a garden. His sister remained at home and was harvesting some sweet potatoes and steam-cooking them. Nikint spoke harshly to her about some matter and then left for the forest in order to clear a space for a garden. When he came back he found that his sister—who was a young, unmarried woman—had gone into the interior of the house, covered herself with her pandanus sleeping mat, and was weeping loudly. He thought that his sister was hungry, and so he raced to their garden and cut a bunch of *keninga* cooking bananas. He dug up yams. He harvested some taro corms and gathered greens. He hurried back with all these foods and peeled the bananas. He collected stones for the oven, dug a hole for it, and lined it with leaves and greens. He cut the firewood. Then he went off and called to his pig, "ants, ants," and a brown-colored pig came. He told it to come to where he had spread out some leaves. He attached a rope to its leg, brought it forward, and struck it with his club and singed the hair from the carcass. Nearby in the brushwood he heard two things disputing with each other. "What are those two things doing?" he wondered; then he saw it was a *mot* bamboo knife from the Melpa area (to the east) and a *teklip* knife from the Kuma area (in the central plains). "Mot, you will just cut in the way you cut, let me try Teklip and see," he said, and so he thrust the bamboo in and the front quarter of the meat looked good, and the hind quarter also. There was so much meat there, it was like mud that builds up at the entranceway to a house.

Ndepana Nikint called out to his sister to come and roast and eat some pieces of pork. But she continued to lie there inside the house, covering herself with her mat. So he roasted some pieces himself and invited her to come and eat. But she stayed inside and refused to move. "Come and wash out the insides of the pig and I will heat up the stones for the oven," he said. But she stayed inside where she was. So the brother went and washed out the entrails and laid them out himself. Then he set fire to the trestle of wood with the cooking stones on it to heat them up. Having done this he called out again to his sister to come and eat some greens and meat from the small cooking hole, while he would prepare the big oven. But she still lay there as ever, crying. So her brother first prepared the small oven, and then the large one. Then he called out, "Sister, come and cook some of the inner parts." But she still lay there crying.

Ndepana Nikint set everything into the oven and then went down to the Jimi Valley area. There he washed himself and his skin glowed like that of the *mopa* banana or the *wenakla* banana. He wore a fine front apron, put on a cassowary headdress and a forehead band of nassa shells along with a conus shell in his nose, and rubbed pig grease on his skin. Then he returned and opened up the earth oven he had left at home. He laid out the pork and called to his sister to come and eat. But she still lay there crying inside the house.

He left a side of pork for her and took one side for himself. He laid out the backbone for himself, and the flaps of meat from the chest for his sister. He took the pig's tail joint for himself. Then he counted out the bananas and other pieces such as the inside and organs and left some for the sister; he did the same with the taro and the yams. Then he put aside two kinds of netbags, wrapped the pork in a *mongndamb* insect's nest, which he gathered onto his shoulder, and took off. His sister came out and saw that her brother had gone. She took up the pork, bananas, and other things he had left, put them in her netbag, and followed him, crying loudly as she went. Nikint meanwhile went on and on and he came to the place where a man called Kukl and his sister lived. His own sister was overtaken by darkness in the forest and she laid out her large *kupin* netbag and lay down on it to sleep. There a large cassowary came along and swallowed her.

Ndepana Nikint stayed with Ndepana Kukl and his sister. One day the two men said they would go into the forest and make a clearing for a garden. So they went off and began to work at this. They heard a sound in a nearby bamboo grove, and it was the cassowary, which had come and was saying, "My brother told me to eat beech nuts, and so I'm eating them. My brother told me to eat wild pandanus nuts, and so I'm eating them." When Nikint heard these words he severed a joint of his forefinger. Ndepana Kukl saw this and asked him, "Why are you crying and lopping off a finger joint?" Nikint replied, "I had a sister, a young unmarried woman whom I left behind at my home when I came here. She must have followed me and this cassowary ate her, and now it has come to the bamboo grove up there and I've heard it speaking."

So the two of them went into the forest nearby and Kukl waited on the lower side of the grove and Nikint went up into the bamboos and began beating them with a stick in Kukl's direction until the cassowary came out just where Kukl was. Kukl seized hold of it and pulled out some of its plumage and there was the young woman. The two men took her home, and Kukl married her while Nikint married Kukl's sister, and took her off to be with him at his own place. Kukl stayed in his own place. When the two of them had a son they planted a casuarina tree, and when they had a daughter they planted a cordyline.

Commentary: Ndepana means "forest" and Nikint means "red parrot." "Red parrot man of the forest," as we have already noted, belongs to the cycle of narratives about the Female and Male Spirits and the magical powers of growth and fertility they can confer, exemplified by their association with the forest and its powers of renewal of life (see Strathern and Stewart 2000a: 79–99). Figures such as Nikint retain this magical aura in some stories, but they also appear as humans in search of a social pattern of living. So, in this narrative, Nikint is living with his sister. Both are adults but unmarried. The cross-sex sibling tie is an important component of social relations, but it cannot constitute these relations in a reproductive way because of the incest taboo. Nikint and his sister are therefore both incomplete components of a set of relationships that constitutes the elementary paradigm for social life. Perhaps this is what is really at issue between them. Nikint goes out to make a forest garden by himself, while his sister stays at home to cook sweet potatoes. Nikint speaks harsh words to her about something before he goes, thus violating notions of respect between the two and treating her wrongly.

The girl, a grown-up but unmarried young woman, retires into her house and sobs inconsolably.

Nikint realizes the error of his ways and hastens to try to make amends. He rushes off to the gardens by himself and gathers up all kinds of foods, doubling up the work of man and woman. He calls out to a pig, as women do, and slaughters and butchers it, as men do. Then he seeks his sister's forgiveness by trying to entice her with delicacies and their aroma. He also asks her to supply her female work (signaling that she has forgiven him and is prepared to work collaboratively with him again) by washing out the pig's entrails for him, but in the end he has to do this for himself. The sister remains out of sight inside her house, covered up with a pandanus mat, wailing. In his perplexity, Nikint divides out the cooked pork and vegetable food, some for himself and some for the sister. Decorating himself finely, he leaves home, in search of a more complete life (one that incorporates sexual relations).

This sequence portrays closely the affective ties between sister and brother, which are constrained by incest taboos. Nikint regrets his cross words and tries to make up for them. The sister cannot overcome her anguish, and so Nikint sadly leaves. He decorates himself, however, in the manner of balladic protagonists who are going off to search for a wife. The storyteller has used some of the formulaic phrases found in sung ballads in the body of the spoken narrative, such as the phrases about the two kinds of bamboo knife for butchering the pig, and the appearance of Nikint's skin when he decorates himself. His skin glows a golden color, indicating he is a light-skinned man, akin to the Sky Beings.

As soon as Nikint goes off, the sister comes outside and is distraught to see he has left her alone. She too gathers up her share of the pork and at once follows him, without him knowing it. But instead of being able to accompany him and find herself a husband, she is ambushed by a forest creature, the cassowary, itself a complex symbolic figure with both male and female associations (see Strathern and Stewart 2000a: 43–58). She is taken back into the forest itself. She has spread out her *kupin* netbag to sleep on, which is the kind of netbag a young woman wears to go to her husband's place on the occasion of her marriage. This detail suggests that the cassowary stands in place of a husband.

Nikint meanwhile finds another forest sibling pair and lives with them. One day he goes to make a clearing for a forest garden, recapitulating the motif with which the story opens, but this time with his male associate, Kukl. The lost sister then reveals herself through the cassowary, coming close to the garden, and saying that her brother made her do what she is doing. That is, he left her behind and she was ambushed by the cassowary, so she has to eat its wild foods, not human ones. The two men now operate together as hunters to ambush the cassowary, just as it ambushed the sister earlier. Kukl pulls off some of its plumage, they rescue the sister, and take her home. A sister exchange ensues and an elementary society is set up, with a folkloristic flourish at the end: when they had sons they planted a casuarina and when they had daughters they planted a cordyline—both signs of reproduction, continuity, gardening, and attachment to place (Stewart and Strathern 2001d; Strathern and Stewart 2001). Each married couple lives virilocally, so sister and brother are separated in space but linked through their respective marriages. From now on they can visit freely.

The story includes the romance of seeking a wife away from home. But it points to the importance of sister to brother as well and implies that the sister exchange satisfies the wishes of both men and women. Nikint wrongly speaks cross words to his sister. He tries to make it up to her with food, taking on the work of both the female and the male in doing so. He shares his food with her. The cassowary further blocks the way for the completion of the male/female relationships, but the sister inside it guides it to the new forest garden and calls out to her brother. This communication causes the brother grief, but the grief also galvanizes the two men and they recover the sister, in a kind of rebirth, from the cassowary's body. The cassowary had tried to consume the sister and kill her reproductive future but through its actions it indirectly gives rise to a sister exchange. Having both male and female characteristics combined in one, the cassowary provides a good symbol for potential differentiation and the creation of a marital alliance from this process.

The next Hagen story mimics the plot sequence of a famous ballad from the Hagen area. It also includes the courting song ritual as part of the events it depicts.

5. The Story of the Young Woman Rangmba of the Place Ambra (Told by K-K. She heard it from her mother. Narrated on June 1, 1964.)

Ambra Rangmba was being courted by men who came to sing to her and to take part in the turning head ceremony. The man Krai of the place Miti said he would go to court her. His mother and father warned him not to go, because the place was one where their own kin had driven people out and killed them in warfare. But he insisted that he would go. So they cooked a pig and gave it to him and he carried it with him. As he drew near to the edge of a sweet potato garden, he met the young woman's mother. She said to him, "Where have you come from?" "I've come from Miti," he replied.

The mother carried the netbag of pork for him and they went on together to her house. Rangmba was busy turning head, but she took a walk outside and she saw Miti Krai arriving. She too went and asked him where he had come from and he told her he had come from Miti. So they turned head together until night fell.

Next morning Rangmba's mother said she was going to give her daughter to Miti Krai. The father, however, said no; but the mother insisted. The father repeated his refusal and beat the mother with a stick, but she still insisted and he still refused, so the young couple turned head again during the night and continued until daybreak. The next morning they gave the young woman to Miti Krai and cooked a pig. Night fell and they put the pork in the house and the two slept. Next morning the mother anointed the bride with cosmetic oil and the two of them carried the pork back to his home. Meeting his mother and father, Krai said, "I've courted Ambra Rangmba and brought her back with me."

His parents said, "Her people are those whom we killed and drove away in warfare, why have you brought her here? What has made you do this?" They divided up the pork and gave some to the people, then they cooked again their own portion and ate it. As they did so, Rangmba's former suitors burned down the house of her mother with the mother inside it. Rangmba was up on the Miti mountain and she looked over and saw the smoke coming up, and she said to Miti Krai, "Those men who turned head with me are burning to death my mother and father in their frustration. I'm going to see." Krai replied, "Let's go together tomorrow, first let's cook a pig together today."

So they prepared to cook a pig. The wife dug up yams and the husband harvested bananas. She peeled the bananas and he cut the firewood for heating the oven stones. They cooked the pig together and when it was in the oven they went down to a stream together to wash themselves. Coming back up from the water they opened up the oven. The wife took the chest flaps, the backbone, and the head, placed them in the netbag, and carried them. The man put the two sides of pork on his shoulder and carried them. They came to the banks of the Gumants River. Many people came with the news that Rangmba's parents had been burned to death. In her grief the wife tipped her netbag of pork into the river and went on without it, wailing. Her husband followed her, still carrying his pork. She went first, crying and wailing, and he followed. There were many mourners at the funeral place, and they received Rangmba into themselves. Her husband came behind, with his load of pork, and went to where his wife was crying and there they all stayed at the funeral.

The next day they cooked pigs, but Rangmba said she wanted to take her own pigs back with her alive. Her husband suggested they cook them there, but she insisted that she would take them with her, so he agreed. They took them off and on the way it grew dark at Kraldung. They realized they could not carry on with all their pigs. The husband told his wife to light a fire and stay in a house while he himself visited the house of an old woman nearby. "Where have you come from?" she asked. She gave him some cooked sweet potatoes that she had, some ripe bananas, and a bunch of cooking bananas, and he took them back to his wife and they ate them together. The old woman then came and asked them for some money in return for the food she had given them. The man said he had not brought any money, but he could get some from his home and give it to her later. She said no to this, so they gave her a piglet from those they had brought with them. So the two of them slept there, and the next morning they carried on their way.

While they were going through the forest Miti Krai caught a marsupial. Ambra Rangmba said to him, "You've been favored by the little spirits of luck [*kor kil köi*], I see, to have shot a marsupial where people go about." She had worn a towel on her head and he wrapped his catch in this and they brought it home. Some of his people had come to meet them on the pathway and they all took the pigs back together. They cooked the marsupial and left it in the oven. His people said, "They have anointed a woman, the one he got by turning head with her, and they've brought her here." Then they opened up the earth-oven and took out the marsupial and gave part of it to the woman's kin. So they slept.

Next morning they said, "Let us give the pigs and shells for the woman." They put red ocher on the shells and attached ropes to the legs of the pigs and prepared them for the woman's kin. Her relatives took these off. The next day the groom's kin killed some pigs and cooked them. Then they slept, and the following morning they took the pork over to the young woman's home place. They shared it with the bride's kin, and part of it they ate themselves. Then as it was dark they slept. Her kin gave them gourds of pig grease and some female pigs and they took them home. So the man's kin had cooked the "pigs of the house" and taken them over to the bride's place and returned home, and it was over.

Commentary: This narrative follows a part of the balladic sequence with the same protagonists, Ambra Rangmba (or Rangkopa) and Miti Krai (or Weipa) (see Strathern and Stewart 1997a). This is perhaps the most well known of the ballad themes in Hagen. The two chief personae are the prototypes of couples who marry out of their own personal preferences, against the odds, and pay a price for doing so.

Ambra and Miti are two actual places, separated by a stretch of swamp, grassland, and rolling plains in the Central Hagen area. Ambra is a hill that projects sharply out of the swampy plains around it. The narrative does not tell us which named groups are involved, but Miti is a mountain pass to the northwest of Ambra, belonging to a range of hills occupied by the populous Minembi tribe. The various clans of the Minembi maintained hostile relations with groups to their south, a circumstance that fits with the sequence in the narrative in which Miti Krai's parents tell him he must not go to woo Rangmba because she is from a hostile area. Courting parties depended on amity or alliance between groups. Krai takes a big risk for the sake of his personal wishes and sets up the possibility of danger for himself and others.

The narrator's version of this theme stresses the agency of both Rangmba and her mother. The mother shows her liking for Krai by offering to carry his netbag of pork, which he has brought as a gift for his visit, when she meets him at the edge of her settlement. It is she who supports his case, against the initial wishes of the father, who may be supposed to have favored a suitor from his own *moka* exchange partners. And the mother prevails, in spite of the fact that her husband tries beating her with a stick to get his way.

The narrative suggests that the courting took place partly in the daytime, but could also happen at night. This is interesting because in historically recorded times the courting dance always takes place only at nighttime, not by day. Vicedom and Tischner, however, as we have noted earlier, record a fragment of information suggesting that in the past matters were different and couples could meet in the daytime by riverbanks to court, sitting on mats (Vicedom and Tischner 1943–48: vol. 2). Balladic and folk tale themes do seem to encapsulate glimpses of earlier times and archaic expressions, and it is partly this that makes them interesting to listeners.

Having boldly made her choice, Rangmba soon realizes the price to be paid for it. The angry and disappointed suitors shift from alliance with her family to hostility and burn her parents to death. This detail dramatizes and intensifies the experience in life by which the failure to win a bride or the breaking off of a marriage by a woman's father invariably results in resentments and angry attempts at revenge, or at least a refusal to remain on speaking terms. Stereotypically in these matters a girl is said to be "greased," that is, persuaded, by her mother; but responsibility is often attributed to the father, since it is he who has to put together the wealth items needed to repay a brideprice and so effect his daughter's divorce from her husband if that subsequently occurs. The mother's action in these instances is described as *kunt rurum*, "she secretly persuaded her"; of the father it is said *"mboklam möngköröm,"* "he took back his daughter," with the implicit idea that the intention was to give her in marriage to another man and get a new brideprice payment for her.

Here in the narrative we see the attempts of parents to influence their offspring's decisions and the mixed results of these efforts. Krai goes against both of his parents in order to court Rangmba. His name, incidentally, suggests how he succeeded: it means "love magic," the magic that is manifested by the light that glows from fireflies in the night and can sometimes be seen on hillsides from a distance. He is the magical lover from the magic mountain of Miti. Rangmba's name means "she/he will pluck/harvest," perhaps also encoding a sense of her strong agency.

The narrative punctuates people's actions with the obligatory cooking of pigs and the standard tableaus of the sexually defined labor that goes with these cookings and the customary division of parts of meat between spouses. Krai and Rangmba have to take pork to the funeral just as Krai had to take a netbag of pork to the courting dance. Finding out about the death of her parents, Rangmba tips her pork out in grief, while Krai must follow behind her, still carrying his own load. Apparently the suitors are content with their revenge, since the two are not molested at the funeral and Rangmba also succeeds in getting some of her own pigs to take back with her.

Up to the point where the suitors burn Rangmba's parents to death, this version of the story follows the balladic theme of retribution closely. From the funeral onward, however, the narrator switches to depicting the actual brideprice and exchanges between the kin of Krai and Rangmba; and here she also introduces a few improvisations and modern elements of her own. Krai and Rangmba are bringing back her pigs and they find a place to stay overnight, at Kraldung. Kraldung is also an actual place, within the territory of the Minembi tribe, in the flatlands or foothills south of the Miti mountain, so this means they are back in an area that is safe for Krai. He requests food from an old woman, presumably a relative, and later she comes and asks him for some money in return. The reference to money here is a contemporary twist in the story, showing how such elements infiltrate into narratives over time. It is interesting, because in the larger corpus of stories collected from both men and women in 1964 that we have analyzed, there were only a few mentions of new elements of this kind. Then, as the two progress on a forest pathway toward Miti, Krai shoots a marsupial and wraps it in the tradestore towel that Rangmba has been wearing over her head in place of the more traditional head covering, a netbag. By the 1960s young women were fond of buying towels in stores if they had money to do so, and the narrator, who was an unmarried girl, was perhaps thinking of Rangmba as someone like herself. In this way, with succeeding generations of narrators, the details of stories may be changed, while other aspects of these stories remain unaltered and can be compared in detail with versions collected both earlier and later.

The marsupial, which Rangmba takes as a mark of Krai's good luck and so as an omen for the success of their marriage and their relationship, is taken home and duly enters into the marriage exchanges. As a creature of the forest belonging to the Minembi, it is given to Rangmba's kin to eat. Marsupials, as we have seen, are said to be "the pigs of the Sky people" who control game in the high forest. The narrator seems to have improvised this element, but it is thoroughly in keeping with the overall framework of the story.

The story is then finished quickly with an account of the exchanges of wealth at the marriage itself. Though Rangmba's parents are dead, her kin in the wider sense are alive, and they come to receive the public payment for her (known as the *penal*, the wealth given at the ceremonial place), followed by the *mangal*, cooked pork, which the groom's kin take to the bride's people, who give her in return flasks of oil and breeding pigs to set her up as a producer of wealth in her husband's place. So the narrative ends quietly, descending into the customary and the everyday. The narrator truncates the retributive structure of the balladic version, to which we will turn in the next chapter.

CONCLUSION

In this chapter we have ranged over a number of themes from a limited set of ethnographic areas in the Highlands. We have cited the Kewa materials from John LeRoy's study because they show strikingly two mythic themes that are brought together in ritual practices and in everyday life: the theme of the Sky Wife and her association with wealth and fertility, and the theme of the interplay between cross-sex sibling and spousal relationships. The Kewa stories we have used here point strongly to a potential opposition between wife and sister. The Sky Wife herself represents a kind of mediation of this opposition because she incorporates both sisterly and wifely attributes in herself. This pattern is quite similar to that found in the Hagen Female Spirit cult.

The Hagen stories we have drawn on further show the interdigitation or interweaving of human concerns with spirit agencies. The stories imply a background awareness of spirit powers, seen via the actions of beings such as Ndepana Nikint, who instantiates both the magical powers of the forest and the sky and at the same time the human circumstances of men in relation to their sisters and their search for spouses.

Taken as a whole, these stories show a number of themes that are best seen as overlapping rather than exactly isomorphic across the different areas. One theme is that of the broken promise: if the human husband breaks his promise to his Sky Wife, disaster will occur and wealth and fertility will be lost. This theme appears strongly among the Duna and the Kewa. In the Kewa case it is intertwined with the theme of the sister's jealousy (sometimes this also appears as a co-wife's jealousy), resulting again in disaster. Some of the Hagen narratives mediate this problem by showing how the wishes of both brother and sister can be attained through a marriage exchange. In Hagen the broken promise theme therefore does not emerge so sharply; but in its place we find the third theme, angry words, in which someone speaks crossly to kin, for example a mother's brother to a sister's son. Disaster, again, or near disaster, results from this. This theme, especially stressed in Hagen, ties in with the Duna broken promise theme, since in the Duna stories the human husband promises not to speak cross or harsh words to his spirit wife. When he does so, she turns into a wild pandanus nut tree, and he in grief changes into a bird (Stewart and Strathern 2001a: 73–74). All three themes—the broken promise, the sister's jealousy, and the angry words—not only structure the mythical domain and its reflections in ritual but also belong vitally to the emotional world of social life today, just as much as in the seemingly timeless mirror of the narratives themselves. The themes present themselves as admonitions of a moral sort as well as artifacts of the aesthetic imagination set into the compass of the forest, the sky, and the land.

Comparing further the themes found in courting songs from Hagen with those displayed in folk tales and myth, we find that the songs tend to have individual expressions of desire at their center; desire constrained by social norms and set into a network of kin relations, but desire nevertheless. The emotion of *kond*, which predominates in the songs, reveals a certain balance of sensibilities, the wish for an ideal outcome combined with a regret that it may not be possible. The folk tales implicitly depend on this same emotion of *kond*, but also display ways in which it is denied or broken, as well as depicting people tied into elementary forms of social relations. Significantly, in the context of courting, it is the nexus of sister-brother-wife relations that is often brought into play. The ideal picture of the wife seems to combine elements of sister and spouse together in the image of the Sky Woman, who is also the prototype for the Female Spirit herself. But attainment of the ideal is often ruptured by jealousy and deceit or disobedience, by the breaking of promises and the uttering of harsh words. The folk tales show accurately how human conduct may conflict with human ideals and despoil them. Motifs of this kind are portrayed vividly in the ballads. Moreover, the idea of retributive action hangs over the drama of the folk tales from different areas, like a cloud ready to descend swiftly from hilltops.

The category of *kang* (folk tales) in Hagen also bridges over to that of the ballads, as we have seen in the last example given here, and which lead us to the next chapter.

Photo 1. Young male participant at a dance in 1967 held on the occasion of a pig-killing festival. He wears a large convex baler shell over his chest and a small baler piece at his forehead. On his left shoulder a netbag is suspended, inlaid with marsupial fur. His feather decorations include a Superb Bird of Paradise crest pinned to his wig, and banks of eagle, cockatoo, and Raggiana plumes. A pandanus strip nicked in a chevron pattern winds around his wig and similarly cut cockatoo feathers protrude from his ears. (Pangia) [Photo from the Stewart/Strathern Photographic Archive]

Photo 2. A line of men march into the ceremonial ground of a host group at a pig-killing festival in 1967. They wear baler shells at the chest and nassa headbands at their foreheads with waving tips of plumes pinned to their wigs. They carry bows, arrows, and axes as a mark of a potentially hostile relationship with their hosts, with whom they nevertheless are likely to be intermarried, since it is marriage ties that largely influence to whom pork is given at these events. (Pangia) [Photo from the Stewart/Strathern Photographic Archive]

Photo 3. Unmarried girl dressed for a dance in which she will link arms with youths and men at Aluni in 1991. She has a brown cassowary headdress and her front is covered by a tightly made netbag with an apron of dried reeds below. Other girls stand prepared for the dance beside her. (Duna) [Photo from the Stewart/Strathern Photographic Archive]

Photo 4. Two young unmarried women flank a man at a dance in Aluni in 1991. The man fingers the skin of his short hourglass drum in anticipation of the fast rhythm he will shortly beat out on it. One young woman wears a tee-shirt, another a draped netbag at her front. The atmosphere is formal, but the occasion is also one of courting behavior. (Duna) [Photo from the Stewart/Strathern Photographic Archive]

Photo 5. Female Spirit cult dance, 1964, among the Ukini Oyambo people. The two leading dancers hold up a set of three large and highly valued pearlshells mounted on resin boards, as marks of the Spirit. Their white Lesser bird of paradise plumes and their whitened headnets also mark the presence of the spirit in their dance. They are practicing inside the cult enclosure for their later emergence into public view. (Hagen) [Photo from the Stewart/Strathern Photographic Archive]

Photo 6. Back view of women dancers, lavishly decorated and in procession at the climactic celebration of the Male Spirit cult (*Kor Wöp*) performance in the Nebilyer Valley among the Epokla Elya people in 1965. Tall head-dresses of Harpyopsis eagle and Raggiana bird of paradise feathers top their costume. Green snail shells hang from their hair, large pearlshells mounted on resin boards covered with red ocher cover their shoulders, and everted pearlshells rest on their crimped red cordyline bustles. As they march they shake seed rattles that provide a swishing sound. (Hagen) [Photo from the Stewart/Strathern Photographic Archive]

Photo 7. Girls and women at the ceremonial ground Maninge among the Kawelka people in 1971, on the occasion of an internal *moka* prestation between two clans. The girl in the center is decorated informally as a spectator at the dance, with neck beads, trade cloth, face paint, and a towel along with her netbag over her head. She has an array of keys at her neck and she holds the tip of a stake set up for tethering a pig that is to be given away on the occasion. (Hagen) [Photo from the Stewart/Strathern Photographic Archive]

Photo 8. Women crowd in to watch a line of male dancers at a *moka* occasion among the Kope people in 1974. Two of them wear capacious decorated netbags, a form of women's wealth, at their backs, while one has draped her head with a large tradestore towel. All wear brightly patterned cloths. The dancers' profuse headdresses of eagle feathers and Raggiana, Lesser, and Sickelbill bird of paradise plumes can be seen over the spectators' heads. Such dances are displays equally of wealth and of powers of attractiveness, seen as related attributes. (Hagen) [Photo from the Stewart/Strathern Photographic Archive]

Photo 9. Young girls dressed for the *mölya*, a playful courting dance, on the occasion of a *moka* in 1971 among the Minembi Yelipi people. They have multiple rows of beads, marsupial fur headbands, plumes, and crimped red cordyline front coverings tucked into belts woven from fiber and beads. (Hagen) [Photo from the Stewart/Strathern Photographic Archive]

Photo 10. Young woman lavishly decorated for the *mölya* dance among the Minembi Yelipi in 1971. She has plastic bangles and bead armbands, chevron face-painting, and decorative leaves in addition to her headdress and shell ornaments. Crimped cordylines are tucked into her woven belts and her skin is oiled to make it shine. (Hagen) [Photo from the Stewart/Strathern Photographic Archive]

Photo 11. Close-up of a man beating his drum at a *moka* among the Minembi Yelipi people in 1971. Above his horned human-hair wig he wears a *köi wal*, a plaque of variegated bird plumes, indicating his status as donor in the *moka*. He has a Superb ruff at the front of his wig to which a piece of baler shell is pinned and a conus shell in his nose with crest plumes of the King of Saxony bird. (Hagen) [Photo from the Stewart/Strathern Photographic Archive]

Photo 12. A *moka* among the Tipuka people in 1974. A man, his long front apron kilted up with a fiber string, displays a set of currency notes neatly arranged on a backing of coffee-tree leaves, to be given away on the occasion. The notes have the Queen's head still depicted on them, since Papua New Guinea's new currency, the Kina, replacing Australian dollars, was introduced only in 1975. Previously, pearlshells were given in *moka*, but by this time they had been replaced by state currency. The display is reminiscent of those used for brideprice occasions in the Wahgi Valley east of the Tipuka. (Hagen) [Photo from the Stewart/Strathern Photographic Archive]

Photo 13. A woman with towering eagle-feather headdress beats on her vertically held hourglass drum at a *moka* among the Tipuka people in 1974. She leads a procession of women dancers performing *werl*, the married women's dance. Both of the two leaders have numerous swathes of tradestore beads around their necks and large baler shells at front. These dancers demonstrate the potency of women in raising pigs for the *moka*. Cassowary pinions are inserted in their nasal septa. (Hagen) [Photo from the Stewart/ Strathern Photographic Archive]

Photo 14. Two young men with elegant horned wigs and Lesser bird of paradise plumes perform at a dance held in honor of the acquisition of a coffee plantation from its former Australian owners by the Dei Local Government Council at Tiki in 1974. The performers come from the groups on whose land the plantation had been established. One man beats an hourglass drum, held horizontally. White face-paint surrounds their eyes while the rest of their faces and beards are heavily charcoaled. They wear long netted front aprons with fur insets, made for them with great care by their female relatives. (Hagen) [Photo from the Stewart/Strathern Photographic Archive]

Photo 15. Tall dancers lead a processional held to celebrate a plantation takeover by the Pipilika Business Group in 1975 at Wurup. One wears a towering headdress of eagle feathers and a long tail of the tree-kangaroo (*kui mokelip*) at his front. The two lead dancers wear conus shells in their noses and hold long spears. This kind of ceremonial recognition of new kinds of business enterprise was popular in the years around Papua New Guinea's acquisition of independence in 1975. An asbestos and tin-roofed building stands at the rear. (Hagen) [Photo from the Stewart/Strathern Photographic Archive]

Photo 16. Dancers from the mid-Wahgi area perform at a celebration for the inauguration of a Lutheran church at the mission-station Ogelbeng north of Mount Hagen township in 1964. These Wahgi men do not wear the large horned wigs characteristic of their western neighbors, the Hagen people. Their forehead bands of nassa shell and green scarab beetles in yellow orchid fibers are topped by fringes of red parrot feathers, with bird of paradise plumes towering above them. They have green snail fragments at their waists to produce a clinking sound along with the beat of their hourglass drums. [Photo from the Stewart/Strathern Photographic Archive]

Chapter 5

Ballads

In this chapter we look at the expressive form of ballads, which have, in addition to enormous artistic appeal, much to say through epic narration about life and love. Long ballads that are performed by popular experts, famed for their detailed descriptive accounts, are found in only a few of the Highlands areas of New Guinea (Strathern and Stewart 1997a, 2000f). They are also known in coastal areas such as the Trobriands and they may be or have been more common than has been recognized.[1] They bring myth, aspects of daily life, and ritual practice vividly alive in the listener's imagination. The plots of these epic tales express the agency of the protagonists, their kin, and spirit beings, and they convey sets of moral messages and commentaries about the vicissitudes of life in the sphere of courtship and marriage. They do so by highly dramatized portrayals of experience in which structures and feelings merge together to produce narrative emplotment. This form of expression has been little studied by ethnographers for its potential contribution to the understanding of sensibilities in the Highlands.

These ballads are relatively lengthy pieces of performance art that are highly esteemed traditionally in the cultures where they are found and are comparable in many ways with oral epic traditions found in the Greek and Balkan areas, as far as in their modes of construction and expressive presentation (Lord 1991). These Highland ballads are significant art forms worthy of study in their own terms. They are a rich source of statements on romantic and/or tragic themes that provide insightful materials on past conditions of society, changing forms of poetic composition, and diverse matters of revenge, love, leadership, and local custom.

We have extensive materials on the little-studied balladic forms known as *kang rom* from the Hagen area of the Western Highlands of PNG and *pikono* from the Duna area. In this chapter we provide excerpts from translations of these ballad forms and summaries of their plots in order to show the development of sensibilities in the two areas. Some of the *pikono* materials are excerpted from all-night performances that are too long to present in their entirety here (Strathern and Stewart n.d.). One can think of these as the *Das Rheingold* of the Duna, sung by a single person who is the narrator of the entire action.

These balladic materials represent an untapped resource for interpreting Highlands cultural themes. In the Hagen *kang rom* the stress is on overcoming distance, the desirability and danger of marrying at a distance, the perils of travel, the uncertain nature of sexual partners, and the nemesis of jealousies resulting from exchange ties that impinge on individual preferences in selecting marriage partners. In the Duna *pikono* the stress, instead, is generally on the alliance between a young male protagonist, who is just learning about life and love, and the Female Spirit, the Payame Ima, who educates him in the ways of human existence and who guides him along the difficult and perilous path toward finding a suitable wife. The Duna emphasis here is in line with the importance of Payame Ima generally, as chapter 7 explores further.

HAGEN: KANG ROM

The Melpa ballads are called *kang rom*, "loud stories" or "stories of praise." *Rom* is a form found also in the expression *ka rom*, "a loud crying or wailing," and *rom rondopa ni*, "to sing a song that marks someone out." It may be cognate with the verb *rui*, "to strike." *Kang rom* are sung by specialists who expect payment for their efforts. Traditionally they would be chanted in a men's or women's house. Both women and men had the knowledge and opportunity to produce ballads. Great care is taken in the intervals of breathing, much as the musical expression in an operatic aria is firmly controlled in order to produce heightened emotional responses in the listener.

Balladic performance was a prime form of entertainment in the past among Melpa speakers. The stories were constructed around a limited set of plots that frequently involved a female and male and their story of courtship, which had favorable or unfavorable consequences for both them and their kinsfolk. These Melpa ballads are a particular genre that exists among the roster of sung genres, for example, courting songs (*amb kenan*) (see chapters 2 and 3 on this form), songs for ceremonial dances (*kenan, mörl, werl, mölya, rom rondoromen*, etc.), and spoken folk tales (see chapter 4 on these). *Kang rom* are chanted in a highly characteristic, stylized, and regular manner in couplets that build into sets of four lines or more that serve as a mnemonic device, enabling the singer to proceed through the lines and build on them.

The themes of these ballads are reminiscent of first origin tales (see chapter 4; Stewart and Strathern 2001d). But in *kang rom* the protagonists are not seen necessarily as "first people": rather, they are portrayed in a sense as archetypes of human character. Individual agency and the consequences of actions are clearly portrayed in these stories—a feature shared with origin stories and courting songs. The various motifs and narrative elements in ballads are identical with those found in the spoken *kang*. It is their sung form and their elaborate poetic vocabulary that make them a distinctive genre, as the examples we give show.

PLOTS OF THREE KANG ROM BALLADS

1. The Story of Kuma Pököt and Kopon Morok

This is a tale of the "romance of exogamy" where Pököt goes in quest of a wife and experiences trials and tribulations in his journey.

Pököt, while at home, sees a column of smoke arising in the distance just at sunset. The smoke rises and mixes with the mists of the hills. Out of curiosity Pököt wants to see what the source of the smoke is. Before leaving on his journey he bathes himself, washing away his dirt, revealing his healthy, full brown skin. He shines brightly like a star, and he carefully decorates himself for the journey with a bark-belt fitted around his waist, cordyline leaves at his back, and a front apron. As he travels toward the column of smoke he sings to himself while crossing rivers and waterways, climbing mountains, and traversing barren plains. Finally he reaches a garden at Mukl Ropanda in the Jimi Valley where he finds a grand house. Here he sees two young women. The father of the two women appears and asks Pököt what he has come for. Pököt explains that he saw the column of smoke and was curious to see who lived there. The father takes Pököt into his grand house and feeds him fresh sugar cane and prepares a fine earth oven feast for him. Pököt spends the night in the house and in the morning declares that he is leaving. The father offers him many fine presents (money, fine shells, and cassowaries) as departing gifts but Pököt does not accept them. So the father presents one of his daughters to him. Pököt prepares a great feast for his new wife and her family. He again washes himself as he had at the beginning of his journey and sets off for his home with his wife at his side. When he arrives home (Mukl Dopaim) he asks his new wife to wait in his house while he goes to tell his kinsfolk to come and greet his bride. But shortly after he leaves her alone the suitors from her own village, who had followed closely behind during the return journey, approach her and in anger ask her why she has left to go to live elsewhere. They say to her, "Come on, let's go." The young bride does what she is asked to do by the suitors but before leaving she cuts off a lock of her hair, moistens it with her tears, and wraps it in a leaf, leaving it for Pököt. When Pököt returns to find his wife gone he becomes crazed and, believing he has nothing to live for, he hangs himself.

"Kuma" here refers to the Central Hagen area, and "Kopon" to the Northern area, including the Jimi Valley, a place of balladic magic and mystery.

2. The Story of Miti Weipa and Kundila Rangkopa

The plot of this ballad is a variant of the previous ballad (Kuma Pököt and Kopon Morok). In this story Weipa, like Pököt, goes in quest of a wife and the story proceeds in essentially the same way up to the point when Weipa leaves with his newly acquired wife to return to his home village.

As Weipa and his wife Rangkopa are traveling home they notice that in the direction from which they have come (Rangkopa's home) a great deal of smoke is rising. Rangkopa is worried that something may have happened in her village and she is concerned for her kinsfolk. Weipa says that he will go back to investigate. When he arrives, he finds that the suitors of Rangkopa, who were angry with her departure, had killed her parents and set the village on fire. Weipa takes revenge on the suitors but one of them succeeds in mortally wounding him with a spear. In concern for his new wife's well-being, Weipa sends his spirit back to her and shows her the way to travel to reach his village safely. Rangkopa is fooled by the appearance of Weipa and does not realize that he is dead and that only a spirit is guiding her. Rangkopa arrives safely at the village of her husband's people only to discover the body of her husband being carried in for burial. In her great grief she takes an axe and cuts off a finger and then another finger and yet another finger. She mourns for his passing for three days while his body is elevated on a funeral platform. Rangkopa stays with Weipa's kinsfolk for the rest of her life.

3. The Story of Miti Krai and Ambra Rangmba

Miti Krai sees a column of smoke in the distance at the Ambra sweet potato garden. He wants to investigate. His mother warns him of the potential dangers ahead of him while traveling to unknown regions. But he goes off, and at Ambra meets Rangmba, and he and she declare that they will always be together with each other as husband and wife. Just as Miti Krai and Rangmba are preparing to leave Ambra to return to Miti Krai's village where they will live, Rangmba transforms herself into an old, ugly female; but Miti Krai had promised always to be loyal to Rangmba, so he takes her on the long journey back home. Upon arrival at his home village his people are revolted by the old woman who is his wife since she is supposed to be a young bride able to work for many years and raise children. Miti Krai is scolded for bringing her home with him and his sister complains loudly and beats Rangmba severely. But Miti Krai takes Rangmba to his house and begins married life with her. One day a "big-man" dies and a funeral is prepared for him. Before attending the funeral Rangmba transforms herself again, this time into a handsome young man. At the funeral Miti Krai's sister, the one who had beaten Rangmba when she first came home with Miti Krai, sees the handsome youth who is really Rangmba in a transformed state, and she falls in love with the youth. Meanwhile, Miti Krai goes ahead and prepares a large bridewealth payment, having seen a speck of red ochre paint on Rangmba's eyelid as a mark of her former appearance. Rangmba eludes Miti Krai's sister and in secret transforms herself back into a young beautiful female—the one that Miti Krai had first seen and fallen in love with. The sister of Miti Krai who had treated Rangmba so badly was heartbroken and never recovered.

Kang rom text lines are highly ordered, with numerous repetitions. The lines tend to fall into couplets with counterbalancing or complementary pieces of information in them. Some lines from the beginning of a version of the Weipa and Rangkopa story (recited by Oke-Koropa in 1965) illustrate this pattern.

> Mukl Miti kang Weipa-e
> Mukl Miti okla murum-e
> Murum omba moklnga moklnga-e
> Pan kil kil int purum-e
> Ui kil kil yand urum-e
> Römndi rup kwun pitim-e
> Untinga nombokla oronga mba titim-e
> Kang mel e kit ni-e
> Murum mba moklp moklp-e
> Pela ming e leil pitim-e
> Tembakl koa leil pitim-e
> Kang mel e kit ni-e
> Tep alt ndurum köndöröm mel-e
> Mukl Kundila al kana-e
> Ndip ni wurlung nurum-e
> Ndip ni arlung nurum-e
> Ma ya amb nam-e
> Ta ya wö nam-e
> Al kona mukl ila-e
> Ndip ti nonom e ya-e
> Na mbo könimb mint-e
> Nimba kumb kelipa purum-e
> Ma ya amb nam-e
> Ta ya wö nam-e

Niminga nin ik-e-ya
Na ya pili napint-e
Al kona ndip nonom ila-e
Mbo kumb kelimb nitim-e
Kang mel e kit ni-e
Pöp kumb ya nitim-e
Pili kumb ya nitim-e
Köni kumb ya nitim-e
Kang mel e kit ni-e
Pen nimba pena purum-e

The translation follows:

Weipa, the boy of Miti mountain,
Was up at Miti his home.
As time went on and on,
The dry days passed away,
The wet days came back.
He stood as straight as an arrow
And walked on the old paths,
That daring youth.
As time went on and on
He played his bamboo flute,
He played his bamboo harp,
That daring youth.
Then, as he looked to the east
On Kundila mountain, see!
A fire burnt to the west,
A fire burnt to the east.
Oh who is my mother,
Oh who is my father?
On that eastern mountain
A fire is burning and
I must go now and see!
He said and finished his talk.
Oh who is my mother,
Oh who is my father?
Whatever it is you say,
I will not listen to you!
The fire that's burning there
I really must go and see!
That daring youth
Spoke his good words.
I want to learn, he said,
I want to see, he said,
That daring youth.
And out he rushed away . . .

The text goes on from this point to describe how Weipa kills and cooks a pig to take with him and then decorates himself for his courting activity.

He cut a *rukmömb* banana,
He gathered some *morok* greens,
He split the casuarina wood,
That daring boy.
He took it to the sacrifice house,
And went right inside
That thing you call the pig's rope,
He tugged firmly at it,
Out of a red, out of a black lake, as in the stories,
Calling, he took hold of it:
A red male pig,
Its big ears flapping,
A depression on its forehead where the club would strike,
Bristles standing up on its head.
Its belly hung down to the ground,
Its feet shook with its own weight.
He applied the pig's rope
To the front leg and
Took it right inside,
That daring boy.
See! right into the sacrifice house
He took it right inside,
Struck it with his club of *milik* wood
And its spirit went down to the banks of the Jimi River,
That daring boy.
Then he singed its hair, it was not like singeing, but more
As though he were clearing a field of tangled weeds.
That boy of Miti, Weipa,
He singed it and laid the skin bare,
And then as he listened, over there he heard
Two things fighting, like fists banging
Against each other, holding tight.
What are those two things? he thought.
One was the bamboo knife of Temboka, Mot,
The other the knife of Melpa, Wat,
Each saying he wanted to eat the pork.
Be quiet, Melpa Wat, he said,
and Temboka Mot came in.
He cut the pig from the tail to the head,
And laid bare the shoulderblade meat.
He cut it again from head to tail,
And pierced the opening to its bowels.
It was not like meat for eating,
It was plentiful as pebbles, on a river bank,

Plentiful as beech nuts that fall from trees.
Like a cluster of red cordyline leaves,
Like a bunch of red *yuimb* tree leaves,
That bold blood of the pig
He made into packs and strung them
Over the fire, as a great leader is lifted
Onto a platform at his funeral.
That daring boy
Said that it was good.
The big pieces of pork he placed in the oven,
Like *konda* bananas, buried to make them ripen,
The little pieces too he buried,
Like *konda* bananas to make them ripen.
Weipa, the boy of Miti hill.
He went down to the banks of the Jimi River,
That daring boy.
He rubbed and rubbed at his skin,
Until it was like the skin of a *mopa* banana.
He rubbed and rubbed at his skin,
Until it was like the skin of a *wenakla* banana.
The fat showed plentiful under his skin,
Even though his body was not so big,
That boy of Miti, Weipa,
And he pulled himself out of the water,
Saying that it was good.
At the entrance to his men's house.
He threw aside the wooden fastening slats,
Took a look about and entered,
That daring boy.
And people who were watching said,
"What is it he's about to get?"
He went for his pack of salt,
That stood up like the Tirikla hill.
He broke off a piece and took it.
And then he grasped a root of ginger,
Round like the head of the *rumbina* bird,
That daring boy.
He pinched off a leaf of *murip kopal*,
Saying that this was good,
That daring boy.
He pinched off a leaf of *woröu kopal*,
That daring boy,
The boy of Miti, Weipa.
When he blew the salt on the pork,
It was like a storm of rain and hail,
That daring boy.
The people on the far side of the Jimi River
Said it was a rainstorm blowing, and

Covered themselves with their pandanus mats
The people on the near side of the Jimi
Knew it was Weipa blowing his salt,
And came to get a lick at it.
Weipa, the boy of Miti hill
He cut and cut at his pork
See now! He gave to his mother and father,
Making a great heap for them,
And telling them to stay there and eat it.
Then, when he had finished,
He briskly entered his house,
He fastened his bark-belt tightly,
Inserted the cordyline sprigs at his back,
That daring boy.
Tight and dry as a rock cave, inside his belt,
The cordyline tops protruding out were like the legs of a wild pig,
And as he walked they swished like the wings of the *poklma* bird,
That daring boy.
The conus shell in his nose
Closed his mouth like the door of a house
    where people with leprosy live,
Like the disk of a full moon in the second month of *Ui*,
That daring boy.
See! How he wore his nassa shell bands
Strung round his cheeks like wraiths of smoke,
Like the fastenings on fences the Koka-Milika make,
That daring boy.
Weipa, the boy of Miti hill,
His headnet, inwoven with possum fur,
Was like a *kepa* marsupial and its young
Up on the fork of a forest beech,
Weipa, the boy of Miti hill.
That was how you might look at it.
His cassowary headdress
Was like the bloom of the *kengla* bush,
See! Riding high on his head, it was also
Like the great mound of an anthill.
Weipa, the boy of Miti hill,
Said that it was good.
He filled his *kupin* apron inside his belt,
Bright like the gushing water of the Wahgi River.
As he walked he dug up the ground
Like a wild pig rooting for tubers.
That daring boy.
The bright green-snail shell
Hung from his ear like a *nggoimnga* fruit,
Clinking at his cheek.
Weipa, the boy of Miti hill,

That daring boy.
His face was red as the cordyline,
That's planted to mark a boundary.
He said, "I'll stand," and he stood;
His skin was as bright as lightning.

Commentary: The elaborate vocabulary, full of precise and evocative images and explicitly fanciful similes, shows clearly enough in the translation. The pig Weipa kills is not just a pig: it is a prize specimen. The passage where he calls to it recalls the context of myths in which pigs were magically called out of a "red" (light-colored) or a "black" (dark-colored) lake. The pig itself is "red" and male. The red color is a mark that it will be dedicated in sacrifice to Sky Beings. Its male character makes it suitable for the comparison with a great leader (*wuö nuim*) placed on a funeral platform. In Hagen, when pork is prepared for the oven, it is customary to put small pieces of fat mixed with blood into long packets of leaves, then to roll these up, fasten them, and cook them above the wooden trestle on which cooking stones are heated for lining the oven. They are hung up in a way that the ballad compares with the placing of a dead leader on a *paka*, a funerary platform, for all to see. The valuable pig Weipa kills is thus further dignified by being compared with such a dead leader.

The interlude with the two types of bamboo knife may be compared with the description in the story given in chapter 4. Here the *mot* knife is described as being from the Nebilyer Valley (the narrator's group's place of origin), and it is the *wat* knife that is said to be from the Wahgi. The local knife is chosen.

In retiring to wash himself, Weipa is said to "go down to the banks of the Jimi River." Earlier in the narration, we are told that this is also where the sacrificed pig's spirit goes. The Jimi, lying to the north of the Hagen area proper, is one of the traditional places marking the boundaries between the living and the dead. Saying that Weipa goes down to this same place to decorate himself is at one level just a conventional form of expression (which was also preserved in the story given in chapter 4). At another level it points out that Weipa is about to engage in a dangerous expedition, which could, and in fact does, lead to his own death.

The epic proportions of his acts show in the idea that when he blew out a mixture of salt and chewed ginger as a condiment for the blood sausages of pork, the spray seemed to distant people (like those in the Jimi) to be a sign of a storm of hail and rain.

The description of his decorations is detailed, and includes a reference to a style of wearing single bands of nassa shells looped across the cheeks and attached to the nose flanges. This was not current fashion in the 1960s in Hagen, but was a marker of the past. The nassa bands on his face are likened to the bindings on fences made by a people who live in the rainy, mountainous Kaimbi area south of Hagen, known for the neat and secure fences they make, the Koka-Milika tribe. The conus shell is compared to both a full moon in one of the months traditionally enumerated in pairs by Hageners as the "elder and the junior" months (*komon akel rakl*), or the first and second months; and, a closed mouth, like the doorway of people who shut themselves firmly away because of their skin condition—of leprosy. Emphasis is placed on his shells and his feather headdress of cassowary plumes. His overall "red" color marks him out as filled with health and beauty but also as possibly in mortal danger.

When he leaves he tells his parents that if a "red" cloud comes up from the place he has gone to, it will mean he has been killed. A red cloud duly appears.

The parallel description of Rangkopa as she decorates herself for her marriage with Weipa, after declaring against all opposition that this is her personal will, is equally striking:

> She went down to the banks of the river Jimi,
> And washed her skin over and over again,
> Until the fat under her skin was glowing,
> Though her body itself was small.
> Her skin was like the *mopa* banana,
> Her skin was like the *wenakla* banana.
> She pushed away the dark color
> Like pebbles in the Nebilyer River,
> She brought back the light color
> Like pebbles in the Komon River.
> Her headnet she wore raised back from her face,
> And the bangles bit deeply into her arm
> The woman of Kundila, Rangkopa,
> To the right she wore the testicles of a pig
> The woman of Kundila, Rangkopa,
> To the left she wore the penis of a pig
> The woman of Kundila, Rangkopa,
> She wore a slim pearlshell at her breast
> The woman of Kundila, Rangkopa,
> She draped herself in long seed-necklaces
> The woman of Kundila, Rangkopa,
> Her cheeks sloped smoothly upward,
> Her cheeks sloped smoothly downward
> The woman of Kundila, Rangkopa,
> Her face was like an iris flower
> The woman of Kundila, Rangkopa,
> Her face was like a sweet flag flower,
> The woman of Kundila, Rangkopa,
> She said that it was good.

Her teeth were like those of girls who sit
In corners of fields with little cane-grass knives.
See how they can chew!
See how they can eat!
When she stood up her genitals were closed,
When she sat down her genitals were opened.
Her upper thigh was smooth as a shield's surface,
Her genitals as fine as the *ndan* tree's bark.
At her front she wore her apron,
Closed over her like dams on the river Nebilyer. . . .
She fastened her belt of *weang* cane until
It was tight on her bottom below it
As she stood up, see, see!
The belt slid loose and rode up.
The woman of Kundila, Rangkopa,
She was such a fine woman,
They touched her skin and tasted their fingers,
They touched her skin and smelled the aroma.
The woman of Kundila, Rangkopa,
She was there,
Her skin was as bright as lightning.

Commentary: Several phrases in this passage exactly repeat those describing Weipa, emphasizing the parallels. Rangkopa (or Rangmba in many versions) goes down to the banks of the Jimi as does Weipa. She, too, is at the edges of life and death. Both decorate themselves finely because their marriage may be the supreme moment in their lives; so finely indeed that it is almost as though their decoration was also to mark their death.

The difference between the descriptions lies in the stress on the physical, bodily attractiveness of Rangkopa, by comparison with the enumeration of the magnificent shell and feather decorations of Weipa. Both, however, are depicted as dazzling: their skins were as bright as lightning. Weipa's archaic style of wearing nassa bands looped on his cheeks is matched by Rangkopa's style of wearing pig's penises as bracelets on her forearms. Early pictures from Hagen confirm that this was indeed a practice in the 1930s.

Rangkopa, like Weipa, is a magical character, supremely full of vitality and a sense of herself. In another passage, the narrator describes how she smokes tobacco:

Rok nomba ol rurum e
Rok wakl prap-prap purum e

Where she smoked tobacco and spat,
Tobacco seedlings sprouted there.

Weipa takes it upon himself to avenge the death of Rangkopa's parents. This is a personal act, induced by his own sense of honor and his feelings for Rangkopa. He would not have been obliged by any rules of kinship or politics to undertake this. He girds himself for battle and goes.

Kundila okapona kota nile
Kang mel e kit ni ya
Woklöui mel nimbö kana
Piling ndopa ropa ropa kitim a
Kang mel e kit ni ya
Wuö nimbö ropa ropa kana
Ropa ropa kumndi mbö mundurum a

At the edge of the Kundila gardens
That daring boy
He took out his arrows
And shot them again and again, until he was satisfied,
That daring boy.
See! He shot and killed, he killed those men
He killed them and piled up their bodies in a great mound, like a mound of
   pork.

But in turn one of the enemy is aiming at Weipa himself:

Nanga wuö nimbö rokon ken a
Nimba pilpa kelpa a
Mbuna-nga karakl ti
Kang mel e warpa-nga nde nila
Pukl tepa moklpa kana
Mukl Miti kang Weipa
Mel ti mbur ndopa köndöröm
Aem mong kikoröm kana
Mukl Miti kang Weipa
Ile poklpa terakl nitim a

"You are killing all of my men,"
He said, and prepared his thoughts,
He drew out his piece of the black-palm tree
And tightened it on his *warpa* bow.
It pierced the nipple of Weipa's breast,
It pierced him straight and he fell back.

Weipa dies, and his ghost, still devoted to Rangkopa, comes to her in order to guide her back safely to his own place. It is a new way for her and she might stray from the path and get lost. She would not be safe at her natal home after the killings. Rangkopa thinks he is still alive, but is perplexed by his appearance:

> Niminga oron e mel a
> Köi kngal kiya na nonom e
> Kokla poke kiya na nonom e
> Nggraem kel kiya na nonom e
> Köng i öit kul kul oklna e
> Niminga köng i kandep nint e

> You do not come as you usually come,
> Your cassowary headdress does not shine,
> Your conus shell, it does not shine,
> Your forehead nassa band is dull,
> Your skin feels cold, so cold,
> What has happened to it, I say?

His ghost guides her on the way but as they reach his home his kin come bearing his dead body and she realizes the truth. Rangkopa is wild with grief and she cuts off three of her finger joints.

> Kundila amb Rangkopa ni ya
> Amb e ruk körkili nitim e
> Nanga wuö mon we ti ka
> Wuö-enga köng kandep ont ndi
> Wuö ndi rong kant e

> The woman of Kundila, Rangkopa,
> Threw herself down in grief.
> "My fine, my beautiful man,
> The man whose body I saw and came,
> I see they have killed him."

After the funeral, at which his body is raised on a platform for the mourning, as befitted his status (a motif that recapitulates the earlier death of the pig that he sacrificed), Rangkopa stays with his parents.

> Mukl Miti kang Weipa
> Ya koklpa elim purum e
> Kundila amb Rangkopa ni ya
> Mukl Miti kang Weipa-nga
> Tepam-na mam rakl-kin a
> Ile pek korong e

> So Weipa, the boy of Miti hill,
> Died and went upon his way.

The woman of Kundila, Rangkopa,
Stayed with the father and mother
Of Weipa, the boy of Miti hill,
Until they all died.

She remained faithful to his memory and stayed as a daughter-in-law with his parents and kin for the rest of her life.

Romantic ideals of this kind are of course not always realized in practice. *Kang rom* are forms of high art and as such they present idealized themes. We would not expect their themes to be literally played out in practice, any more than we would expect people's lives exactly to follow the sorrows of Orpheus and Eurydice or Dido and Aeneas. However, these chanted epics and the spoken folk tales on which they drew certainly influenced people's horizons of experience in the past. And they would not have appealed to their listeners, as they assuredly did, unless their themes were meaningful and expressed the inchoate wishes and desires of ordinary people, and in a general way their own lives also.

This can be said a fortiori of the Duna *pikono* traditions, since the *pikono* ballads formed, during the 1990s, a highly popular medium and nocturnal performances of them were frequently held at Hagu settlement in the Aluni Valley.

DUNA: *PIKONO*

Pikono is an art form that details in heroic mythical proportions practices such as the *palena anda* (boy's seclusion, growth house) (for further details of Duna ritual practices see Stewart and Strathern 2002; Strathern and Stewart 2000a). *Pikono* are sung by men and to men who gather at night in special men's houses to listen to the singing of a solitary performer, which lasts well into the morning hours (Strathern and Stewart 2000f). The journey of the ballad takes the listener across the landscape from the edges of the familiar to the depths of the underworld (on the significance of landscape to the Duna, see Stewart and Strathern 2000d). Local mountains, lakes, streams, rivers, and landmarks are named as the heroic figures move through the action of the story. A special stylized archaic form of the Duna language is used to enrich the performative aspects of presentation. This form of entertainment gives its listeners much pleasure because it is contextualized in the landscape of the day to day, which is transformed into the landscape of the extraordinary, and inhabited by powerful beings.

Duna *pikono*, like the Hagen *kang rom*, are based on stories that are also told as spoken folk tales, *hapiapo*, "stories of things that happened long ago." The recitations are long, taking place in communal houses or lean-to areas shared by men. The best narrators tend to be mature men who have plenty of knowledge of other aspects of cultural and political life. From time to time a youth may begin to try his hand at the genre, gaining experience as he goes. The audience encourages the narrator with expressions of interest, amazement, approval, and amusement. Old and young are equally engaged in the process of active audience participation. Although Duna women and girls are not formally supposed to be in the audience, they do know the *pikono* stories also and greatly enjoy hearing the songs being sung in the men's house as they listen from outside.

One of the experts at narrating *pikono* was Pake-Kombara, a senior man from the parish next to Hagu, Haiyuwi. Pake was able to summarize the plots of the *pikono* he knew, and he did so for us. Like the Hagen *kang* stories, Duna *hapiapo* and *pikono* often feature the activities of cannibal monsters of the forest, people who are not true humans (Stewart and Strathern 2000d). The *pikono*, however, often pit a human protagonist known as the *pikono nane*, "the balladic youth," against the cannibals, known as the *auwape*, interspersing the account of his struggles with these creatures with his adventures in search of a girl to marry.

The form of language used in *pikono*, like that in *kang rom*, is elevated.

The following excerpt will demonstrate something of the character of the poetic expression in these narratives.

> Yerepi range rakini yarita
> Ayu inu honda hongwa tata ruana
> Yerepi range rakini wa Kali
> Hu pakoru konarua rita
> Atili hu pakoru konarua rita
> Mali ra hu pakoru konarua rita
> E-e karo ko tinani
> Antia pi ame pi
> Ndu naraiya o
> Kulu kelo pi ndu naraiya o
> . . .
> Apima hu ya ulundu pakoru konarua rita
> Ateli huya ulundu pakoru konarua rita
> Akepi katani keto karoko ndolu pi
> Romokane pokoro mea ipa kaya hongi wangi
> . . .
> Kimatangata hongi rangi
> . . .
> Yakombata ngata hondita tale rane
>
> I sing of the man Yerepi Rangerakini,
> As we sit here and I tell you the story.
> Yerepi stayed at the place Kali,
> Where the water rushes and makes a noise.
> He stayed at the place Atili,
> Where the water rushes and makes a noise.

At the place Mali, where the water rushes,
There he stayed, he was an orphan,
No mother, no father,
No one to help him care for pigs or stake bananas. . . .
So he set out from the place Apima,
Where water rang loudly, from Ateli, from Akepi,
Where water rang loudly, he went up the hill,
In the dry season, when people searched for fish
In the shallow streams, beating the water with *mbata* sticks . . .

(Pake-Kombara Oct. 31, 1991)

A summary of the story in this *pikono* was given by its narrator, Pake: Yerepirangerakini and his younger brother Yerepindokope lived together. They were orphans, and without kin, since the *auwape* cannibals had killed their relatives. One day the weather was dry and the younger brother suggested they should hunt for marsupials in the forest. The elder brother said no, because the *auwape* might find them and kill them, and so they stayed at home.

Ipakurukuyako came to their settlement, and she stayed with them for two or three years. One day the elder brother left the house and went into the forest by himself. He found a rock shelter in which he might stay but there was smoke coming from it. What was it? A huge *auwape* man was there, sleeping, after he had prepared an earth oven.

Yerepirangerakini was big too, and they were both afraid of each other. They greeted each other politely enough, and Yerepirangerakini opened up the earth oven. He found that it contained human flesh, which the *auwape* offered to share with him. Yerepirangerakini tasted it and it was good, so they ate it together. The *auwape* told him to savor the flesh and not eat it too quickly. Then Yerepirangerakini drew his bow and tried to shoot the *auwape*, but he could not, and they now went together to find more victims.

They killed a man who was wearing cowrie shells and a pearlshell at his neck, and Yerepirangerakini took these and put them on, then they cooked the man together. Yerepirangerakini returned to the garden in his own settlement to get some sweet potatoes to eat, and he gave the shells to the woman Ipakurukuyako. She saw that the shells were ones that belonged to her brother and she cried because Yerepirangerakini had become a cannibal and had eaten her brother.

Ipakurukuyako and the younger brother went off to her own place, Pikonotindi. Meanwhile the *auwape* and his accomplice steam-cooked the meat from the man and ate him. Their bellies became large and their feet and hands became small because they had gorged themselves on the meat, and they could not walk but lay there as if dead. After a while Yerepirangerakini released his bowstring and used his bow as a stick to help him walk. He hobbled off and the *auwape* followed him. The two went to Yerepirangerakini's house, but they could find nothing, the house and garden were all gone. The younger brother had found the footprints of these two and had followed them, and taking the pinion of a cassowary he had planted it in their footprints, which had caused them both to be bloated and the settlement to disappear. But Yerepirangerakini found the pinion and pulled it out, so that the settlement reappeared. He then pushed the pinion into his own back so that the two of them recovered their proper form.

They killed a pig belonging to Yerepirangerakini and took it back to the *auwape*'s place. Many *auwape* were there, gathered beside a pool of water. At the *auwape*'s place, two of his many children said to their father, whose name was Kirapaiyeni, "Don't kill the human man, let him live with us instead." The father said, "All right, he eats with us, so I won't kill him." Kirapaiyeni then made a *yekea* (courting-house) feast and called to all the *auwape* to kill pigs for it. They cooked many pigs together, and in the afternoon held the courting occasion, singing loudly. Kirapaiyeni himself killed a huge pig and laid half of it aside.

Yerepirangerakini had heard that a big courting occasion was to be held in the area of the Huli people (south of the Duna) and he asked to take the big side of pork over there as a gift so that he could join it. When he arrived there he shook hands with the people and smiled, but he sensed that they were unfriendly. The people gave him shoulderblades of pork as a gift and two old men, Iruwangipa and Sapaisiapa, warned him that the men at the *yekea* planned to kill him later that night. Realizing his fate, Yerepirangerakini said that this was all right, because he himself had done wrong (i.e., eating human flesh). The families of the two old men stayed to look after him and just before daybreak the men came and shot him with arrows. He was full of these arrows, but early in the morning he stood up and asked who had done this. Then he shot fourteen men of a single group and finished them off. He went back to the *auwape*'s place and together with the cannibals there they defeated all the *pikono nane* (human youths or men, ordinarily the heroes in these narratives).

But the younger brother and the woman Ipakurukuyako stayed together, while Yerepirangerakini stayed with the *auwape* and married one of their daughters.

Commentary: This narrative reverses the more usual order of events in *pikono*, in which the *pikono nane*, the human youths who have become mature in the *palena* house, defeat the cannibal giants. The *pikono* narrators are free to vary their plots, since their purpose is not to articulate strict origin myths (*malu*) but simply to entertain their listeners while at the same time conveying "morality" tales of social interaction. In this regard they seem to exercise more license in fact than the singers of *kang rom* in Hagen did. This impression may, however, simply result from the fact that the art of singing *kang rom* has been on the decline in Hagen, whereas among the

Duna of the Aluni Valley *pikono* are popular and often are still performed. This probably has to do with the much greater degree of urbanization in Hagen by comparison with the relatively remote Aluni Valley.

This *pikono* downplays any element of a romantic search but it does carry a number of significant messages, the most important of which is that there is a clear divide between human (*pikono*) and cannibal giant (*auwape*) society. Persons, however, can choose to cross the divide as the elder brother did by agreeing to eat human flesh. Then they may get a taste for it and turn into cannibal hunters themselves.

At the beginning of the story the two brothers are presented as orphans. This is a classic motif, found also in Hagen *kang* stories, indicating that the subjects of the story are outside of society and have the potential to make good or bad choices in life for themselves, without mentors to guide them. They are in a liminal state, to use Victor Turner's terminology (Turner 1977). The story then plays on another classic motif (again, found in Hagen), the division between the elder brother and the younger brother. Here at first the elder brother assumes the socially responsible, quasi-parental role and warns his younger sibling not to go into the forest where the *auwape* live. But when the female figure who here stands for the Female Spirit, the Payame Ima, comes to be with them, after a while the roles change. (The woman's name means "she who dances at the water," a reference to the *Payame Ima*'s association with sacred lakes.)

Implicitly the Spirit has chosen the younger brother to be with her and has given him magical powers, shown by his ability to make the settlement disappear, a power that the Payame Ima herself was supposed to exercise if any of her rules were broken by the men she had been helping. The elder brother now goes out into the forest, meets an *auwape*, agrees to share in eating cooked human meat, and from that time on cannot succeed in killing his cannibal host. Nor can the cannibals undertake to kill him. Cannibal commensality has brought him across the threshold and into *auwape* society. His identity, however, is labile. Now he asks to join in a celebration among the humans of a neighboring language area, the Huli. Yet he has a kind of "mark of Cain" upon himself, which the humans recognize, and they plan to murder him. Showing the human side of his nature, he agrees that this is only right because he has broken the taboo against eating people.

He accepts a gift of pork from the humans. The fact that it is a shoulderblade indicates that it is one of the cuts regularly offered in cult sacrifices. Perhaps this marks him out also as destined to be "sacrificed" for what he has done. His *auwape* host is also called "shoulderblade of the Kira Cult" (*Kira Paiyeni*), perhaps indicating a symbolic shift in this cult from cannibalism to pig sacrifice.

But Yerepirangerakini's consumption of humans has also given him magical strength. He shakes out the arrows of his foes and slays them. His transformation is completed by his marriage to a cannibal girl.

The other side of the story is that the younger brother remains faithful to the Spirit Woman. She has taken him to *pikono tindi*, the land of the ballads. There he, too, lives an enchanted life with her. He becomes human while his brother becomes a cannibal, hunting humans to eat them. Thus, the story demonstrates the potential for humans to become like cannibal monsters or to adhere to "proper" human sociality. The two brothers stand here for two types of human characters.

The Spirit Woman recognizes that the elder brother has become a cannibal when she sees him wearing the ornaments of her own brother as a decoration. He attempts inappropriately to give them to her, causing her to cry bitterly for her brother, and to take the younger brother away. His actions are even more inappropriate because he in fact has joined with the murderers of his own parents, betraying his responsibility to take revenge on their behalf: the *auwape* has seduced him into changing his identity by offering him the forbidden meat. The overall message here is that if you eat with someone, you may become one of their group, so be careful about accepting offerings from those with whom you may not wish to be fully associated later on.

The story also underscores the ambiguity of hospitality. Yerepirangerakini goes out ostensibly to take an honorable revenge on the *auwape*, but he is offered hospitality and is seduced by it. Later on in the story, his Huli hosts also offer him hospitality with pork, but their intention is to "sacrifice" him. Hospitality and dangers of death or social transformation are mingled together.

Pake's *pikono* can be compared with one narrated by another acknowledged master artist in the Aluni Valley, Kiliya-Hipuya (July 10th, 1998).

Kiliya's *Pikono* Story

A man and his wife were living in the forest and an *auwape* came and killed them. Their son and daughter were left as orphans, and they worked together to make gardens and take care of the pigs. The daughter was the elder of the two and she cared for her younger brother as he grew up. There came a time of dry weather and the boy went into the high forest, where the wild pandanus nut trees grow, to hunt for marsupials, but he did not see any. Then he tried to find his way back home, but he got lost, and he came across an old garden site belonging to his father and used in the *palena* growth-rituals for boys. There was an old cult house there, and as it was nighttime he slept in it. In his dreams he learned things about the *palena*, for example, about the *manda kaluwa*, the special upturned wigs rubbed with red ocher that the *palena* initiates used to wear.

His sister waited for him at home but he did not come. She was anxious and began to cry, and she cut off a finger joint in her grief. She wondered if an *auwape* had killed him. "He was so small and I looked after him until he was big and now he is lost," she thought. Two or three years passed by as she waited there.

One day, a youth called Luya, who was the son of an *auwape*, came by and saw the sister and realized that she had no man with her. He decided to befriend her, so he came nearby and said that he was hungry and asked if she had any sweet potato. She said, "You look like a youth who's staying in the *palena* house, so you shouldn't be taking food from a girl like me." But he said it did not matter, he ate food like that anyway, so she gave him some and he ate it. From that time on they were friends. They lay together. When he left he said that she should stay in the house and he would keep coming back to see her.

Meanwhile her brother grew into a man, just like the *auwape* youth in appearance, and he too made his way back to see her. His appearance had changed, and when she saw him she thought that it was her lover who had come, so she called out to him, "Hello! Come over here and sleep with me now!" Her brother was upset. "What kind of talk is this?" he thought. "I am a *palena nane* (growth-house boy) and this is bad talk for me to hear." In his anger he shot her with an arrow and she died.

He buried her in the garden, thinking, "Something spoiled my sister's thoughts. She used not to speak like that." He killed a pig and cooked it in an earth oven. The sun went down and he slept, and in his dreams a woman came to him. She made a noise near the house and called out to him. Then he awoke and he saw that it was his sister's spirit (*tini*). She said to him, "I've come back. You killed me and I died but I've come back. The only reason I spoke to you the way I did was because I thought you were my lover. So now you've killed a pig and baked it but I didn't get any to eat. Give some to me now. There are many other ghosts that have come with me here and they're hungry too."

He put some pork in her netbag, and she ate it along with the other ghosts. Then she said, "We will go back now. We cannot stay here. To-morrow an *auwape*'s son will come to see me. Shoot him and kill him. We must go back now to the place of the dead. Take the other half of the pig and go up into the mountains where the wild nut pandanus tree grows. There you will see three *auwape* women who will try to befriend you. Go up there and cook the pig again where those three women will come. I am dead and must go now."

At dawn the *auwape* youth appeared and looked for the man's sister. He saw the new burial place in the garden, and wondered what had happened. Then he saw the woman's brother in the house. The brother said, "Hello. Have you just come?" Deceiving him, the *auwape* said, "Yes, I've not been here before. I don't know this place." The brother replied, "Wait, I'll throw you a burning stick so you can light some tobacco and smoke." But instead he strung his arrow and shot him dead. He threw the body into a deep limestone sinkhole.

Then he took the side of pork with him up into the wild pandanus nut forest and re-cooked it there by himself. He saw a nut tree there, which he thought was growing wild, so he cut a cluster of nuts from it and cooked them too. But as he did so he heard a cry from the treetop and a young woman came down, a fine-looking young woman, who said, "Who has cut my pandanus fruit?" "I did it," he replied. "I thought it was a wild one with no owner. I didn't see any signs of anyone having cleared the area at the base of the tree to mark it as theirs. She said, "Well, I planted it. Are you going to pay me for it?"

"I will, but I don't have any cowries to pay you with. I'll give you my armband and my cassowary feather headdress. You can take them and some-one will give you cowries for them."

"All right. I'll take these and I'll go. You and I are friends now. I slept and I had a dream. A fruit bat came to me and said that it was the sister of a boy down the hill and asked me to go and look after him. Now you stay here and look along the pathway. Three women will come and greet you as their in-law, saying two of them are to be married to you. This will be a trick. They are not true women but *auwape*, and they only want to kill and eat you. Don't sleep with them. If you do they will trick you and eat you. You can take them with you but have them sleep separately from you in the women's house. Here, I'll give you something to help you," she said, and gave him some feathers of the *urungauwe* parakeet. She added, "When you've killed the *auwape*, I'll give you something else [i.e., a wife]. When you go to their place and they try to kill you, put these feathers in your wig and fly away like a bird and then you'll come to the place where I am."

The *auwape* women came and stayed at his place. In a week they had finished up all of his food, and all the produce of his gardens, and then they asked to go. The next morning, refusing to let them go first, he led them up a stony hill and he saw that their eyes had become red and their finger-nails long and they wanted to eat him. Using his magic feathers he flew up to a treetop and when two of them came to get him the branches broke and they fell down on top of the third and they died.

The youth flew off to the place of the young woman. She was the Payame Ima. He landed there. She had his pigs and was looking after them for him. His pigs smelled him coming and broke their leg ropes to come running out and greet him. On the way he had met a girl who gave him directions and said she would befriend him later. He stayed in the settlement, taking the place of an old man's son, who had died. Girls fought over him at dances, including the one who had said she would befriend him. The old man had said he should go and kill in revenge the *auwape* who had killed his own son. This same girl helped him to accomplish this feat by changing his arrows into good ones. She knew the place of the *auwape* and helped him kill them off. The Payame Ima protected them. In fact, one of the *auwape* girls whose father was an *auwape* but whose mother was of the *pikono* side also helped him. So he married them both, and they went back to his place and had many children together there.

Commentary: The story presents us with an initial retributive structure, followed by the adventure against the *auwape*, also encompassed in a retributive schema or scenario (see Schieffelin 1976 on this concept). Into these sequences fit the striking interventions of the Payame Ima and the progression of the protagonist through his trials of outwitting the cannibal women and killing the cannibal men. At every stage the agency of women protects and guides the protagonist. There is a transition from his sister to the Payame Ima, who herself appears as an amalgam of a sister and a bride, and from the Payame Ima to the two young women who help the protagonist kill the cannibal men and who eventually marry him.

The first phase of the narrative portrays the magical growing up of the boy in the *palena* house of his father, which he finds in the forest. It also depicts the growing up of the sister; left by herself she becomes a woman and finds a lover, though she is careful to warn him against breaking any *palena* rules. If he were human, his actions would have constituted breaking these. And by befriending a human girl, he is attempting to cross the *auwape*/human boundary: a dangerous process. The sister seems to think that he is human and accepts his approach to her (thus she already mistakes an identity). Then follows a further sequence of mistaken identity (the *hamartia*, or error, in Aristotelian terms), recognition (*anagnorisis*), and role reversal (*peripeteia*):

1. The sister mistakes her brother for her lover.
2. After he kills her, they both recognize their errors.
3. The brother takes the place of his sister and kills the *auwape* rather than befriending him.

In her death, the sister acquires a special knowledge and realizes that Luya was an *auwape*. Just as the boy's dead father has been able to help him acquire *palena* knowledge in a dream, so the sister is able to appear to the youth in a dream and warn him of impending events. She does the same by entering into the Payame Ima's dreams and persuading her to help her brother, even though he has mistakenly killed her. The cannibal women are implicitly coming to avenge the death of the *auwape* lover, so the retribution scenario continues.

The Payame Ima is mistress over the domain of the wild, especially the wild pandanus nut trees. The presents the young man gives her include an armband, which is the kind of object a youth might give to a girl he is befriending. But she is more like his guardian spirit. The *urungauwe* bird is an instantiation of the spirit herself, so it is a part of herself that she gives him to assist him in escaping the cannibal women. These cannibal women's greed is akin to witchcraft: all-consuming, without any giving at all, a characteristic amusingly conveyed by the picture of them gobbling up all the garden produce of the young protagonist. They ask him also about his pigs, but the Payame Ima has taken them away to her own place and is keeping them there for him as the nucleus for his true brideprice payment. Her role throughout is to be the sisterly protector.

Just as the *auwape* boy tried to make himself humanlike by deceiving the sister into being his lover, so an *auwape* girl tricks her paternal kin by helping the human brother kill them. The *auwape* boy pays for his transgression, however, with his life; while the *auwape* girl is rewarded by marrying into her *pikono* side and becoming human. The *pikono* side thus prevails. And it is the Payame Ima who stands on that side against the *auwape*. Given that in the *palena* rituals, she was the patroness of the youths in the growth-house, her role in this *pikono* is remarkably consistent with her historically conceived role in the actual *palena* traditions. The *pikono* stories preserve this role and give it continued relevance, even though the actual rituals have not been practiced for many years. The *pikono* genre also reveals to us that the *palena* rituals had to do not only with the creation of handsome young men who were ready to be married, but also with the creation of human beings who were ready to fit into the acceptable social order, a process in which humanity and morality are defined as the antithesis of the greed of cannibalism and witchcraft. Since witchcraft is seen as a contemporary threat, protection by spirit beings such as the Payame Ima still serves as an important model of acceptable versus nonacceptable social actions. The protagonist also has to kill the "anti-human" side of the *auwape* in order to achieve his own maturity as a human being: a ritual killing that is a necessary precursor to his own entry into the world of marriage.

Both the Hagen *kang rom* and the Duna *pikono* combine together the themes of maturation/initiation and the perils and pleasures of courting and marriage. This combination of themes amounts to a set of orientations or overall sensibilities toward marriage itself and the reproduction of social relations through the regeneration of the emotions of desire and the frameworks of obligation. In the next chapter we look at some aspects of decorations in this same context.

NOTE

1. Epic ballads from the Trobriand islands have been translated and discussed by John Kasaipwalova and Ulli Beier (1978) and by Jerry Leach (1981). For the Highlands, Melpa and Duna ballads have been briefly described by us (see Strathern and Stewart 1997a, 2000f; Stewart and Strathern 2000d). Alan Rumsey has also done some analysis of Temboka ballads that he has collected in the Nebilyer Valley (2001). Also Huli *bí tè*, which are comparable to the Duna *pikono*, have been described by Jacqueline Pugh-Kitingan (1981).

Pugh-Kitingan (1981) points out that the Huli equivalent of *pikono*, *bí tè*, "are composed extemporaneously as make-believe stories akin to the fairy tales of the west." They are distinguished clearly from origin stories, she argues (even though one of her examples merges with an origin story [origin stories, *bi henene*, "true stories," are usually not sung melodically]). They are for entertainment, but they may also instruct. She adds: "Despite the encroachment of transistor radios due to the current tradestore boom in certain areas, *bí tè* continue to be one of the major forms of nightly fireside amusement." This is also true for the Duna area since radio transmission is weak, if audible at all, without shortwave receivers.

Huli *bí tè* are long "fireside" stories. They are melodic, with three main pitches, and their duration varies. Listeners interject "e" at the end of lines to show they are not asleep. This contextual feature is like that of the *pikono*.

In one story a brother and a sister live together. The brother goes to the Enga area and tells Kandime, his sister, to drink and eat in the ways he instructs her and to stay in her place. She disobeys him, and goes downhill, finds clay and paints her body, and discovers a parrot's egg, which she swallows. On return she gave birth to a boy who grew up quickly and was called Clay Ground Boy. When his uncle returned with salt packs and pigs, he made a bridge over the river for him and told his mother to tell him not to fall as he stood in its middle and shook it. But she did not call out to him and some parrots came and took him away. His arms turned into wings. He said, "Break off my wings and give them to mother." "Children and kin should not be taken for granted" is the moral of this story. The story here is reminiscent of a wide class of stories in which human beings turn into wild creatures as a result of blockages, difficulties, shortcomings, and problems in their human lives. Jacqueline Pugh-Kitingan, who has studied the Huli stories as melodic forms, argues that they are forms of prose expression that from time to time resolve into poetry. By this she means that the variable length of utterances resolves into more formulaic and stylized sequences that she calls poetry. The distinction is thus like a prose/verse distinction rather than a broader prose/poetry one as the expression "prose poem" shows, since poetry can be a state of the imagination rather than a form of words (cf. also "free verse" as an expression).

Pugh-Kitingan also comments interestingly on the content of *bí tè* stories. In one story a senior ritual bachelor tricks five young men in his charge and marries a woman who comes to their seclusion place. Pugh-Kitingan comments: "[W]hile such behaviour would be considered outrageous in everyday life, it is interesting story-telling material. *Bí tè* characters frequently fall in love, yet this is not openly discussed in Huli life" (p. 348). One can see the stories, therefore, as projective devices, and this helps to explain their popularity also.

She also notes that "characters frequently perform impossible feats." A woman swallows a parrot's egg in one gulp and becomes pregnant, for example.

Chapter 6

Body Decoration

The sensibilities, desires, and ideals associated with sexual display are expressed in body decorations as well as in song, folk tales, and balladic forms. This chapter looks at this aspect of body decoration for some of the Highlands cultures. The themes involved here have to do with colors (e.g., red and white), the movement of items (skirts, plumes), the significance of substances (e.g., tree oil, pig fat), dance steps (stomping, jumping), and the overall connections between wealth, health, and fertility discussed earlier and brought out clearly in the themes of folk tales and ballads. Plumes and feather assemblages are of obvious importance, as are symbolic associations with birds generally. These have been discussed in earlier works, so we will not duplicate their discussions here (see A. Strathern 1985; Sillitoe 1988; O'Hanlon 1989).

In both the historical and contemporary arenas what is at issue is the healthy, attractive body and its extensions. We will examine some of the phenomenology of this topic for the Hagen case, looking briefly also at the significance of the concept of *noman* or "mind" (see Stewart and Strathern 2001a: 113–38 for a more detailed discussion), and returning to the context of folk tales at the end of this chapter.

The decoration of the body is a means of communicating emotions and desires nonverbally (Sillitoe 1988; see also Stewart and Strathern 1999d). The human body can be a platform on which displays of morality, self-worth, ideals, and sexuality are played out in day-to-day living as well as the ritual and ceremonial context (see, for example, O'Hanlon 1989, 1993). Self-decoration can provoke language or eclipse it, determining what we think we know and what we feel is worth knowing about the person under the skin. Physical accessories may include colored pigments, items that express emotion through movement (e.g., skirts, plumes, netbags), substances that heighten the contours of musculature (e.g., oil, pig fat), shell valuables, beads, and other objects that carry "culturally" coded meanings.

The decoration of the body in New Guinea involves the use of various components of local flora and fauna (e.g., leaves, bark, moss, earth pigments, insects, snakeskin, animal fur, bird plumes, bones, tusks, and varieties of shells) as well as items (e.g., tree oil to make the skin glisten) obtained through trading partners from other areas (Strathern and Stewart 1999c, 2000b). Many meanings can be encoded into the decorated body: messages about ghosts and spirits, bodily attractiveness, social power and status, the roles of women and men, group membership, alliances, hostilities, and the progression of initiates from one stage of existence to another, including the movement from life to death. The Hagen people say that one cannot know what is in another person's mind. But they say that people's minds are socially revealed by the beauty of the decorations they wear for ceremonial dances. Their ways of interpreting what they see in these bright decorations worn on the body and in the condition of the human body itself are aptly summed up in Michael O'Hanlon's memorable title of his classic study on the Wahgi people, eastern neighbors of the Hageners: *Reading the Skin* (O'Hanlon 1989).

Wealth items, which may also be used to decorate the body (e.g., pearl-shells and cowrie shells), were deeply involved in life-cycle rituals marking birth, weaning, adolescence, marriage, maturity, old age, and death. These rituals wove people and their places together in a tapestry of kinship and marriage, seen as a product of the flow of life-giving and life-enhancing substances. Wealth items themselves, such as shells that could be worn as decoration, were seen as equivalents of these flows of substance through channels of kinship, explaining their prominence in life-cycle exchanges.

Part of the stress on personal decoration and display that is found in Highlands societies is linked to contexts of exchange occasions and other celebrations as previously noted. Body decoration was used to impress spectators at festivals. Wealth items worn on the body reflected aspects of the person and the networks of trading influence through which wealth items could be obtained. Some of the most elaborate body decoration was found in the central Highlands valleys of PNG, where wealthy groups invested much effort into obtaining feathers, plumes, and shells from trading partners in the less heavily populated areas to their north and south where the marsupials and birds were found in greater abundance (Healey 1990).

The stones used in rituals were decorated as well as the people who danced for the spirits (Stewart and Strathern 1999c). Nowadays most of the rituals and festivals for which people once decorated themselves are gone, but people still decorate and dance for cultural shows and on some other occasions (e.g., national Independence day celebrations). Particular parts of the body carry a weight of symbolic meanings. One of these parts is head hair.

HAIR

One main purpose of initiation rites and puberty rituals in the Highlands was to enhance the beauty and attractiveness of those who took part in them, including, especially, their hair.

In the precolonial past boys in the Duna area (Southern Highlands, PNG) would be prepared for adult life by entering the *palena anda* (boy's growth-houses) (see chapter 7). During their time in seclusion they would be taught how to make their bodies strong and beautiful with a healthy skin. This knowledge was bestowed upon an adult male bachelor who had been chosen as a "husband" by the powerful Female Spirit, Payame Ima (see chapters 5 and 7). This adult male would then teach the boys in the *palena anda* (Strathern and Stewart 2000a: 79–99).

A particular focus of attention for the *palena* boys was their hair. Spells to make the boys' hair grow long and strong would be chanted by the bachelor ritual expert as he combed out their hair. The Payame Ima was said to have provided these spells (*mini mindi kao*) to the ritual expert.

An example of these spells follows:

> Be straight! Rub it with fat
> Rub it with fat
> The Payame Ima does it this way,
> Take it and pull at it now!
> Hold it and pull
> Hold it and pull
> Tip water from the bamboo on the hair
> Tip it up
> Pull the hair
> Pull the hair
> Pull it now.
>
> (Strathern and Stewart 1999e)

Also seen here is the significance of hair in sensibilities of sexuality (cf. Leach 1954), in addition to the connection of head hair with the head itself and the substance of the head. For the Kwoma of the East Sepik Province (PNG), the head is identified in a number of contexts with fertility and masculine sexuality (Bowden 1984), as it is also among the Huli of the Southern Highlands (Glasse 1968). And for the Hagen people *peng konya* (head substance) is linked directly to the spinal fluid and reproductive fluids (Stewart and Strathern 2001a). Likewise, for the Etoro people of the Strickland-Bosavi region the male fluids ingested by youths during initiation ceremonies are said to alter the minds of the recipients by transmitting personal capabilities derived from the donors (Kelly 1976: 45–53). A part, assuredly, of these capabilities has to do with physical maturation itself.

The connections of sexuality and fertility with the head and head hair are quite marked throughout New Guinea. Strauss and Tischner (1962: chap. 48) explain that in the Hagen area boys had their hair bound into a barkcloth hat when they reached the age of ten to fourteen. This would be done only after the hair had grown well and thick and strong. Thus, the boys would be concerned about the condition of their hair (*peng ndi*). The head hair is seen as a seat of power. "The hair is of the utmost importance, for it is the delicate web which constitutes the individual's relationship with the spirits. This is why the Mbowamb [Hageners] are particularly concerned about their hair. Cutting off a man's hair is the equivalent of cutting off his link with the spirits" (p. 321). Funeral feasts in which pigs are cooked for the spirit of a dead person are called *peng ndi kng*, "the pigs for the head hair." In this instance the reference is to the return of the person and the vitality of the person's hair to the realm of the dead.

Like specific forms of initiation ceremonies, the time when the barkcloth head covering was put on was a time when a boy was given advice on how to begin assuming the role of an adult male, including the presentation of a bow and arrow to facilitate his adult contributions to warfare as well as his eligibility to begin taking part in turning head ceremonies. The boy was now called *wönö pöki*, "the one with a head cloth," as opposed to *wönö-nö-pöki*, "the one without a head cloth" (A. Strathern 1989). Girls at their time of transition from girlhood to womanhood put on an adult headnet. In the past pigs' penises would be wound around their wrists, indicating their fertility and marriageability. We have seen an example of this in the chapter on ballads, with reference to Ambra Rangkopa. Headnets and wigs are artifacts that were used to enhance the body as an extension of the person. Shells provide another example.

SHELLS

For the Hageners, the pearlshell (*kokla kin*) was the most admired and sought after valuable from at least the 1930s until its demise in the 1970s. It was used in exchange transactions (*moka*), for brideprice payments, and as a decorative display item on and off the body. Many other shell types were used in exchange and as decoration. These included the baler (*raem*); cowrie ropes (*ranggel*); nassa shells (*nuin, pikti*) sewn into mats (*pela öi*) with a central diamond shape called a navel (*uklimb*) from which the shells radiated outward in a design; and green-snail (*kötö, örpi*), used largely as ornaments, attached to the ears and ringlets of hair, primarily by women.

Shells in the highlands and surrounding regions may have quite complex symbolic associations. One association that is made is between shells and eggs, as happens with the Foi (Weiner 1988). Jeffrey Clark also found complex linkages of ideas between pearlshells and fertility in the Pangia area (Clark 1991). The place of shells in brideprice transactions and compensation payments for killings is therefore easy to understand. It is important, however, to look here at the specifics of appearance. Shells are bright, and their shining quality is universally associated with the idea of "a good skin," one that is able to attract others. The "good skin" of the shell is compared to the smooth skin of healthy people, so that a kind of isomorphism is established between shell and person. Some shell types, such as cowries, are white, although cowries can also be mottled white and brown (in Hagen *kokla rangkel nder-mbar*). The pearlshells, however, in particular should be a ruddy, yellow color, and their color is enhanced further by rubbing them with red ocher. This kind of preference holds universally in the Western Highlands and the Southern Highlands Provinces. As we have seen in a number of references earlier, red ocher is a mark of the vitality of the Sky Beings. We suggest that even if this is not an explicit association that is made in a given area, it is an implicit or hidden kind of meaning that is disclosed in mythology and folk tales. The Sky Beings were also supposed to be light skinned, and the color of the skin of balladic protagonists in Hagen, at any rate, is compared to the deep yellow color of types of sweet bananas. One of these kinds of bananas (*rua mopa*) also appears in folk tales as the typical food given to people to help them recover from a coma-like or traumatized condition of near-death. From all this it is reasonable to suggest that there is a special connection between pearlshells and the Sky Beings. Certainly, in Hagen, the pearlshell was one of the emblems of the Female Spirit herself, and if we recall that this Spirit was imaged as an attractive, decorated young woman coming to a set of men as their collective bride, the connection between shells and a female realm of attractiveness is strengthened (Stewart and Strathern 1999a; Strathern and Stewart 1997b, 1999e). The Sky Women are in fact the prototypes of attractive beings, even though they themselves are not viewed as sexually active generally. (We are not arguing here that shells are simply "female," only that the complex sensibilities that surround them *include* the features we have remarked on here. In a completely different sense, shells in Hagen belonged also to a male sphere, because they were kept in men's houses and magic to "pull" them into these houses was in the control of men. This, in fact, fits with our argument that pearlshells themselves have strong female associations. Furthermore, "female" here needs to be specified more closely as "reproductive female" and connected with the notion of "sexual attraction.")

An abundance of wealth items is also connected with the same value of attractiveness and is linked aesthetically in spells to the attractive power of blossoms on certain trees. For example, in one Hagen spell there is an image of the *kilt* tree, which produces numerous pink- or mauve-colored blossoms in season. Parakeets flock to these blossoms in order to sip the nectar from them. The image is used to create a spell for pearlshells to come into the men's houses of the groups: they will be attracted to the group as birds are to tree blossoms. But the tree here also stands in another sense for the shells themselves, since its sweet-smelling resin was used to provide a setting for the pearlshells employed in bridewealth and *moka* exchanges. Another kind of complex association between bird plumes and pearlshells is found in the Duna notion that the ruff of the Lophorina Superba bird can be spoken of as its *kuriapa*, or pearlshell. Elements of display, courtship, maturation, and climactic patterns of behavior are inscribed generally in Melpa ideas regarding the mutual mimesis of birds of paradise and human dancers generally (see A. Strathern 1985).

Wearing an abundance of shells was therefore a sign of wealth; but it was also a sign of magical attraction.

SUBSTANCES AND PAINT

The substances of the human body, and earth paints and other materials, all formed an amalgam of symbolic, cognitive, and affective sensibilities that constituted the meanings of decorations. Red earth paint for example was a mark of Sky Beings as we have seen; it also was a mimetic equivalent of blood. White pigment was equated with *kopong* or "grease" in Hagen, and examples of such grease were semen and breast milk. Black charcoal signified war, disguise, group hostility. Red and white together mimicked the mixing of reproductive substances, blood and semen. Although people did not readily give specific exegeses to this effect, ritual contexts in Hagen disclosed the background meanings of each paint and their connections with the human body and a reproductive model of the cosmos (Stewart and Strathern 2001a). The state of the skin revealed the harmonious plenitude and balance between substances in the body, or the disturbance of such a balance operating on people's *noman* or mind.

This model of the body, the cosmos, and substances used in decorations belongs in particular to Hagen, but the principles involved in it hold much more widely in the Highlands and New Guinea generally (see Knauft 1999: 21–83). The colors of artifacts such as shells formed a part of this cosmic view as did the treatment of body parts such as hair with red ocher and pig grease; or the oiling of the skin itself with pig fat or vegetable tree oil to make it shine like the skin of the mythical Sky Beings themselves. The Hagen term for the Campnosperma tree oil, which was traded into the Western Highlands from the Southern Highlands and was highly valued as a cosmetic, was *kopong keta kae*, "the grease for a good face," or "oil for beauty," based on its own ruddy yellowish color.

MOVEMENT

It is also important to notice that the display of decorative items on festive occasions was not just static. Instead it was created by the dancing body itself. So it was that the crest plumes of the King of Saxony bird were especially said to sway about with the dancers who wore them. The front aprons of male dancers were supposed to swish forward and backward. Green-snail pieces worn at the neck by either men or women, but especially by women, were said to clink together as the dancers moved. The faces and identities of dancers were partially disguised; but this was done also to accentuate the interest they generated and the recognition of their identity through the mass of decorations. Lining around the eyes (in Hagen *mong akeremen*, "they dig out the eyes") was designed both to highlight the significance of the eyes and to obscure their appearance (cf. Howes 1991b: 190). Folk tales play on the idea of the decorated person coming as a stranger to dances, thereby generating excitement and interest. Decorations, like masks, both disguise and reveal identity.

Elements of courtship entered into all, or most, dancing occasions. In many parts of the Highlands, girls could indicate their active, even aggressive and competitive, interest in male dancers whom they admired by breaking into a line of dancing males and joining hands with the ones whom they chose. In the Kewa area it appears that there were some constraints on this practice: a girl could hold the upraised axe of the man, displayed in the dance, only if he were unmarried. No doubt, there were ambiguities about this. In Hagen, also, a young woman could display herself in a dancing line of her own male kin, to be seen by possible male admirers from elsewhere.

Some dances were explicitly connected with courtship behavior. In Hagen *mölya* dances were of this kind. They took place at the same time as, or shortly after, a formal dance to mark a set of wealth transactions was completed—either the men's *mörl* and women's *werl* dances or the men's *nde mbo kenan* dance. In *mölya* men and women, married or unmarried, freely linked hands and danced in a circle, singing songs that frequently had an explicitly sexual content and were performed antiphonally by the females and males (see also chapter 2). The *mölya* dance was vigorous. After a round of singing, a set of girls dancing by themselves might jump up and down, their decorations swinging, clinking, and swaying together, their bodies expressing great concentration. When the men and women joined together in *mölya*, the sound of their singing and the stamping of their feet as they spun around would often rise above the ceremonial oratory of leading men in other parts of the ceremonial ground. These men would complain about the noise, but to no effect. The sexual and political aspects of the occasions were therefore in some sense poised against each other; but they were also intimately linked, because out of marriage came political alliance.

NETBAGS

Women's and men's netbags have been in the past, and still are today, significant elements of self-display, artifacts to be considered along with shells and plumes. With the decline in dancing and decoration in the Highlands occasioned by Christian mission teaching, we find that sensuous expression has to some extent been infused into the bright-colored clothing and netbags worn by women that simulate the colors of decorations previously used for traditional dances.

Netbags in New Guinea generally are decorative objects that have an enormous potential for communication and self-expression (MacKenzie 1991; Stewart and Strathern 1997b). They are functional components of dress and adornment that can be used to conceal or advertise particular facets of identity. They carry social and political significance in marriage bestowal and exchange contexts and form a part of life-cycle celebrations and rituals of death. Netbags carry many sorts of objects: pigs, infants, the bones of a dead person, vegetables, private belongings, items of wealth, and so forth. Different kinds are used by both men and women.

Carrying persons or objects in a netbag can signify their translocation from one place to another or from one state of being to another. The following myth from the Hagen area (PNG) shows how a wealth item (a pearlshell) is hidden and then revealed in a sequence signaling the "birth" of an object:

The pearlshell acquires a marked religious and cultic significance through its use in the Female Spirit Cult [see chapter 7; Strathern and Stewart 1998b,1999e] and in the closing scenes of a *moka* exchange ceremony [see Strathern and Stewart 2000b for a discussion of *moka* exchange]. . . . According to a myth these valuables were at one time stolen by bad people of the Underworld. A brave woman, along with a few men, risked herself in going down to the underworld and brought the valuables back. This act is represented at the end of the *moka* festival. In order to display this return of the shells in a truly dramatic manner, they were first hidden from view in large carefully prepared grass-filled netbags, with their shiny sides exposed. At the ceremony men with distinctive decorations carried the shells into the dancing place with many shouts and yells, and were received there with great jubilation. Later the shells were handed to the recipients of the *moka*. (Vicedom and Tischner 1943–48; vol. 1, 120, translated from the German)

The myth tells of a "brave" woman who went to the underworld. She is the wife of a polygynous man, and it was a pale-skinned cannibal woman who stole the man's sons, Eklimb and Kuklup. The "brave" woman was called Kopona Nde (perhaps derived from the term *kopong nde*, for the bamboo tubes of Campnosperma oil, which were used in decoration of the skin), and it was she who made her way into the underworld through a rock face and an underground lake. Kopona Nde burned the cannibal inside of her house and rescued the two boys, as well as the other men who were being kept there. She took the possessions, valuables, cassowaries, and pigs of the cannibal woman and returned to her above-ground home. After this the two boys who had been rescued made the *moka* shell festival, using the shells that the woman brought back with her (Vicedom and Tischner 1943–48: vol. 3, 37–38).

The myth gives the active role to the female, whose bravery is commemorated by hanging the shells in a netbag when they are brought into the dancing ground.

In Hagen, women's netbags (*wal omb* and *wal kupin*, "work" and "ceremonial" versions) are distinguished from *wal kumbana*, which traditionally were carried only be men and had shoulder-strap handles. The manufacture of netbags is replete with overtones of sexuality, reproduction, and in further metaphorical forms political associations.

The action of pulling the long thread through each netted loop is described as *walinga rui*, "to strike backwards and forwards," and this is the same term that is used for the sinuous inflection of the head by partners in the *amb kenan* (courting ceremony for unmarried girls) (see chapter 3). In the *amb kenan* the male sits cross-legged beside the female, who sits with her legs bent underneath her. The foreheads and noses of the two partners come together and roll rhythmically back and forth as their bodies sway. During this action the partners listen to the courting songs sung by the spectators, which provide a beat to which their actions can be attuned.

The needle employed for pulling the thread to make the netbag is traditionally made of flying-fox bone and is called *ngal aipa*, "flying-fox bone needle." The spun thread is called *kan röngi*, "manufactured rope." In a phrase used to express political alliance between male exchange partners, the image of thread and needle is invoked: *nim kan röngi, na ngal aipa*, "you will be the thread, I will be the needle" (and together we will make the netbag, i.e., the *moka* exchange). Thread and needle also carry a sexual significance here.

This combination of sexual and political meanings can be seen in the context of widow's wear also, since the widows of war victims were supposed to wear piled-up netted materials over their heads so as to provide a "house" for the dead man's spirit until it was revenged by his clansmen. (The widow's role here is both "domestic" and "political," and the netbag again expresses both aspects, just as the netbag used for shells in *moka* did) (Vicedom and Tischner 1943–48: vol. 2, 225). The netbag as a home for the newly born spirit of the dead mirrors its role as the container for a newborn baby, and also the term for the placenta, *kunung wal*, the "covering netbag," in the Melpa language. This term also applies to the netbag worn as a head and back cover for protection against rain and excessive exposure to sunlight.

In the Ok region immediately to the west of the Duna people, men make the bird feather netbags worn for initiation ceremonies, adding these feathers to a bag made by the initiate's mother (MacKenzie 1991: 113). Usually a man presents his wife with prepared fibers from which she loops a bag. The man then decorates this bag with feathers (e.g., hornbill, eagle, or brush turkey feathers). The netbag thus created is therefore a composite product of their shared interactive labor, representing also the fertility of their sexual alliance. MacKenzie refers to this in her phrase "androgynous objects"; alternatively we may see these composite bags as expressions of a cross-sex alliance of inner and outer form.

In the contemporary context netbags may be used to make statements about personal desirability and worth. The highly colored and decorative netbags that women make stress their beauty rather than their utility, by contrast with the work netbags used for carrying foods. The decorative netbags are often carried with shoulder straps rather than suspended in the traditional fashion on the head. If they are worn from the head they may have multiple pastel-colored, light-weight scarves attached to them that fall to one side of the woman's face or flutter in the wind as she moves. The netbags are often woven out of brightly colored fibers with criss-crossing geometric shapes woven into them. These patterns are reminiscent of the face coloring done by young girls and women in the past for exchanges and nowadays for "cultural" shows where young people demonstrate their regional decorative variations and dance and music traditions.

Among the Daribi people of Chimbu Province (PNG) the decorative motifs (stylized geometrical symbols) and the talent and skill involved in making netbags were thought to be acquired through dreams (Wagner 1972: 77). The metaphorical character of the geometric patterns utilized in Daribi netbags is linked to the structural codification seen in dreams themselves. This attribution of creative knowledge to dreaming is similar to that seen among some Australian Aborigines, for example, the Pintupi (Myers 1986: 242). A Daribi who saw a poorly crafted product would conclude that the maker had not had a dream that would have provided inspiration to produce a well-made, functional, and attractive product. The knowledge that is accrued through dreaming comes for the Daribi from *izara-we*, women living under the surface of the earth. These women live without men and have skins that are said to be slippery, coated with a whitish substance like saliva, from which an odor is emitted. Through the interpretation of dreams the Daribi bring the capacities revealed in dreaming to bear on the events of day-to-day life; and the knowledge acquired through encounters with *izara-we* in dreams is creatively depicted through netbag design and decoration (Wagner 1972: 72–77). Daribi myths further indicate that netbags are also associated with contexts of fertility, life and death, and regeneration. Our point here is that they have been connected, too, with attractive self-display, primarily by women.

The decorative netbag has been woven into myths, legends, songs, and poems throughout the Highlands. Myths from many regions tell of spirit women who possess netbags (Biersack 1982: 244; Brumbaugh 1980: 440). In one Duna story, two Payame Ima female spirits give a man meat in a netbag to take home, warning him not to let his wife see it. The wife finds the netbag and dirties it, and when the man returns it to the spirits, they kill him. Courting songs also may refer to these important objects.

A Melpa courting song (see chapter 2) demonstrates a boy singing to a girl that she should leave the flatlands of the valley area where she lives and come with him to his mountainous land to live. The song also reveals the boy's offer of what were desirable "modern" foods to her, which metaphorically is equivalent to offering her sexual intercourse: the netbag being a container for food and she herself being a receptacle for his sexual gifts.

> Girl, why are you here
> On the empty grasslands?
> This is no place for you.
> Let me take you off to Mbukl.
> Open your netbag.
> I'll give you meat and rice
> To fill up and carry away.
> (No. 19, A. Strathern [trans.] 1974: 53)

The following *amb kenan* shows a singer referring to the weight of two types of stone axe blades that he has obtained and must carry to his home. He asks a girl whom he likes if she will carry them for him in his netbag (and thus go with him to his place), or if she will lift the load up for him to swing it onto his back, as a wife might help her husband. Thus, the netbag appears as a technical carrying instrument of great strength, sufficient to hold heavy stone blades, but the suggested context is also intimate and bodily; helping someone of the opposite sex to load such a bag may be taken as an intimacy, displaying both sympathy (*kaemb*) and the freedom to make bodily contact.

> My netbag of *kontin*,
> My netbag of *nggaema*:
> They are so heavy
> Will you take it?
> Or shall I take it?
> Help me and lift it
> Onto my back.
> (No. 22, A. Strathern [trans.] 1974)

The decorative netbags of women are important in establishing relationships of many sorts. When an Orokolo (Gulf Province, PNG) bride was led to her husband's house she carried a special bag that contained her coconut spoons, betelnut, and lime with which she would entertain in her new house. This *avoa* (conjugal bilum) was decorated by her parents with rows of shell valuables; the top row she would keep for her personal decorations, the rest she would distribute to her new affines (Maori Kiki and Beier 1969: 18).

In the Goroka area (Eastern Highlands Province, PNG) during the betrothal ceremony a netbag (*owu*, meaning womb) is symbolically displayed
on a wooden post, the netbag being the primary symbol of the bride's
fertility. As the bride stands next to the post with its attached netbag, the
girl's male relatives make speeches about her future marriage and the
bridewealth they will receive. The bride is accompanied in the ceremony by
one or two of her female relatives who carry netbags filled with pork to be
given as gifts to the groom's relatives. In addition, the bride's mother may
also be given a netbag filled with pork or sweet potatoes (Sexton 1986).

Another arena in which the netbag plays an important role is in the yam
festival in the Sepik area of PNG. It is worthwhile to mention this here,
even though the Sepik is beyond our main focus in this book, because it
shows how the Highlands patterns are not isolated but are typical of a wider
area. Bowden (1984) discusses this for the Kwoma people of the East Sepik
Province whose yam harvest ceremonies are performed annually in every
village. Special sculptures are used in the ceremonies: *yena*, *mija*, and
nowkwi. Each of these types of sculptures represent "spirits." In the *yena*
ceremony the sculptures are displayed along with newly harvested yams and
large women's netbags. The stage for this display is likened by the people
to a womb (*kow*). Kwoma men say that the *yena* figures themselves are
powerful spirits that are responsible for and preside over the fertility of yam
gardens. At the end of the ceremony when the stage is dismantled and the
yams are removed, the men say that "they are taking 'eggs' out of 'wild
fowl' nests, wild fowls being thought of as 'female' (*mima*) birds" (p. 456).

Not only is the netbag displayed with the yams on the ceremonial platform but it is also used as a significant part of the construction of the *yena*
sculpture as a ritual object: "[W]hen the figures are being painted (one of
a series of acts that magically activates them with the spirits they represent)
the figures must be placed on pillows made from rolled-up women's netbags
(*kow*), objects which in ordinary social life are not only directly associated
with women, but are linguistically equated with wombs, the receptacles in
which unborn children are carried" (p. 457). Men said that if the sculptures
were not placed onto these "female" objects "the designs would not 'go on
straight', and the figures would remain lifeless and sterile, devoid of the
spirits that gave them power" (p. 457). The myths of the Kwoma relate that
the yam ceremonies and the powerful ceremonial objects used in them were
"originally invented by women" (p. 457). This is a common theme in various areas in New Guinea, as we have seen. Myths often present men as the
ones who "stole" secrets from women, or "tricked" them into giving them
up, or simply forced them to do so. Whatever we make of this theme in
general, it certainly recognizes the importance of women and female symbolism to the concerns expressed in what have been called "male" rituals
(Strathern and Stewart 1999f). In turn this symbolism usually has to do
with powers of attraction and regeneration.

FOLK TALES

The following Hagen story, like those presented earlier in the chapter on myths and stories, tells of a remembered time prior to many of the changes brought by the colonial forces from the 1930s onward. This particular story interweaves details of bodily decoration, desire, and attire. We present it here to convey the importance of these objects in the day-to-day contexts as narrated in this story. The story was narrated by a young man of the Kawelka group in 1964. It encapsulates many of the points touched on in this chapter, linking them to the discussion of folk tales in chapter 4.

The Story of Nggömbi Kan

A brother and a sister lived together. The brother allowed his sister to be idle. He worked in the sweet potato gardens by himself, cooked food, and fetched water and gave it to her, and she had all her time to herself. Once when he was off to work in the bush he said to her, "I haven't brought you any water to drink, but if you get thirsty later don't go up to the place where the *kengena* and *kindöpit* plants grow and the good sweet water flows, go to the place where the pigs have been treading and drink the muddy water there." He went away and during the day she grew thirsty and decided against going to the muddied water where the pigs had been. She went up and drank from the sweet water. The man worked and brought back sugar cane, bananas, short pitpit (*Setaria palmaefolia*), sweet potato, and firewood, hung about on his shoulders. As he came home he saw that his sister had put some clay on her navel and he said to her, "Before I wanted you to live a leisurely life, now I see you yourself want to work and produce your own food to eat"—and he gave her an axe and a knife, adding, "I see you didn't want me to bring your food to you, you want to work your own gardens and cook your own sweet potato." So she went and worked her own gardens and while she was at this, she became pregnant, although she was an unmarried girl. She bore a boy and called him Nggömbi Kan.

When he grew big and could grasp a bow and arrow or axe he went into the sweet potato garden with his mother and he stayed at the side of the field where his mother's pandanus cape and things had been laid. The boy's head decoration of marsupial fur, bow and arrow and small axe together with a round of tree-bark for his belt were placed there and left for him (by his spirit father). The boy then grew up rapidly and spent his time turning head, he was never at home. One day, while he was not present, his mother's brother spoke harsh words about him. "He's always gadding about turning head, is he? Does he think his father will come and buy him several wives or something?"

Nggömbi Kan had crept close to the rear of the men's house and listened to what his mother's brother was saying, then he crept back and returned, talking loudly and treading heavily. His mother's brother had gone into the house, and he said to his mother, "Oh, mother, tomorrow morning you must bring some taro for me and cook it before the sun rises." He said this and cried bitterly. Next morning he took his headnet, front apron, rear-covering, spear, axe, cropped cassowary plume, and dance decorations, and told his mother that he was going to go to a distant place, so she should pack up some food in a barkcloth for him. The mother, knowing that her son was intending to go, had herself already prepared two netbags, and said to him, "I will carry your food for you part of the way and then you can carry on and I will go back." So the two went off, straight on the path to the Jimi area. They walked on and on and came to the place of the Tipuka Ndikambo, in the Pakakla Pass. As they arrived a company of people were cooking food together at the turning head for a young girl, and they said to the two, "Tomorrow you can carry on your journey, now we will sing the turning-head songs, eat food together and sleep here." But the two said, "No, now we must continue, when we come back we can stay with you, turn head, and on the next day go." So they next came to the place Rolna, where food was being cooked for a Klamakae and a Palke girl, and the people said to them, "Where are you two going to? It's getting dark now, stay with us and turn head tonight and tomorrow you can carry on to the place you are going to." But the two said, "No, now we must go on, when we come back we can sing with you." They journeyed on, crossed the river Ökl and the river Mokla, climbed up on Ngönde Mbakamanga, and found the people cooking food for a Maplke girl, and the people said to them, "Where are you two going to? Darkness is falling, now stay with us and turn head, tomorrow you can go." But the two replied, "When we come back we can stay with you, sing, and then return home, but now we must be on our way."

They walked on, and the young man said, "Mother, you have come far enough now, you go back, it was your brother who spoke hard words to me, and I said I would go off by myself. Nevertheless you've come all this way with me, but now your brother is living in the Wahgi while you've come down to the Jimi, go back to him. I'm a man without a father, I'll go on by myself." So saying, he gave her his battle axe. She said, "Did he speak of a lap-pig and you're giving it to me now? Well, I'll put it in my netbag and carry it for you." She put it in her netbag and carried it. He said to her, "I'm going to a distant place, you go back." He took out the conus shell decoration from his nose and gave it to her. She said, "It hurts your nose, so you are giving it to me, I'll carry it for you"—and so they went on. They came up close to the place where the Murip lake is and he said to her, "Mother, why have you followed me here? This is where I have been traveling to, your brother is on the other side of the mountain divide (between the Wahgi Valley and the Jimi), you go back to him." He told her this but she would not listen to him and so the two went on until they could hear the roar (*nggon-nggon*) of the waters underneath. They passed on into groves of sticks of the *kui* tree and small bushes of *el pil*. Coming up to the water, the young man took his spear and divided the waters with it and went in underneath the surface.

She wanted to follow him but found herself alone on the dry shore where the small pebbles lay. She searched and searched among the leaves on the forest floor but could not find his footsteps, and then she cut off all her fingers (an extreme expression or sign of grief) and slept without food for three days beside the water, crying all the time. Then she got up and traveled the long journey back to the place of the Maplke and reached Ngönde. The Maplke girls said to her, "Old mother, you took a fine young man with you, we saw you two on your way, and now you've left him behind and come back by yourself." They said this and went into mourning for him, crying, cutting off their long ringlets of hair, and folding it up, while the mother carried off the fingers she had severed and came up to Rolna, where the Palke and Klamakae girls saw her and said to her, "Mother, we saw you on your way with a fine young man and now he has gone off and you yourself have come back alone, with the fingers you have cut off." They said this and cut off their hair and went into mourning for him. She traveled on and came to the place of the Ndikambo at Pakakla where the girls of the place said to her, "You took a fine young man off with you and now you've come back without him we see." They said this and cut off their hair and went into mourning for him. She carried on and reached home. Her brother had left off his head covering, and his cordyline rear covering, belt, and apron were all awry. He had put some sweet potato in a netbag and was carrying it in spite of his exposed state, when he heard a woman coming crying along the mountain path and wondered who was coming along the way, crying as she went. Then he saw it was his sister, who was crying as she came. "Oh my sister's son," he said, and pulled at his hair and cut off a finger.

Kawelka Kundmbo folk had come to turn head and they now went into mourning, their women brought food for the mourners, other women brought food in this same way too, and two young girls with whom the young man had turned head before said to the mother, "Let us bind up your hand and put the *ui nggoa* [dark mud of mourning] on your face and stay with you for good." Later there was a big dance put on among the Maplke, and the Tipuka and Kawelka people all attended it. The mother said, "The weather is good today, and everyone is going to the Maplke place to look at the big dance, I will go with them all to look at it and come back, you two girls stay for a while in my house." So she went, along with a company of them, and then as they all dispersed to sleep in the houses of their friends, she went near to the river Kokla and there a woman was washing yams, taro, and other good food in the water. It was her sister, long ago dead, who was washing the food there, but there was a cloud over the eyes of the living woman and she could not recognize her sister. However, the dead sister recognized her living sister, and said, "My sister, where are you going to?" The living woman replied, "Everyone was going to the Maplke dance, so I came with them and am here." "Well, have you any friends here or not?" she asked her. "No, they were all going and I came because I wanted to go as well, I haven't any friends here," she replied. "Now where will I go to sleep?" Her dead sister replied, "My sister, I do not cook human meat, I have an earth oven for cooking beans in only. Tomorrow you can go on and see the dance, now you shall stay with me and we will go to spend the night together." She counted out some taro and red yams and gave these to her, saying, "You have killed your man, mother, but my two men will be dancing tomorrow, so you make up a package of food for one of them and take it for him and I will peel some food for my man and cook it and give it to him."

So that night they cooked the food and the dead sister said, "Mother, you have killed your man and now you are a widow, let us two twist some thread of mine into a rope." So she said and they worked to produce a long rope, and then she took a nest of grub-cocoons and rolled up the spool of rope into this. Next morning they cooked pig, and she wrapped up a pig's tongue and red taro and yams along with the spool, cut up the pig, and gave it to her sister. The following day was the final day of the dance, and Roka of Kopon and his son Nggömbi Kan, wearing different kinds of decorations came, and as the news spread everyone came round to look at them. The dead sister said, "Give me the spool and food I gave to you to bring, and as you are a widow if you go along the road you may feel you grow tired, so here are some stinging nettles to scratch your skin with." The living sister gave the dead sister the food and the spool and the special digging stick she had given to her. She took these and gave one end of the spool to her living sister, and the other she went and put in the hands of Nggömbi Kan, pulling it out and giving it to him. After the dancing men took off their marsupial skins and feather decorations, and Nggömbi Kan and his father performed the *ware* dance as two men of Kopon (Jimi) might do. When all the men had removed their decorations, the dead sister said, "Take the end of the rope and go home with it, if it gets dark as you go, you go inside a house and sleep, Nggömbi Kan will stay outside and do the *ware* dance, take the thread now and see how it goes." She did so and Nggömbi Kan tipped over slightly (as if in a trance) and came.

She took a straight road back, and as they came up to Rolna night fell, so the mother went inside and slept while the son stayed outside and danced the *ware*. His father, Kopon Roka, said, "Oh, my son, Nggömbi Kan, [has] gone away," and saying this he went off into the forest, uprooting forest trees, dislodging rocks that knocked over as he went—he went wild in the forest and died there. Nggömbi Kan and his mother came home. The two young girls were saying, "The people who went to see the dance all came back yesterday, our mother will be back today," and so they cooked food and held some bananas ready on the fence stile and waited there. Then they saw the mother coming first down the pathway and her son coming behind her, decorated with fine palm cockatoo feathers, hornbill feathers, parrot feathers, Sicklebill feathers, Red Bird of Paradise feathers, all fastened to his head, and tails of the *kokla* marsupial and skins of the *rakop* marsupial bound around his forehead too. He was performing a dance as he came. As the two neared the girls said, "Mother, you've brought your son with you." They came up close and shook their hands in delight, and they all went inside and ate the cooked food, while the son himself stayed near the doorway outside and remained dancing the *ware* dance for a day and a night. The next day they cooked food and the mother took a piece of burning barkcloth and put it to his nose. He walked about steadily now and she took her special digging stick and struck the back of his knees with it. The two young girls came close to and removed his decorations and marsupial fur and feathers and rubbed his skin with stinging nettles so that he woke up again. When this was done the mother gave the brideprice for the two girls and he married them and they lived on eating their food and sleeping until they died.

Commentary: From the point of view of the overall structure of the story, this tale has a similar plot line to many of those we have looked at in the chapter on myths and narratives (chapter 4). A boy is born through the magical fertilization of a human woman by water identified with a forest spirit or Sky Being of the Ndepana Nikint kind or the Male Spirit, the Kor Wöp. The boy has magical powers about him, but he lacks a complete human parentage. The mother's brother stands in for the father. But, instead of nurturing the boy, he speaks harshly of him when the boy grows up. The boy overhears him and goes on a quest to find his progenitor, beneath a lake where he lives. His loyal mother insists on going with him. She does not let the ties that bind go, either metaphorically or, later in the story, literally.

The drama of attraction and courtship occurs as mother and son pass through succeeding settlements where the people are impressed by the looks and demeanor of the young stranger and ask them to stay so he can join in their courting ceremonies. The youth and his mother refuse to do so and pass on. The son tries to tell his mother to go back home but she will not.

Nggömbi Kan vanishes beneath the lake and the mother, being only human, cannot follow him. He enters the world of the spirits. Brokenhearted, she lops off her finger joints and retraces her steps to the lake, and all the girls who longed to turn head with Nggömbi Kan are also upset, and in their grief cut off ringlets of their hair, like the ringlets found by the man in another folk tale, which he used to trace a girl and marry her. They destroy a part of their own beauty in their mourning: a part also of their own overall vitality and maturity, as we have seen earlier in this chapter in the section on hair. Locks of hair are sacrificed by the potential but thwarted brides and presented by them to the woman who bore him.

Nggömbi Kan's movement along the trail is like a movement of initiation or a pilgrimage quest, a sacred journey. He has to find his father before he can become a man. The finding of the spirit father will also, however, lead to the father's complete death or his final disappearance in the forest.

It is the mother's brother's harsh words, denying a responsibility to pay a brideprice, that confirm the boy's feeling he is being treated like an orphan, without a father (*pokndame* in the Melpa language). Both the father, who impregnated the mother through water, and the mother's brother are destined for destruction. In fact we learn that the mother has in a way entailed or caused the death of the spirit husband, or at least his disappearance, by drinking his magical water.

The mother's access to the knowledge that her son is still alive, although held in an entranced state, is given to her by her own dead sister; an emphasis on female as opposed to male links, since her brother had repudiated his ties to her earlier, by cursing her son.

Father and son appear at the dance the mother attends, and they astonish their viewers, where, as strangers, they perform an unusual dance: this means also that they wore different eye-catching decorations for the *ware* dance, known from old times among the northern Melpa speakers among whom the story is set, and associated particularly with the Jimi Valley, as is the case here. The son appears in the guise of the handsome, stranger youth. His mother now pulls him back with her spirit-given thread, the female thread shown to her by her dead sister, until he reaches home where two young women, already in the role of daughters-in-law, have been keeping her company. So he reaches his maturity, with the help of all the females. His father and mother's brother are both deranged, but he achieves his own manhood. His brilliant decorations and dancing mark him as having been given a spiritual enhancement by his father. It is his mother, however, with her netbag thread, who pulls him back home to human life, to his *manga-ambnga*, his "woman's house," leaving the "men's house" of the magical forest and lake behind. And it is the *kond*, or "sympathy," of the young women along the trail that also pulls him to them and away from his own *kond*, "sorrow," for his spirit father.

In the next chapter we look again at female powers and male initiations in order further to contextualize our findings in this chapter on decorations. The folk tale we have given explicates particularly well the point that decorations not only make political statements about persons and groups but also signify deep emotions and desires connected with the life cycle in general and courtship in particular.

Chapter 7

Female Spirits and Initiation

Anthropological writings about regions develop their own stereotypical baselines that tend to persist over time in spite of certain recensions and modifications. A major trope employed in ethnographic comparisons on the Highlands of Papua New Guinea was set in hand by a chain of writings, from Ward Goodenough (1953), R. F. Salisbury (1962), Michael Allen (1967), Lew Langness (1967), and Kenneth Read (1965) through to the synthetic work by Daryl Feil (1987), all of whom, though in varying modalities, expounded a range of putative differences between Eastern and Western Highlands societies. One stereotype, particularly established by Allen, was that Eastern Highlands societies stressed male domination, male initiation, warfare, patrilineal social structure, and sexual antagonism, while the Western Highlands societies were seen to stress exchange practices, alliance, flexible social affiliation, and fertility cults as opposed to male initiation. Feil systematized many of these contrasts and related them to differences in the intensification of horticultural production, pig rearing, dependence on female labor, and the development of the "big-manship" style of male leadership based on exchange.

Many aspects of these contrasts have continued to be expressed in subsequent writings. The contrast, for example, between male initiation in Eastern Highlands societies such as Gahuku-Gama, Bena Bena, the Fore complex, the Gururumba, and others, and combinations of fertility cults and "bachelors' cults" in the Western Highlands, is, for the most part, applicable. However, every contrast leaves out some aspect of similarity, and every conglomeration of cases leaves out some aspect of difference. To recognize this point is not to go so far as to suggest that comparisons cannot validly be made because all cases shade into one another so as to become merged. It is, however, to accept that comparisons are inevitably perspectival and thematic, all picking on matters of interest in order to place them in a foreground or background of discussion (Strathern and Stewart 2000a). In the present context the contrast between male initiation in the Eastern Highlands and its absence and "replacement" by fertility cults and bachelors' cults in the Western Highlands has obscured two cross-cutting aspects of similarity between these parts of the Highlands region. First, there are obvious concerns with overall fertility in the Eastern Highlands cases; and second, there are equally analogous concerns with initiation in the Western Highlands cases. These two considerations can help us to modify the somewhat artificial appearances of clear difference that have been set up by earlier writings.

We are dealing here not with sharply bounded differences, but with clines and nuances of similarity and difference. Female Spirit cults, of the kind that we find in the Hagen, Pangia, Enga, Huli, and Duna areas, were apparently not in existence in the Eastern Highlands. Yet the Fore, as we have seen, had a picture of a creative Female Being, Jugumishanta, who resembled the figure of Afek, which we find in the Ok region just to the west of the Duna. Elements of erotic and heterosexual symbolism entered deeply into practices concerned with the flutes used in initiation ceremonies among the Gahuku-Gama in their Nama cult (Read 1954, 1965), and analogues of these ideas are found extending right across to the Duna wherever we encounter the ritual use of flutes and other musical instruments such as mouth-harps. And the bachelors' cults of the Western and Southern Highlands societies were tied in explicitly or implicitly with the fertility cults centering on the powers of Sky Beings. The precise way in which this tying-in occurred was through the idea of the spirit marriage, which we have explored in earlier publications (see Strathern and Stewart 2000a, for example) and have discussed also in chapter 4 of this book. In this chapter our aim is to draw together some observations on these themes and therefore to link together aspects of "initiation" practice, broadly conceived, in different parts of the Highlands.

We look at the role that female spirits in some societies were said to play in assisting boys to become men and the knowledge that these spirits imparted to males for the ultimate reproduction of the group at large. We look at the emotional tone of such meanings and how they were conceived of in counterpoint to human marriage and sexuality, illuminating the values and tensions of these forms of marriage.

Spirit marriages may be seen as extreme versions of exogamy, like those portrayed in Hagen ballads, exhibiting its advantages and its dangers. Exogamy involves crossing boundaries, and when the boundary is that between humans and spirits, both of these aspects of advantage and danger are increased. Danger also characterizes the relationship between living and dead spouses: since the dead are on the side of the spirit world, they too can become like spirit spouses. The emotional tie with a dead spouse is feared by the living, since the dead are said to want to take the living to be with them—to the other side of existence. Such a notion presents one of the emotional aspects of memory, making it important to forget the dead so that dreaming about them does not occur too frequently, for dreaming can be a time when a person is vulnerable to attacks by spirits. These examples demonstrate through several diverse themes the presence of strong emotional ties between spouses—human/human or human/spirit, as also demonstrated by Duna narratives of the Female Spirit (Payame Ima). In the cases of the Payame Ima and the Hagen Amb Kor, dreams are held to reveal their power but also their ability to assist the living and to bring young people to a state of maturity and health as well as to inflict sickness on them if humans do not show the spirits proper respect (Stewart and Strathern 2000e).

In the Female Spirit (Amb Kor) cult in Hagen (Western Highlands, PNG) male performers in the cult's activities were said to have entered into a collaborative relationship with the Spirit as her husbands. In part, their male strength was seen as deriving from her ritual protection and the capacities that she gave the community at large (Strathern and Stewart 1997b, 1998b, 1999e, 2000a: chapter 6; Stewart and Strathern 1999a).

The theme of a Female Spirit as a partner to human men is replicated in a number of areas: Pangia, Enga, Huli, Paiela, and Duna, for example (Stewart and Strathern 1999a; Wiessner and Tumu 1998; Frankel 1986; Biersack 1982, 2001). Many of these Female Spirits are linked with the idea of Sky Beings who are associated with water, seen as rain or as the source of rivers and lakes (Strathern and Stewart 1999e, 2000a).

The Eimb cult in Hagen is another example of the significance of water in cult activity. The spring water in this cult is described as both "male" and "female" (Strauss and Tischner 1962: 404–424). In one account of the Eimb the ritual expert brought in to guide the group had to locate the specific sacred water source to be used (Strauss and Tischner 1962: 414). The male cult adherents had to drink this water and transform it into semen, which their wives would then transform into children.

Strauss and Tischner (1962) describe "an Eimb legend" deriving from the Mundika area near Tambul, where so many of the complexes of spirit cults appear to have originated. A man was out hunting in the forest for marsupials, and as he tried to seize one of the type called *kepa*, he fell into a pool and was carried into a subterranean river and deposited into a hollow *mara* tree. The log eventually floated up to the surface and the man called out for help until another man came by and took him out. He realized that the spirit of the pool had wished to seize hold of him (*eimb mugli*) and keep him safe. First, he had to close his eyes (*kumbili*), then he could open them again (*mökili*). In commemoration, he and his clansmen went back to the forest, and their ritual expert dug two holes with his cassowary bone dagger. Water gushed from these and he called them the opening and closing of the spirit's eyes. They decorated the place finely with ornamental shrubs and built two cult houses, in which they sacrificed to the Eimb spirit (Strauss and Tischner 1962; see also Strathern and Stewart 1999f).

This origin story is interesting for a number of reasons. It reads like a typical folk tale or *kang*, with a man going alone into the forest to hunt marsupials. The *kepa* marsupial he tries to catch may have been a form of the Eimb spirit itself. He tries to catch it but is himself caught, a hunter who in a sense becomes prey to the powers of the wild. He plunges into a pool, but does not die. Folk tales tell that the underwater regions of pools are places of spirits. In one story a woman is saved by being caught in a fish or eel trap set by a man, who finds and revives her, then marries her. The experience is one of death and rebirth. In another story, a group of boys hide from a hostile spirit in a log, and when they emerge they find brides for themselves. They are in fact discovered by a girl, who restores them to life and leads them to maturity as men. Thus, the theme of death and rebirth is combined with the theme of initiation or life-cycle passage as we saw to be implicitly present in the Nggömbi Kan story (chapter 6).

Strauss, in his own analysis of the origin story, stresses the creative, fructifying power of water, and links it to the *okla wamb*, the "beings up above," that is, the Sky Beings, since rain comes from the sky. He suggests that in trying to catch the marsupial, the hunter is infringing on the rights of the Tei or Sky People, and so he falls into the pool. This idea certainly corresponds to a general notion prevalent in Hagen and elsewhere that marsupials are the Sky Spirits' pigs. But, with proper ritual respect, marsupials may be caught. We suggest that the spirit Eimb, who "catches" the man, does so in order to teach people the right rituals to ensure that they can safely hunt. The power of water belongs both to the male and the female domains of existence, Strauss argues, and it can overcome all threats to group prosperity and harmony. In establishing the ritual, then, the men were setting up the proper harmony between themselves and the spirit itself. Water brings fertility. It also brings unity.

Strauss further points out that, as with all of these fertility cults in the Western Highlands, an element, at least, of initiation is preserved within the overall ritual sequence. The youths, who are being brought into the cult performance for the first time, pass beyond the internal fence in the cult enclosure known as "the fence of the boys" (*kang röprö*) into the inner enclosure where the major sacrifices will be held, and where they, like the other men, will drink from the sacred spring water. Strauss's manner of writing about this sequence indicates that he is aware that the "initiation" element, rather than being dominant, is encapsulated within the aims of the group as a whole, and the youths are not made a central object of interest as ritual actors. They have already been taught how to sing the proper incantations, so no special attempt is made to terrify them, and they are simply made part of the overall ritual process itself. They are, however, subsequently called the *koepa-köni kang*, "the youths who have cooked and seen," and in the course of the cult they do much of the cooking itself. They take sweet potatoes handed through the main fence of the cult area by women and girls and wash them in the spring water. Two of the boys also help the ritual experts collect spring water in bamboo tubes and give it to the seated rows of cult participants for drinking. These two are called *el-rup kang*, "bird arrow boys," suggesting a connection with the forest. (Strauss goes further and suggests there is a connection with the founding myth of the Female Spirit cult, but perhaps the association is simply a broad one with the magical arena of the forest generally and its male aspects.) The sung incantation or invocation to the Spirit that Strauss gives includes a command to pigs to come (red pigs, black pigs, and parti-colored pigs are called on); and an invocation to the Beings of the Above, including Nung Nung (thunder) and two Sky Women, Yuwin and Yawin (probably seen as sources of rain). Water generally is called by a term that does not belong to Melpa at all, *ipa*, which is found far to the west among the Huli and the Duna peoples (Strauss and Tischner 1962: 404–424). Forest pools are a part of the domain of the Duna Female Spirit. Spells migrate across language boundaries.

The Duna Female Spirit (Payame Ima) was said to come to a man who was a bachelor and whom she had selected to be a ritual leader. The Payame Ima remained with the man as his help-mate and companion. He did not take a human wife during the time that the Payame Ima was with him. He used the knowledge that he gained from the Female Spirit wife to instruct the boys during the ritual time when they were enclosed in the *palena anda* (boys' growth-house) (see Strathern and Stewart 1999e, 2000a for further discussions of these Duna practices).

The Payame Ima also gave protective powers to other men selected and instructed by her on how to use the *ndele rowa* (divining stick) to determine who was guilty of acts of witchcraft (see Strathern and Stewart 1999a, 2000a: 101–24; Stewart and Strathern 1997c). Witchcraft is said to have originated among the Duna from a male ancestral spirit and is subsequently passed on to humans through mothers or fathers (Stewart and Strathern 1999b). But it is a female spirit entity that provides protection from witchcraft.

The Payame Ima is a pervasive figure in the imagination and folk tales as the source of special powers for men (see Stewart and Strathern 2002). In order to receive favors from the Payame Ima, the men had to adhere to the terms of the relational contract established between them. She was said to be able to punish men who disobeyed her or present them with wealth and power if she deemed them worthy. Biersack (1982) describes a similar practice among the Paiela (Southern Highlands Province, PNG), who have a bachelors' cult in which the young boys are said to enter into a relationship with a female spirit who is like a wife to them during their time of seclusion. This spirit is referred to as Ginger Woman. In the Duna case, however, the Spirit is seen as the wife of the senior bachelor expert, and is therefore more like a mother to the youths in the *palena* house.

In the Strickland-Bosavi region of the Western Province of PNG the Be-damuni people have a strong history of a female spirit called Dunumuni (Isao Hayashi, personal communication 2000) who gave rise to plants and animals through her body parts after her death. Dwyer and Minnegal have also recorded narratives of the myth of Dunumuni (2000). One of these narratives states that "Dunumuni told the men [who had captured her] to carry her to the land of Lugumari people. These men, if they used a stick made from a particular kind of tree, would be able to kill her. And that is what happened. The Lugumari men killed Dunumuni. Then they butchered her and, in doing so, released many of the animals and plants that [the] Bedamuni know today" (p. 261). Her urine and blood were said to have formed the streams and rivers in the Bedamuni landscape. Clark (2000) recounts more of this story as told to him by Isao Hayashi: "When her [Dunumuni's] skirt was removed prior to dismemberment, it was discovered that Dunumuni did not possess a vagina. The men tried to cut her open with a bamboo knife but failed repeatedly until they used a stone knife. A wind emerged from her vagina and birds and animals were also released, finally two things—life and death. . . . Men wanted to copulate with the dead body but failed until the oil from various trees was used as a lubricant" (p. 14).

The oil involved here was probably that of the Campnosperma tree, which was so important as a decorative substance for the human skin in the South-ern and Western Highlands and was traded northward from Kutubu. It was this same oil that Huli men were supposed to apply to the genitals of their wives when the married pairs first engaged in sexual activity. This is the oil that Glasse (1968: 59) called "foul-smelling." In fact, not only was it con-sidered to be sweet smelling or aromatic by those who used it, but from this passage we learn that among the Bedamuni it figured as a primal or mythical substance used to facilitate intercourse with the Female Spirit whose body had released wild creatures of the forest. Bedamuni narratives also linked this spirit with the creation of streams and rivers, parts of the overall landscape. Her body and its flowing substances thus helped to define the environment itself.

We see a parallel here with the Duna people where trackways were estab-lished through the local landscape along which rituals were held that in-voked the spirits of the earth such as the Payame Ima. The limestone outcrops and sinkholes that define the landscape are said to be the ossified remains of giant cannibalistic ancestral beings (*auwape*). *Auwape* figure as main characters in *pikono* ballads (see chapter 5). They were said to take human spouses sometimes. Many of the Duna ancestral beings are featured as characters in origin stories (*malu*) of the people (see Modjeska 1977, 1995; Stewart and Strathern 2000d, 2002). Some of these beings are said to live within the ground and to require sacrifices at particular times to ensure the renewal of the fertility of people, animals, and crops. The Duna incorporate these creatures of the spirit world into their spatial divisions of the landscape: zones of varied powers that inform the people's sense of the cosmos at large and their own placement and function within it. After a person dies the *tini* (soul) moves upward to the forested areas, which are looked after in part by the Payame Ima, and the substance or "grease" (*ngwani*) of the body is absorbed by the ground. Thus, the sum total of the person becomes bound to the landscape.

During life Duna people traverse their landscape along walking trails maintained by persistent use. Extended kin ties link the people throughout the area. Each local area has its specific origin story (*malu*) that details the connectedness of the people of that group to the ground (*rindi*) in a unique way, thereby differentiating people by their varied ties to the landscape. In the past it was thought that the ground became depleted at regular cyclic intervals and that rituals such as the *rindi kiniya* acted to prevent the complete decay of the earth (Stewart and Strathern 2002; Strathern and Stewart 1998b, 1999a; Stewart 1998).

Two of these rituals involved the movement of bodily substances along specific pathways that had ritual sites positioned at varying intervals along the way where specific sacrifices would be given to spirits within the ground (Strathern and Stewart 1997c; Stewart and Strathern 2000d).

One of the rituals involved the use of a virgin's menstrual blood (see the following section). Another, called the *hambua hatya*, involved the movement of Duna men into an area west of the Duna area where a young man from this place (Oksapmin) would be captured and killed. After the body had been exposed on a burial platform for some days pieces of the victim's flesh would be distributed throughout the community and people would be told to plant the pieces so as to induce better growth of garden crops—imbuing the *rindi* with fertility. Other pieces of the man's body would be placed inside of a bamboo tube and carried along a ritual trackway that was said to have been originally established by the character, Hambua, a cannibal being who was said to live in a hole in the ground at the end of the *hambua hatya* trackway and to whom offerings of human sacrifices were given. The cycle of activities was conducted to restore fertility to the soil, the people, and the animals (Strathern and Stewart 1998b; Stewart and Strathern 2002). The younger brother of Hambua was said to have brought salt from Koroba and persuaded the people to give up cannibalism in favor of eating pork sprinkled with salt (Strathern and Stewart 1999a).

Within this landscape the Payame Ima is associated with pools of water at both high and low altitudes and also the Strickland River itself. Sacrifices to her were made in the *Timako* cult, which included casting pieces of pork into the pools that she inhabited. Another name for a variant of this cult was *Imanenda* ("the house of the woman"). Either version of the cult could be performed at the site of a pool associated with the spirit, *ipa ane*. Sometimes such a pool was said to be the female spirit's and an associated pool was said to be her brother's. These pools were also called *ipa raiyanda* ("water sky house") and putatively had the ability to disappear and reappear again at a different location.

For the *Timako* a small cane house was specially constructed and an earth oven was made inside of it to cook a sacrificed pig. Upon removal of the meat from the cooking oven a male and a female dancer or in some instances two female dancers (one representing the agnatic or male side and the other representing the cognatic or female side of the group) came to the house. The female dancer entered the house and uncovered the meat in the earth oven. The male dancer followed behind and ate part of the meat. Cuts of the meat, including the shoulderblades, were thrown into the pools as offerings to the Female Spirit. All of those participating in the cult had joined in clubbing the sacrificial pigs to death. The sticks used to do this were then thrown into the direction of sunrise and sunset as protection against enemy groups. Then the Female Spirit would be invoked, with the cult members saying, "Send us good sweet potatoes and make people's skins good."

The Payame Ima is also said to grant men the ability to discover *ipu rei* crystals, which are used by them to keep their skin in good condition when they are traveling. The crystals are said to be found in the *yukulini* marsupial's stomach. This animal is said to live in the high forest and is one of the Female Spirit's manifestations. Another one of her transforms is the Yuro Ima, the spirit of the Strickland River. The Yuro Ima directs wild game of the grasslands and forest, wild pigs and cassowaries, so that hunters can catch them. In 1999 we were told that this Female Spirit had gone away as a protest, renouncing her protective powers, including her guardianship of the resources previously available from the Strickland River, because she was angry over the "pollution" of her water by mine tailings from the Porgera Joint Venture Gold Mining Company. Her departure was given as a reason why the company should pay compensation to the Duna. The narratives that we collected in 1999 made it clear that the Yuro Ima was protesting the unsanctioned use and potential contamination of the area under her control and supervision (i.e., the Strickland River and its resources). (For a further in-depth discussion of these issues, see Stewart and Strathern 2002).

One senior Duna man put the story this way:

I have heard about the Yuro Ima. She makes the lightning. She is the same as the Payame Ima but she follows the river, and she causes the lightning [which often flashes from storms in the river gorge and is visible from the whole upland area]. The Yuro Ima used to be plainly identified in her presence before the Porgera Joint Venture Company began its operations. Since then, however, we have not seen the evidence of her, and that is why we have talked so strongly to Porgera Joint Venture about compensation. The river is her home, it is her house, so if her home has been spoilt that means she has been made sick and has gone away. When she was there before she helped us to find various kinds of game and wild pigs to hunt, but now the people do not find these any more. Also, she used to help people when they threw canes over the water to make a bridge across the Strickland so as to go to the Oksapmin side. She helped those on the other side to catch the lengths of cane and not fall into the river. This doesn't happen any more and they think she is gone. They are afraid also that if they try to swim across they will drown because she is angry. The river's color has changed now, it is a muddy color, and we think the spirit woman is dead or has run away. Previously she would guide people while they were making a bridge and even if the bridge was in bad repair she would hold it up for them and they would not fall down into the Strickland River. (Stewart and Strathern 2002: 170)

Another senior Duna man added that the Yuro Ima was actually thought to have made her own invisible magical bridge, known as the *hiwa soko*, "the black-palm bridge," near where the Porgera Joint Venture Company has its water-monitoring station (called SG3) on the Strickland River. He said that she had a pond there that was the same one into which an ancestor's heart (that later would turn into an *auwi* [ancestral] stone) had been thrown. But the water, he said, had been ruined by chemicals and "it looks as though she has been killed by these chemicals. That is really why we asked Porgera Joint Venture for compensation and why they paid us" (Stewart and Strathern 2002: 171). We have cited all these details regarding the Payame Ima because this was the spirit who was also thought to facilitate the growth of boys in the *palena anda*. Her specific role in this regard depended on her cosmic significance.

Another female spirit who is said to look after the environment and is thought to live in bodies of water is Horwar Saliyn among the Wola people of the Southern Highlands Province. The *iyshponda* ritual among the Wola was performed to appease the spirit in times of drought or when climatic conditions were negatively impacting crop production (Sillitoe 1993). Larger or smaller versions of the ritual were performed depending on the severity of the situation. The Wola ritual contains elements common to the Hagen Amb Kor celebration. These cults belong to a larger, related complex of ideas about females, fertility, sacrifice, and wealth (see Strathern and Stewart 2000a for a comparative discussion of female spirits in Melanesia and Indonesia).

Our excursus here on the wider cosmic significance of the Duna Payame Ima and comparable figures such as Dunumuni and Horwar Saliyn has been designed to show that these figures are comparable to the Sky Beings invoked in Hagen cults, particularly through their connections with environmental forces. The Duna Payame Ima was central to the *palena anda* or "bachelor cults" in the past. Our conclusion is that elements of initiation and elements of fertility cults are ultimately related in a single complex of ideas regarding overall societal reproduction and the environment. The same is true for the Enga area.

The Enga people practiced growth rituals for boys in the *sangai* (or *Sandalu* in the Eastern Enga area) bachelors' cult. A special chanted poem of praise (*titi pingi*) was recited to the boys while in seclusion as were protective spells (*sangai nemongo*). Lacey (1975) describes these practices in his "Oral Traditions as History" (pp. 199–244). The ritual leaders (*isingi akali*) in the *sangai* are senior bachelors "who have had much experience with the rites and were appointed as guardians of the ritual objects by their predecessors before those men moved from bachelorhood to the married state" (p. 205). Bachelors ranging in age from those entering into puberty to those in their late twenties would be taken to the *sangai* seclusion hut at night.

The first action that would be taken on by the boys would be the "cleaning" of their eyes with water from a sacred spring. This would be accompanied by *nemongo* (spell) chanting by the senior bachelor. The theme of this particular chant was that the boys needed to avoid seeing "male and female sexual organs and intercourse" (p. 206). After the eye washing the boys remove their clothes, wash, put on fresh clothing, and enter the seclusion house. Lacey refers to what he calls the main aim of the ritual: "to open the participants to the power emanating from the sacred objects so that they may have clear and significant dreams" (p. 208). Lacey explains that his informants stressed that the importance of the *sangai* rites was to make boys ready for adult life: "The purpose of the *sangai* is to help youths grow into strong young warriors. They must be strong if they are to defend their clan" (p. 209).

In addition to dreaming and interpreting their dreams, the secluded boys learned special *nemongo* spells that were recited by the senior bachelor. Some of the more frequently recited *nemongo* that Lacey recorded were "*lenge pingi* (the washing of the eyes), *kalya* (*kai*) *pingi* (the rubbing of the skin with the leaves and bark of the sacred *lepe* plant), *enda ita lelya miningi* (recited as a spell to attract women as lovers while stirring the ashes of the fire) and *titi pingi* (praise poems for the *lepe* plant)" (p. 223). The final stage of the ritual is when the boys emerge from the seclusion house as "beautiful, purified, and powerful young bachelors and warriors" (p. 211). It is at this point that the boys are greeted by rows of young women who have come to view them, singing and taunting the youths. A girl marks out the one whom she thinks is most handsome and strong as a potential future husband. Courting rituals and marriage negotiations may follow this event.

During the time of seclusion the Enga boys were said to be married to a spirit woman who gave them the power to grow (Wiessner and Tumu 1998: 226). This closely parallels the *palena anda* (boys' seclusion) cult among the Duna, in which the Payame Ima is said to become the spirit wife to the ritual bachelor expert who teaches the boys. For the *sangai* cult, one narrative tells how the sacred plants used in the seclusion house to make the boys grow and become strong, *Acorus calamus* (Enga *lepe*), sprang from the breasts of the Female Spirit. Likewise, the bamboo containers that contained sacred fluids used in the *sangai* ritual were planted by the bachelors. Half of these containers were seen as female while the other half were male. Their co-planting represented a second marriage and marked the interdependence of the genders (Wiessner and Tumu 1998: 227; see also Strathern and Stewart 2000a).

Wiessner and Tumu, in their discussion of the Enga *mote* initiation cults of the past, note that "the *mote* boys' initiation appears to have been directed at the "*molopai* python and the sky people (*yalyakali*). For example, the sacred plaques revealed to the initiates depicted sun, moon, snake, rainbow, and specific sky people, and the water of life (*yalipa*, "sky water) partaken to confer health and long life stemmed from the sky people" (1998: 194). They further note that the water of life "symbolized the breast milk of two sky women, Yongalume (dawn) and Kulume (evening), who in Enga cosmology appear as the evening and morning stars respectively" (p. 207). (We may be reminded here of the two springs *mökili*, "open," and *kumbili*, "close," in the origin myth of the Hagen Eimb cult.) Drinking this breast milk of the spirits was supposed to free the boys from the breast milk of their human mothers. We may interpret this as an expression for maturation, not as an expression for becoming free of "female contamination." The *yalyakali*'s role here is, however, generally comparable to the power of the Hagen Female Spirit to strengthen men's skin and stomachs against the potentially dangerous power of female blood. The attribution of the meaning of the water of life to the breast milk of the spirits is startling in the context of the supposed association of "females" with "pollution" (see Goldman 1983: 93 on Huli ideas). It fits, however, with the detail reported by Lacey that the *lepe* plants sprang from the breasts of the Female Spirit, which we have noted above. This detail is confirmed by Wiessner and Tumu (1998: 228), reporting on a myth collected in Laiagam by Gray (1973). In this myth a young man goes to the bush to perform his own growth rites. He falls asleep in a makeshift hut and the next morning a beautiful woman appears outside of this hut and offers him pandanus nuts. She lines the nuts up on her outstretched leg and tells him to eat them without using his hands. He does so, and they make love. The following morning he finds himself transformed into a handsome man. The spirit woman gives him magnificent decorations and sends him home. When the other young men try to follow his example they grow angry because the spirit woman offers to make love to them, and they kill her and cut her to pieces. Her spirit appears to the first young man and, as he weeps over her body, she tells him to cut off her breasts and bury them. "The sacred *lepe* plant for the Sangai grows out of the earth where the breasts were buried" (Wiessner and Tumu 1998: 228).

"Male cults" as a category (usually referring to initiations) were a center-piece of anthropological theorizing on the Highlands of New Guinea in the 1960s and 1970s. They were interpreted as being the symbolic locus of separation between the sexes, of antagonism, and of domination. In more recent years this category has been deconstructed, along with a re-evaluation of the earlier ethnography on gender relations (Strathern and Stewart 1999f). Differences between Highlands societies were in fact recognized from early on, along with the distinction between male initiation rituals, bachelors' cults, and cults centered on community aims of fertility and prosperity. Here, however, we have sought to point out similarities among these practices in terms of underlying cosmological notions.

We have emphasized the significance of a Collaborative Model rather than a "Male Exclusivity" Model for understanding the broader patterns of co-operation between females and males that exist within some of the societies labeled as marked by "male cults," in particular those centered on fertility in general (Stewart and Strathern 1997a, 1999a). The exposition of the importance of Female Spirits as an object of ritual practices in these "male cults" has played a part in helping to develop this model. Here we explore the further relevance of these findings for the understanding of ideas about sexual relations, in the context of social reproduction.

These cults would be initiated at times of environmental stress or prolonged sickness among the people. The female spirit who was honored in the Pangia cult was the Laiyeroa (Strathern and Stewart 1999e). Two complementary cult houses would be built when the ceremony was to be held. One was the "men's house" and the other was called the "women's house"—both were only for the male participants of the cult. Stones that represented the power of the Female Spirit were placed in both houses. In the men's house long stones that had been decorated with bands of colored pigments (i.e., red, black, and yellow) were placed beside a log and rested on top of a bed of leaves. In the women's house stones shaped like mortar bowls were placed. In these bowl-shaped stones cassowary feces were cooked. The stones were then rubbed with these heated feces.

Another house, called the *ombolo* house, was built. At this point it was said the Laiyeroa had come, and the night was spent chanting to the spirit. As with the Amb Kor cult in Hagen, the sacred chants and spells traced the pathways of the cult from its putative origin places. In one of these spells, the names of rivers and streams were called on because water spirits in the stones of the stream beds were said to have caused sickness and the Female Spirit was asked to make this sickness go away—back into the water from which it had come. Some spells were chanted while the pork meat was cooking for the feast. These spells asked that gardens and pigs be made to grow well and women to remain healthy. The next day the cult participants prepared a large pig kill and the men decorated themselves for a dance to the spirit (see Strathern and Stewart 1999e).

The Amb Kor (Female Spirit) cult in Hagen was directed toward ridding the community of sickness and restoring the environment to a healthy and fertile state, as was the Laiyeroa cult. Strauss (1962: 436–39) recounts an origin story of the cult. In it a severe drought was said to have devastated the central Hagen area—streams and rivers had completely dried up. The people were said to have observed rain clouds to their southwest. Two men traveled to where the clouds were seen in the mountainous and rainy Kaugel region, which is said to be the cult's origin place. There the men met two young women who gave them magical plants including red cordylines (this plant is one of the sacred plants associated with the Female Spirit and is used as decoration during the cult performance). The women told the men that they would come to them later. When the men returned they planted the cordylines, and that night a storm arose with lightning and thunder. In the morning the men found two long stones behind their men's house that were manifestations of the Amb Kor. These stones were said to have given rise to "children stones." Each of the men who would be participating in the celebration to the Amb Kor took one of these children stones for himself so as to consecrate it in the cult performance. After doing this, it was said that the people in this group were healthy and fertile and crops and pigs grew well.

When it was time for an Amb Kor performance to be held, the Female Spirit was said to appear to the man who would initiate the ceremony. She might be seen by him as a decorated female, a stone, or a white bird of paradise (Strathern and Stewart 1997b). She imparted to this man the knowledge that he would need in order to ensure that the appropriate sequences of events were followed in the performance.

The male cult performers were divided into two groups: *rapa* ("men's house") and *amb-nga* ("women's house"). (The term "house" here does not refer to a separate building. Both the *rapa* and the *amb-nga* were located physically within the same structure.) The performers from the two "houses" were paired with each other and each pair was required to act in complete unity. These pairs usually consisted of father and son or classificatory brothers but not full brothers.

The actual planning and completing of the Amb Kor performance could take months or years to complete. The stones that were used in the ritual were rubbed with fat and painted with red ocher. Some of these stones were displayed on the *rapa* side of the cult house while others were shown on the *amb-nga* side. On the *rapa* side a pig's uterus was buried, marking the end of the ritual inside of the cult house. Then the men danced in pairs to celebrate the successful completion of the ritual. Many spectators came to observe this and receive the pork meat that was distributed from the huge cooking (see Strathern and Stewart 1999e for further details of the Amb Kor celebration). In both the Hagen and Pangia cults there are elements that relate to the theme of initiation and purification of the body. In Pangia the participants were described as *more*, a term that is synonymous with the term for an earlier initiation cult among the Enga, the *mote*, mentioned earlier. The presence of this term in Pangia attests to a widespread distribution of ideas about initiation that are embedded in fertility cults within those language areas cognate with the Enga language (see in this connection in Goldman 1983: 237 on the Huli phrase *igiri more*, "virgin boys"). In Hagen, young boys were taken into the inner part of the Spirit's enclosure and shown the sacred stones for the first time as their induction into the cult and the powers of fertility it represented. They also became *mowi*, "set apart" from the rest of the community, observing food taboos, and eating only food cooked inside the cult enclosure as boys also did in the Duna *palena* cult.

Central in importance in many of the Highlands cult activities, devoted toward stimulating or ensuring growth of young boys, was a "purification" or removal of bodily "impurities" and the taking in of substances considered to be "pure" or life giving, such as water. A temporary physical separation of these young boys from sexually active adults would also occur. What have been called "bachelors' cults" in the Southern Highlands in the Huli and Duna areas of PNG (Ballard 1998; Glasse 1968; Modjeska 1977; Strathern and Stewart 1999a, 1999e) and in the Enga Province of PNG (Biersack 1982, 2001; Meggitt 1964; Wiessner and Tumu 1998) involved preparing young men to enter into adult activities, which included marriage and sexual activity.

Both bachelors' cult rituals and male initiation ceremonies were temporary points of transition in which boys were prepared for adult life. During these phases boys were separated from male-female sexual activities and entered into a milieu of seclusion where they were taught by other males how to "grow" in body and mind and to become "responsible" male actors in their society. This was a time when the boys learned to be self-sufficient and to rely on their abilities to take care of themselves. Male bodily substances were sometimes transferred from senior males to youths to assist in the maturation process of the boys. These events were aimed at completing the boys' development so that they could become mature males who would marry and begin procreating by joining their energies to those of women. The time in the seclusion houses demonstrated to the youths the extensive labor required to produce their own foods without the assistance of females. It also demonstrated the potential for males to be self-sufficient while highlighting the fact that women are required to procreate, an important theme in the myths of Highlanders. The need for collaboration between man and women to reproduce and produce was a strong message of these rituals. Frequently, female imagery was presented throughout the seclusion phase for these youths through spirit forces invoked in myths or otherwise, as we have already seen.

These ceremonies always took place in forested areas away from the settlements, thus demonstrating the boys' temporary removal from social action as practiced in general. The relationship established by the men participating in these ceremonies would last throughout the years and be expressed in group allegiance in fighting and hunting, assistance in group activities such as ceremonial exchange occasions, and in some instances establishing affinal ties. These youths, for the most part, would go on to enter into marriage after completing the growth rituals. Part of the function of these ceremonies may well have been to cement male-to-male relationships through male participation in the boys' maturation, which could serve as a counter to the sustained relationship that the boys would have to their mothers through the maternal role in the boys' growth. This process of strengthening male-to-male bonds would perhaps readjust the flow of wealth items and distribution of goods between the youths and men, and the youths and women and mother's kin. Another aspect of the lessons taught in the seclusion period was the definition of "correct" and desirable patterns of adult behavior as defined by the society itself. Limiting relations of young boys with their mother and sister(s) reduced the likehood of incestuous relationships.

In the Duna area the *palena anda* was a bachelors' cult in which a Female Spirit (Payame Ima) worked collaboratively with an adult male bachelor as his spirit wife (see chapter 5; Strathern and Stewart 1999e, 2000a). The Payame Ima was said to come to the bachelor who was to become the ritual leader in the *palena anda* to assist him in training the boys to become adult males who would be ready to marry, fight bravely in local disputes, and avoid "inappropriate" sexual interactions such as incestuous relationships. Duna youths were not supposed to have sexual intercourse outside of socially prescribed relationships. Senior Duna men who are knowledgeable about the *palena anda* practices have told us that in the past young people would be killed for engaging in uncondoned sexual liaisons.

In addition to providing knowledge to the ritual expert in general, the Payame Ima revealed to him the sacred *palena* plants that ensured the boys' growth and gave them a healthy skin. The equivalent among the neighboring Huli are the *ibagiya* (water-given) plants. *Ibagiya* were said to have emerged from the body of a young woman who entered into a Huli bachelors' cult enclosure and was killed (Frankel 1986). The story is a multilayered, complex tale with themes common to the Duna Payame Ima as well as the story of Dunumuni among the Bedamini and the Enga stories of the *lepe* plant. An initial sequence in the story involves a young man who receives mysterious help each night with a new garden. He eventually ambushes the last of a line of young women who he believes is responsible for these mysterious events. The woman is a transformer figure (see Stewart and Strathern 2001a: 73–74) who goes through a number of physical alterations when the man takes hold of her but eventually reveals herself as a young woman. Through a sequence of events involving seduction, seclusion, neglect, and error, the man shoots her for supposedly "intruding" on the bachelors' cult enclosure. When this happens she tells him to pour her blood into two different kinds of bamboo tubes. These were to be hidden and surrounded by a protective fence. After doing this he finds that from her body on the eighth day (the customary day of a woman's return from a menstrual hut) the *ibagiya* plants had sprung up in addition to the magic plants that are good for making pigs grow (Frankel 1986: 99). The Huli tradition parallels in several ways the stories of the Payame Ima providing the *palena* plants to the *palena* boys to help them. Likewise, among the Paiela a female spirit called Ginger Woman provides the magical "ginger" plant to the boys in the bachelors' cult, which enables them to become attractive to females (Biersack 1982). According to Biersack, the ginger plant is chosen because of its regenerative capacities, which are said to resemble those of hair.

The magical spells (*mini mindi kāo*) that the boys sang while in seclusion were aimed at ensuring their attractiveness and good health, making them fit for adult duties. Themes invoked in these spells included:

1. Hair preparation by combing, and applying water, pig fat, and intertwining sections of vines to reinforce the hairdo.
2. Calling on birds such as the parakeet and the honeyeater to assist in making the boys' hair strong like bird feathers.
3. Invoking clouds and water sources to make the boys' hair damp and large and pouring water into the hair from bamboo tubes.
4. Spells to make the boys' decorations look fine when they leave the seclusion area and dance for the young girls and the rest of the community.

SPELLS (*MINI MINDI KĀO*)

Knowledge that the Payame Ima spirit gave the ritual experts among the Duna facilitated their task of making boys grow properly into mature, healthy men who would be prepared to marry and lead adult lives. In the not too distant past (prior to 1960) this included preparation to be a warrior in tribal fighting. The Payame Ima would putatively show the ritual expert how to use water to enhance the masculinizing aspects of the boys' bodies (e.g., their hair growth) and how to grow the magical plants that the boys would look after while they were in seclusion in the high forest away from the women and children of the community. The following is an example of a spell recited by a ritual expert to the boys while in their seclusion (Stewart and Strathern 2000d), comparable to that given in chapter 6.

> Iruli tane tane pondo pondo
> Kope ta ko wero
> Apane kope ta ko perako

Andane kope ta ko wero
Andane kondo kondo wero
Andane kondo kondo wero
Apane kondo kondo kope ta ko wero
Tapane kondo kondo kope ta ko wero
Kayame kondo kondo kope ta ko wero
Andane kondo kondo kope ta ko wero
Tali tali ndoko ndoko kondo kondo . . .
Andande ndoko ndoko sangwa . . .
Kayame ndoko ndoko sangwa . . .
Malu pa ipa pi
Malu pa ipa limu lama ipa
Peipa pi ipa limu lama ipa
Ape pi ipa limu lama ipa
Alupa ipa pi limu lama ipa
Kokora ipa pi limu lama ipa
Ape mane ngisako ipa kuli yu kuya
Aluka mane ngisako . . .
Kokora mane ngisako . . .

He teases out the long hair
Like a cloud, he anoints it with fat and water drops
Whistling and singing
Whistling and singing of kidney fat
Whistling and singing at ease
He combs the hair at ease
He applies pig-fat at ease
Combs it with a bamboo comb
The comb is sharp
He combs the hair at ease

Looking for the hair, he prods and prods
He says, "I will get the hair [and pull it out]
With the sharp comb.
I make the *malu* wig, I make it with water.
I make it with water and a vine from the forest
I make the *peipa* wig with water and a vine
I make the *ape* wig with water and a vine
I make the *alupa* wig with water and a vine
Now morning comes
Morning comes and I sprinkle water on the hair
I sprinkle water with a red cordyline leaf
Give me this in the morning
Give me this at dawn."

In terms of spatial distribution, the important thing to note about the *palena anda* was that it was constructed in forest areas above the areas of settlement: that is, in a liminal area in between garden zones and the limestone caves where bones of the dead were placed. This part of the forest is especially associated with clean streams and pools of water, which the expert called on in his spells (*mini mindi kāo*) (Stewart and Strathern 2000d). (Further examples of some of these spells can be found in Strathern and Stewart 1999e.)

FURTHER FEMALE SPIRITS

Powerful female spirits like the Payame Ima are important figures in ethnographic accounts across a geographic span from Hagen to the Ok area. For example, in the Strickland-Bosavi region among the Kaluli people we find that a *mamul* (spirit) woman was spoken of as married to the male leader of the *bau aa* ritual (bachelors' cult). The cult was aimed at making boys grow into manhood (as was the Duna *palena anda*) (Schieffelin 1976: 126–27). As in the *palena anda*, the boys left the seclusion house, where the *bau aa* had taken place, "decked in their brightest finery, so handsome and so much grown in a few months [after leaving the *bau aa*], many of the bachelors got married" (p. 126). This parallels ways in which the *palena anda* cult in Duna grew boys so that they would be beautiful and thus selected by women for marriage (Strathern and Stewart 1999e; Stewart and Strathern 1999d; see also chapter 6 on body decoration).

It is important to note that it was the Kaluli girls who were expected to choose handsome men to marry after they left the *bau aa*. Thus male agency is exemplified through display and female agency is expressed through selection.

The *mamul* spirit woman was said to be from Mt. Bosavi and came in the guise of an oddly shaped stone. The Female Spirit, Amb Kor, at the center of the Amb Kor fertility cult in Hagen is also said to show herself to men in the form of special stones, as we have seen (Strathern and Stewart 1999a, 1999e). The female stone figure's role in the *bau aa* is not elaborated on further by Schieffelin. For the Ipili (Paiela) of the Southern Highlands (PNG) the *kepele* fertility cult also involved gendered stones. Philip Gibbs (1978) has described the *kepele* as being performed in times of environmental crisis as a means of ritually restimulating the fertility of the ground. The ritual was performed by men who were guided by special experts. Two stones were at the core of the ritual. One was the *ewa*, a round black stone said to be the head of an original ancestor. This stone would be buried along with pork belly fat by a ritual expert so that it would "keep its eyes closed and sleep," that is, not make people sick (Gibbs 1978: 439). The second stone was the *kepele* stone, described by Gibbs (p. 439) as "a large white vulva shaped stone." To this stone would be brought a male figure constructed out of wood and cane, a *yupini*. This figurine was made to dance up and down, showing its genitals, and when it was taken to the back of the cult house it was used to simulate sexual intercourse with the *kepele* stone. Then the stone would be burnished with pig fat, leaves, and tree oil. The *kepele* cult belongs to the widespread class of "fertility-crisis" cults, but shares with these an overall concern for social reproduction and the use of symbolic sexual union to stimulate fertility for the community as a whole. The *yupini*, we suggest, is like a human male, and the *kepele* is like the female spirit. The *kepele* ritual's structure corresponds to the same elementary focus that is at the heart of the collaborative scenario of the genders in which cosmic renewal is paramount in the struggle to retain fertility and health. (Further discussion of the *yupini* can be found in Dosedla 1984; Wiessner and Tumu 1998: 204, 207, 209.)

A practice similar to the *kepele* among the Enga people was the *aeatee anda* ritual of renewal, which was performed at cycles of approximately ten years (Lacey 1975: 120–56). Lacey, who recorded oral traditions of the Enga people, explains that in the ritual's "legitimating myth" the "protagonists in this legend are understood to be sky people (*yalyakali*), beings of great beauty and power who intervene in the life of human beings." These spirits are associated with the sacred stones used in the ritual itself. The myth that he collected tells of a mother and daughter who were traveling together. The daughter walked ahead of the mother and at dark she met a man named Kapeali of Talyulu who asked her if she would like to rest in his house. He prepared foods for her to eat and they decided to have sexual intercourse, but before they did so "Kapeali asked the woman if she knew any spells (*nemongo*) which they could recite for their protection. The woman said to Kapeali that they should recite a *nemongo* which contained the names of all the food crops" (p. 121). The two decided to stay together and Kapeali's brother went to cut the tree that would be the center post of their house. This action is repeated by the men in the *aeatee anda* ritual when they build the cult house. "This house became their dwelling place and she later became the sacred stones which live in that house. Her name is *aeatee* and the house is the *aeatee anda*. In times when there is drought or food shortage or widespread disease, then the woman will be seen again in the region of her house. When she appears, then men know that it is time to build her house again to ensure that Apulini people will prosper" (p. 121).

It is the *nemongo* that the woman gave to her human partner that the ritual specialists are said to use to ensure fertility through the *aeatee anda* performance. These experts are said to be the direct agnatic male descendants of Kapeali. Lacey explains further that among the Apulini and Yanaitini Enga peoples it "is the belief that the continuity and health of the groups and the fertility of their crops depend on the renewal of a correct ritual relationship with the women-stones" (p. 122).

The cyclical performance of the ritual itself was intertwined with the *tee* exchange system, linking the fertility ceremonies with the exchange rituals

(p. 122). During the preparations for the *aeatee anda* ritual the house itself was constructed and while the roofing materials were drying a male leader would initiate a *tee* pig exchange with allies by presenting them with gifts that began the cycle of exchange that might run over years.

During the *aeatee anda* ritual the male participants crawled into the ritual house, bringing foods that represented all their crops. This act of crawling parallels that of participants in the Hagen Female Spirit performances. Then the ritual expert revealed the stones to the participants. The main one "is shaped like a woman and this is the *aeatee* woman" (p. 124). This stone was encircled by smaller stones said to be her children. All of the stones were rubbed with pig fat and subsequently buried along with samples of the food crops.

OTHER CASES

The model of gender symbolism that we have proposed is exemplified in the Enga practices and is further represented in Andrew Lattas's ethnographic descriptions of the Kaliai (West New Britain, PNG) practices: "Nearly all the major male mythic heroes of this culture belong to the female gendered moiety" and express "symbolic femaleness" (Lattas 1989: 456). The original creator figure for the Kaliai is the cassowary (a creature that encompasses both male and female imagery, see Strathern and Stewart 2000a: chap. 4). As we have done occasionally earlier in this book, we cite here materials from outside of the Highlands in order to point up comparisons between the Highlands and other regions of PNG. We also include further examples of materials from other areas (see also Lipset 1997).

Kaliai myths tell of a time when women discovered how to create terrifying masks and other *tambaran* (masks, bull roarers, bamboo wind instruments, etc.). These items belong now to the *tambaran* cult, which men perform (see Lattas 1998). At that time "women and not men had beards, whereas men had breasts, which women did not possess. Women gave birth to children, but they then passed their children on to be wet-nursed by their husbands" (p. 155). A Kaliai male ancestor who was said to have taken the *tambaran* cult away from women supposedly originated from the cassowary's left, or female side, wing (Lattas 1989: 465). Lattas continues that this ancestor was "physically male" but "symbolically female, his very person representing a unity of gender opposites." The cassowary is said to have taken the bull roarer from its female inventor, to have taken women's beards and given them to men, and to have removed men's breasts and given them to women (p. 457). These mythical events are matched in ritual practice when the actions of females and males function collaboratively to express what in day-to-day life is the negotiation of gender relations. Lattas concludes that "the tambaran embodies and reifies the social power of female reproduction" (p. 466).

Lattas argues that for the Kaliai "female sexuality represents both the mythical source of male power and yet that which threatens male strength in the present" (Lattas 1989: 466). This perceptive observation can also be taken to hold for parts of the Highlands of New Guinea. It resonates well with the significance of the "scheme of potentiality" in Highlands rituals that is a design feature aimed at recognizing and resolving the contradiction involved. It resonates also with the "double-gendered" character of mythical creator figures such as the cassowary (Strathern and Stewart 2000a) and with the Ok region (PNG) and its traditions and practices centered on the female ancestor Afek.

The story of Afek "belongs to the range of secret knowledge revealed gradually to men in the course of initiation. It reveals the meaning behind ritual, the rationale behind custom, a reality behind the surface appearance of the world" (Brumbaugh 1990: 54). The myth of Afek is common among the Mountain-Ok people and versions of it are revealed as men move through the levels of initiation. One of the first aspects of her myth that Telefolmin men in the Ok area learn about is her travels into the Ok area from the east. She is credited with inventing sexual intercourse and she releases crops and animals to fill the land from her reproductive organs. "The men's cult and its initiation sequence come from Afek . . . just at the point when they [the initiants] are first severed from their mothers and sisters [to enter the initiation sequence] and brought over sharply into male society, Telefolmin boys find themselves in a woman's world, designed by Afek" (p. 68).

Roy Wagner (1978) has described gender relations among the Daribi of Chimbu Province in Papua New Guinea as expressing sexual complementarity designed to maintain a balance in social functioning (p. 76). In the myths of the Daribi this balancing of female powers with male desires is recounted. In the story of Tumani People, women are seen as creating man's sexuality. "In a myth called 'Siapagewe' ('Firebase Woman'), a completely sufficient woman lives alone, the heat of her genitals being sufficient to kill potential sex partners. When a male intruder succeeds in excising her genitals, the genders take complementary roles in gardening and other activities" (p. 77).

Wagner uses his notion of complementarity to construct a picture of Daribi society in which women and men work together to create a functional social existence, or one in which the procreative powers of women are balanced with the roles that men play. Various aspects of food intake are regulated when boys undergo initiation. They are first separated from the community and do not eat food that has been cooked by their own mothers or other women of the clan but consume special foods provided to them by the male leaders in charge of the initiation of the boys. After the initiation is completed the boys leave the initiation house, and they are then given a feast where they are reintegrated into social life and receive food cooked by the women of the clan (Wagner 1972: 47–48).

Male initiation among the Etoro as described by Raymond Kelly (1993: 157–74) is another expression of gender balancing that prepares youths for adult male roles in their social structure. The youths are initiated while in their teens or early twenties. At this point they enter a seclusion house at the border of the primary forest. The initiates who have been through the rituals of initiation previously but remain bachelors enter the seclusion house along with the uninitiated youths. They hunt and trap together and plant bachelor gardens during this time away from the other members of their group. The relations between the youths and the men in the seclusion house also serve to protect them against witchcraft accusations. "Confirmed witches are excluded from the seclusion lodge proceedings, and the men who participate are presumed to be free of witchcraft. Young men who are subsequently accused are thought to have secretly consorted with witches outside this context" (p. 158). Here we see a fear of male witchcraft as a central concern for those involved in the initiation ceremony.

However, we also learn of the importance of the mother and maternal kin in the development of the youths in the ceremony that follows the emergence of the boys from the seclusion house. "About five months later [after leaving seclusion] there is a second ceremony at which the initiates' heads are anointed with tree oil by an older man, typically a mother's brother (or member of the latter's lineage)" (p. 161). "[T]he tree oil connotes female substance in that it is *heare*, an analogue of blood" (p. 162). This implies that it is in fact Campnosperma oil, which the Foi people associate with menstrual blood and fertility (Weiner 1995: 159). After this ceremony the boys are ready to enter marriage. Most of the men did not marry until they had mentored boys in the seclusion house in another cycle of initiations. The mentoring males were also establishing marriage ties for themselves. The initiation was "one component of an exchange in which a man transmits life force to a youth and then receives the latter's true or classificatory sister in marriage" (p. 162). A similar but inverted exchange has been reported for the Kamula in which the mentor of the youth is the future father-in-law or eldest brother-in-law (Wood 1982: 80).

The initiation of boys begins with their separation from their mothers and sisters. This is the beginning of the boys' relationship with their future wife-givers (p. 221). The first phase of the initiation ceremony is a ritual known as *boropa mu*, "see the old woman." In this stage an uncooked pig is shown to the boys in addition to the other meats for the celebration. One account suggests that this pig serves as a substitute for the novices themselves being consumed (a familiar theme in Highlands mythology, for example among the Duna).

Kaiyarno was going to hold *boropa mu* by killing and eating his son. But his wife said "Don't do that! Use a pig instead!" So he put a pig there instead of his son. (p. 232)

After the consumption of this pig the boys prepare themselves for the dance. The next phase of the ceremony is a raid on non-Kamula. Women could accompany the men and would assist in carrying the flesh back to Kamula territory. "The preconditions to a successful raid are a performance of 'seeing the old woman' [*boropa mu*] and the agreement of the spirits of the head that it is auspicious to hold the raid" (p. 236). Upon their return from the raid, a feast is held. At this time "anyone who is in mourning for a recent death may remove all the special decorations associated with mourning and burn them in the fires cooking the flesh" (p. 236). It is said that the consumption of some of the flesh of these victims "makes the novices 'grow' " (p. 240). The last phase of the ceremony is when the novices are presented with chest bands and other decorations and a ceremonial pig kill is held. It is remarkable that in myth the opportunity to grow up rather than being sacrificed is finessed for the boy by his mother: surely a significant feature here.

Initiation ceremonies among the Samo of the East Strickland Plain (PNG) have been described by R. Daniel Shaw (1990). The Samo *kandila* is a three-day ceremony in which males and females are co-initiated in a condensation or "microcosm that can be applied to the macrocosm in which the Samo live" (p. 15). The initiands are eighteen to twenty-five years old and interact as a group in a public demonstration of specific gendered roles. Shaw states that "*kandila* provides an opportunity for those older than the initiates to reinforce cultural themes and demonstrate the value of alliance" (p. 161). The *kandila* ceremony is preceded by two years of preparation and training of the young people in their roles as members of society at large. On the first day of the ceremony allies are received and at night a feast is shared. The second day consists of the boy initiands dressing. "This ceremonial regalia enables them to counteract supernatural forces for the rest of their lives" (p. 8). Female initiands mingle with the male initiates, and married women instruct both these young men and women to dance. On the third day a military charade is enacted with the male initiates entering into mock battle with the groups of allies that have come for the celebration. The significant role of senior women is clear in this account of Samo initiation practices (pp. 137–54).

Among the Ilaga Dani of the Irian Jaya Highlands special spirits called *amulok*, "umbilical cords," serve as protective guardian spirits to men (Larson 1987: 65–68). At birth the child's umbilical cord is burned or thrown into a stream along with the afterbirth. The locale of this deposit is said to be the birth place of the child. "Soon after a boy is born his mother ties on him an identification bracelet made of string for his *amulok* spirits to see" (p. 66). At around the age of five a boy's father will take him to an oak (*teno*) grove and sacrifice a pig to his *amulok* spirits. After the pork is cooked the father removes the boy's identification bracelet that his mother had put on him, and ties it, together with a piece of charred firewood that had been used to heat the cooking stones, to the trunk of a large tree in the grove. The father then reveals the names of the *amulok* spirits to his son. "Most [of the spirits] are female and their names reflect some circumstances of his birth or activity of early childhood" (p. 66). "For example, Fence Blood (*Negerabon*) is the name of a guardian of those born outside in a hamlet courtyard. Another is called *Nggut*-sounding Woman (*Ngguroone Kwe*) because she is identified with a bird called *Kunggut* found in nearby forests where boys first learn to hunt small game" (p. 82). This sort of sacrifice will not be repeated again until the boy is ready for marriage or if he becomes sick and an attempt is made through the ceremony to appease his guardian spirits. When the ceremony is held prior to marriage the father reveals further information: the names of all the birth spirits of his local patrilineage. These other spirits have the role of "instilling bravery in battle and bringing healing to the wounded during warfare" (p. 67).

The examples we have given in this section are various. We have adduced them not to "prove" our case for the importance of female imagery and female participation at the heart of "male" cults in parts of the Highlands region of New Guinea, but rather to show that in many areas complex ideas about gender relations, complementarity, balance, and the importance of male and female collaboration tend to show at the edges of ethnographic descriptions even when these ideas are not foregrounded by the ethnographers themselves. One of our particular arguments in this chapter has been to show the intertwining of notions regarding male initiation or boys' maturation rites with ideas regarding Female Spirits and their cosmic significance. Such an intertwining of ideas and practices influenced the overall tenor of gender relations and the emotions associated with these. We have not, of course, attempted to annul the obvious differences in tone, emphasis, and customary particularity among these cases. Our general point has been that an overall emphasis on gender complementarity is a hidden narrative within the narratives of male cult activities in the Highlands. And an important part of this narrative is that the secret context of male growth is itself either presided over by a female spirit, as among the Duna, or is at any rate seen as a prelude to the moment in gender relations that we have been concerned with, the time of courtship and marriage. This moment was powerfully infused with the kinds of ritual practices and religious images we have been describing. Initiation for manhood had as much to do with sexual maturation, attractiveness, and the ability to obtain a wife as with other social aims such as the ability to fight.

MENSTRUAL POWERS

The interpretation of ideas about menstrual blood has been central to many assessments of gender relations in the New Guinea Highlands. Here we look at the place of menstrual blood in the imagination and its significance in shifting expressions of gender relations and in regard to its physical manifestations. Menstrual blood is seen as a powerful bodily fluid in many contexts, especially in its recognized role as a source of fertility and as part of the cosmic cycle of fertility. Buckley and Gottlieb (1988a) point out that the category "menstrual taboos" covers a diverse set of practices, and is therefore multivalent (1988b: 7). In spite of this, they remark, theories to explain the widespread occurrence of these taboos have tended either to see them simply as a source of male oppression, or as evidence of psychological complexes; or perhaps in both terms, taken together, we might add. They go on to note that these taboos regulate the behavior of others as well as the menstruating woman, and that rules of taboo should be regarded as having "cosmological ramifications" (p. 9), and also that these practices may include the aim of protecting women, or of giving them social spaces in which they can relax and perhaps socialize with one another or enjoy relief from garden work and cooking for men. Buckley and Gottlieb add that there is a kind of androcentric bias in the interpretations anthropologists have made of taboos generally. For example, if women are tabooed from touching male hunting gear, this is interpreted as a mark of male dominance; whereas if men may not touch something in the female domain, it is interpreted as a sign of female inferiority. In other words, whatever the direction of the taboos, they are interpreted by some anthropologists as demonstrating male dominance (p. 14). This is a shrewd and significant point. Commenting on it further, we suggest that such taboos do not necessarily mark out a linear form of status at all; that is, they do not have to be unambiguous marks of the overall superiority/inferiority of either gender group. Rather, as Buckley and Gottlieb also counsel, they should be interpreted in specific ways appropriate to local cultural logics. Here the most productive clue is their observation that menstrual taboos have "cosmological ramifications" (p. 9). It is within this domain also that the issue of "pollution" has to be settled. Our discussions of cosmology and Female Spirits have prepared us to consider this issue, which has been made central to the evaluation of gender relations.

Buckley and Gottlieb survey the development of theories on this issue from Durkheim and Mauss onward. They cite Mary Douglas's famous theory of "dirt" as matter out of place (pp. 26–27), and her identification of questions of power as central to the interpretation of menstrual rules of seclusion. Seeing menstrual flows of blood as an example of "anomaly," Douglas argued that such anomalies may be seen as dangerous if their power contradicts other power structures in the society (p. 29). Menstrual taboos will then signal this contradiction. To this line of reasoning belong propositions of the kind that Buckley and Gottlieb attribute to Raymond Kelly, to the effect that "women are viewed as polluting in societies in which men are dependent on them as sources of prestige" (p. 29, drawing on Ortner and Whitehead 1981b: 20). Here it is being suggested that men's dependency sets up a contradiction between their claim to power over others and their actual dependency on others; hence in the case of women this is marked by menstrual taboos. The language here generalizes matters to the point of arguing that "women are viewed as polluting," rather than making the more modest claim that "menstrual flows are regarded as dangerous if they are not properly channeled." By this logic also, since leading men in New Guinea Highlands societies are in fact dependent on the labor of other men as well as that of their wives, we might have expected comparable sorts of taboos in relation to the male body and its substances to apply to these men, which we do not in fact find, although we do find that leaders were sometimes afraid their male subordinates might kill them by sorcery.

Mervyn Meggitt's argument provided another putative correlate of menstrual taboos. He proposed for the Mae Enga of the Papua New Guinea Highlands that the practice of these taboos was a reflection of inter-group hostilities, since Enga men marry women of enemy clans (Meggitt 1964: 218–19). Meggitt's argument was an extreme case of sociological determinism. The taboos themselves were held to emerge directly from the structure of society. Such a form of argument is at risk to cases where men also marry into enemy clans but do not hold strong fears of menstrual blood or enforce strong menstrual taboos, such as in the Pangia area of the Southern Highlands Province. Perhaps it is better to accept that ideas about the potentially dangerous powers of menstrual blood are widespread and run across a number of different social configurations. The fears that men have as to the likelihood that their own wives may use these powers to harm them may well, then, be correlated with the extent to which they think their wives may be inclined to use menstrual blood to kill them; and this may vary personally also. In other words, the question of fear belongs to the moral and interpersonal domain, and is distinct from the question of cosmological meanings. In societies where menstrual blood is held to be dangerous to men if ingested in food, therefore, women are enjoined, and indeed enjoin one another, to look after their husbands by refusing them food and intercourse at this time (see Marx 1994). The cosmological danger in fact becomes a source of collaborative interaction and sympathy between wife and husband. Meggitt's hypothesis, then, properly understood, is unlikely to predict the digital presence or absence of ideas about menstrual blood; it does predict circumstances in which there may be less interpersonal conjugal sympathy and hence a greater sense of danger on the part of men. On the other hand, it is likely that Mae Enga women, like Hagen women, were enjoined to take care of any problems arising from their menstrual powers and were blamed if they did not do so (see Kyakas and Wiessner 1992). Such a perspective also accords agency to women and grants them responsibility and social personhood. As well, it recognizes the point Buckley and Gottlieb also make, that spouses are thought to "share substance" and are therefore vulnerable to the reciprocal powers of these substances. We may cite here the point that in Hagen it was thought that the husband's semen could kill his infant child if the husband and wife had intercourse while the child was being breast-fed, since the "grease" (*kopong*) of the semen would enter inappropriately into the "grease" of the mother's milk and so make it lethal to the child's body and destroy it. This example forces us again to rethink the arguments regarding pollution and status that have surrounded discussions of menstrual blood (as we discuss further below). It is moral action by either gender that, in fact, is the focus in these "taboos," and the same substances may be life giving when "in place" and life threatening when "out of place" (see also Goldman and Ballard 1998). Meggitt (1964) also seems to have been unaware of the female associations of the sacred iris plants the Enga bachelors tended.

At the broadest level, the "shared substances" of the genders have to be regarded as embodiments of life forces (Buckley and Gottlieb 1988a, p. 36). Buckley and Gottlieb cite here the former Tiv ritual of mixing menstrual blood with the blood of a sacrificial child in a ritual pipe in order to bless the fertility of farms and women (p. 36). The *kirao hatya* rituals of the Duna area of Highlands Papua New Guinea show the same broad logic, as do notions regarding ways in which the Female Spirit in Hagen could manifest her powerful presence by the overnight appearance of her menstrual blood beside the house of a male leader to whom she chose to come as a "wife" (P. J. Stewart 1998; Stewart and Strathern 2002; Strathern and Stewart 1999e). Such life-forces can be either beneficial or dangerous, depending on how people behave toward them. The agency of both genders has to be taken into account in following this point through. One of the contributors to the Buckley and Gottlieb volume (C. Knight) takes this point much further by stressing greatly female agency in line with his own general speculative argument.

Chris Knight in *Blood Relations* (1991) further developed a general theory of the development of culture in hunter-gatherer times out of his interpretation of the category of "menstrual taboos." We are not concerned here with the evolutionary aspect of his ideas, but his analytical formulations fit with our discussions. These formulations are conveniently found in chapter 11 of his book (1991: 374–416). He begins with a recitation of well-known anthropological accounts, including three from the Highlands of Papua New Guinea, the Gimi, the Baruya, and the Mae Enga (Gillison 1980; Godelier 1986; Meggitt 1964), in which the ethnographers highlight the dangers to men of menstrual blood, and its power to neutralize the fertility of the earth (pp. 374–76). He notes, while rejecting as general explanations, the contradictory psychological theories of William Stephens and Bruno Bettelheim (pp. 376–77). Then he acknowledges the more recent influence exercised by Buckley and Gottlieb (1988a). The first point here is that things forbidden or holy may also be considered dangerous, and that a menstruating woman goes into seclusion "precisely because of the peculiar intensity of her presumed magical powers at this time" (Knight 1991: 385). Knight further argues for the agency that women may express through menstruation, and he interprets hunting taboos, by which men may not engage in intercourse while hunting game for fear of failure in the hunt, to be a result of women's agency rather than simply that of men (pp. 389–398). In this view, women impose the rule so that men will go out to hunt and bring back meat. (A theme that is often in fact seen in the mythology from the Highlands expresses the idea of Sky Women telling men that they need to go out and hunt meat for them to eat, see chapter 4.) Knight also suggests that the reason why the blood of hunted animals has to be kept separate from menstrual blood is precisely because of their potential similarity, since all shed blood is considered dangerous (p. 403). He also links this theme to women's agency.

Rephrasing his position, without its evolutionary emphasis, we can suggest the following. Blood "out of place," that is, shed from the body and flowing from a cut or wound, is in general considered dangerous and taboo. Blood "in place," doing its work in the body, for example, in the womb, is considered sacred and life giving. Hunting taboos require a mutual and complementary exercise of agency on the part of both men and women. The taboo on intercourse should be interpreted in this way here, as it should also be in relation to taboos observed in Female Spirit cults: in order for one important enterprise to succeed, another must be suspended, and this can happen only through collaborative efforts involving both women and men. Shedding the blood of an animal by shooting it with an arrow is similar to the way in which the moon is often said, for example, among the Hagen people, to shoot women so as to cause them to menstruate. These actions can be seen therefore as analogous or parallel to each other. The reason why they should be kept separate is that women's blood "out of place" could negate men's power to shed the blood of animals and cause it to be "out of place" or flow from the animals' bodies. With regard to hunting, then, women's power could negate that of men. Hunting is therefore the reverse of procreation, in which the powers of women and men combine to produce fertility. As opposites, however, they are also symbolically linked, hence the idea that if a man dreams of catching a marsupial this may signify that he will have intercourse with a woman (Wagner 1972; Stewart and Strathern 2000e).

Whether the details of such an interpretation are followed or not, two general conclusions hold. Menstrual blood, like all blood, can be seen as dangerous or powerfully beneficent according to context. And "menstrual taboos" work through the collaborative agency of the women and men rather than simply through domination or the imposition of rules by one sex on the other. A third point also needs to be emphasized. Menstrual blood has to be interpreted in the light of a people's general ideologies and practices regarding blood; and, we may add, other important humors and substances of the body (see Stewart and Strathern 2001a).

The most important points that emerge from this consideration of the work of Buckley and Gottlieb and of Knight are generalizing and methodological in character. First, menstrual blood is a body substance and like all such substances is seen as a locus of power. Its life-force may be used for beneficent or lethal ends. It may be in place or out of place. In interpreting its use and meanings attributed to it we have to take the agency of both women and men into account. Menstrual or other taboos should not be interpreted simply in terms of notions of pollution or the relative status of the genders, although Mary Douglas's notion that they reflect ideas about power is accurate. Cosmological contexts are very important, and here we ourselves have stressed the importance of looking at taboos and rules regarding body substances as reflections of ideas of the collaborative agency of persons, particularly spouses, across different domains of social activity in which they may otherwise be separated, for example, in cult practices, hunting, or fishing in sea waters.

Janet Hoskins explored this topic of menstrual powers in various geographical places at a conference where we also contributed a paper (Stewart and Strathern 2000c). In this chapter we support our arguments with data from various practices and by looking closely at ethnographic materials. The highlighting of the concept of "pollution" in relation to menstrual blood in many of the early anthropological accounts does not always sit easily with the broader ethnographic materials, which often present a very different portrait of gender relations. We argue that ideas surrounding menstruation must ideally be examined in their total context and not partially. This total context would include the whole life cycle of the body, including death rituals and the recycling of aspects of the body and the person in the cosmos.

In terms of gender relations early ethnographies about the Highlands of Papua New Guinea tended to start from the premise of antagonism between women and men as well as the separate aspects of their lives. These themes were frequently connected in the literature with male initiation and fighting conducted between males in intermarrying clans or local groups. The analysis of the role of inter-group fighting in social structure was extended to gender relations. A model of menstrual "pollution" was applied as an encompassing explanatory device that supposedly reflected and explained the implied hierarchical character of gendered interactions. Since the 1960s this overall model has been considerably modified, although, as with many entrenched models, writers have frequently persisted in invoking the model even when it does not fit their own ethnographic materials.

It has been recognized that gendered separation, as seen in initiation practices and like forms of protracted physical separation, does not necessarily mean antagonism. In fact, as we have discussed elsewhere (Stewart and Strathern 2000c; Strathern and Stewart 1999f), separation was sometimes a means of supporting particular actions, thus demonstrating social collaboration between women and men. We have extended the point made by Feil (1987: 168–232) that men's and women's economic activities, for example, "are complementary yet largely independent" in some cases, and that in the Western Highlands of Papua New Guinea there is "an interdependence of male-female roles," which he interprets as a means of achieving high agricultural production for exchange (pp. 168–232). Sillitoe (1985) has also discussed gendered complementarity in production among the Wola people of the Southern Highlands of PNG. Works by scholars such as Anna Meigs (1984), M. Strathern (1988), Rena Lederman (1986), and Bruce Knauft (1999) on gendered aspects of life among the Highlanders of PNG have helped to make gender relations a topic of further careful scrutiny.[1]

We ourselves have looked at the sphere of ritual, especially with regard to Female Spirit cults, and have argued that these cults overtly recognized gender complementarity in symbolic terms and that cult performances "were successful only with the full collaboration and co-operation of both males and females in the communities" (Stewart and Strathern 1999a: 351). We have extended our argument further to the analysis of the Male Spirit cult of Mount Hagen in the Western Highlands Province, PNG (Stewart and Strathern 2001a).

Anthropologists have noted generally that where ties of social alliance and exchange between persons and groups were emphasized the values given to the female domain and to bonds established through women were greater than where these ties were weaker or less important (e.g., Feil 1987). Nonetheless, as we have noted, the motif of menstrual "pollution" was often retained throughout anthropological accounts even though it was detached from the other elements of the original narrowly defined and limited model that had been modified as more focus on the ethnographic materials was utilized in analytical formulations.

We will take a closer look at this topic and develop overall perspectives within which ideas pertaining to menstruation can be resituated. We do this in terms of ideas expressed in ethnographic materials about blood practices and the power dynamics surrounding such important bodily fluids. We accept Mary Douglas's (1966) overall concept of the negative or positive values and powers associated with objects and substances that are placed outside of their "properly" prescribed context. "If we can abstract pathogenicity and hygiene from our notion of dirt, we are left with the old definition of dirt as matter out of place" (Douglas [1966] 1984: 35). Thus, either semen or menstrual blood, if not kept in its culturally prescribed "proper" place, can be very dangerous. Powerful substances require managed flow and use within and between bodies, within time, and within space, in order for them to produce their desired effects and to avoid undesired consequences.

Douglas's work has been criticized for associating the body with the idea of a bounded system, whereas in some societies (e.g., South India and according to some scholars in Melanesia) bodies supposedly "included wider processes and substances than those directly tangible or limited to their own bodily boundaries" (Lamb 2000: 13). Lamb agrees that from a phenomenological viewpoint we can assume that people do experience "some sense of a unique body-self" (p. 13), but she is concerned with the level of social constructions about personhood and the body that may be inter-individual in their focus. Arguments of this sort ultimately depend on some kind of philosophical standpoint. However, it is possible to recognize both individual and social aspects of ideas about the body as operating in a single field of relations, rather than dealing with one aspect or level to the exclusion of the other. Thus, there may be a perception of boundaries and flows of substance across these boundaries, in a way that is analogous to what Fredrik Barth (1969) suggested for ethnic groups: that is, that boundaries continue to exist in spite of transactions across them, and transactions continue in spite of boundaries being set up. Douglas's work concentrated on the idea of boundaries, but it did not deny the flow of substances across them. Indeed her whole theory depended precisely on the idea of such flows. It is also important in this context to make a distinction between substance and agency (A. Strathern 1996: 108–11). Substances may flow, but it is agency that controls them. This distinction is necessary in order to understand the ideas in Highlands societies regarding the flows of substances, including both blood and semen.

We suggest that it is critical for our analyses to look at blood ideologies and practices in general within the overall framework of indigenous ideas about the cosmos in which notions about reproduction and fertility (and also death) are of overarching importance. If this is done then it becomes much less plausible to look on ideas about menstrual blood in solely negative terms, since blood itself is a reproductive element of great power in indigenous thinking. The negative connotations of the English word "pollution" in terms of an encompassing value for menstrual fluid are ones that become difficult to support (see Wiessner and Tumu 1998: 217, 447). Semantic difficulties emerge through the process of translation of indigenous terms as words for "pollution," especially since indigenous words that indicate negative and positive powers of substances may have expanding or contracting meanings that are contextually applied.[2]

Our approach is in line with that taken by others who have written on the topic. As we have seen, Buckley and Gottlieb (1988a), for example, rejected a simple sociological explanation for menstrual practices and advocated that attention must be paid to ethnobiology, which we do here in ideas about the reproductive cosmos. Also, Anna Meigs (1984) pointed out that the gendered characteristics of individuals among the Hua of the Eastern Highlands of PNG were seen as varying over time within the life cycle and that balance was sought in gender relations.[3] We relate this point to the notion of the cosmos and its underpinning by collaborative processes. The discussion that follows is intended to advance an understanding of certain historical aspects of Highlands New Guinea societies that resituates the topic of menstrual blood in terms of ideas of power, placement, and communication. In some instances this model can be extended to include other bodily fluids such as semen, the exudates of corpses, and the powerful residue left from the sexual mixing of bodily fluids. What is important to keep in mind is the duality of these substances (potentially dangerous and harmful or beneficial and renewing). We find in the examples below that both female and male substances, and correspondingly female and male actions and symbolic values, were constantly seen as combined together in these societies in the pursuit of their overall reproduction. These materials fit well with our overall viewpoint, which identifies the tendency to retain balanced relations between the genders within the cosmological nexus, one that must be seen as underpinning everyday life also, even if this is not always evident on the surface of behavioral patterns.

When we are discussing bodily substances, such as menstrual fluid, in New Guinea societies concepts of power dynamics are paramount (see Stewart and Strathern 2001a; Strathern and Stewart 1999a, for example). We use the word "power" to signify "strength to alter," including both "positive" or "negative" alteration in any particular instance. Menstrual blood is recognized as an extremely powerful substance. It is a definitive signal of the potential for individual reproductive capacity. Without menstruation a group cannot be sustained and that is one of the reasons why it is recognized as powerful. The Siane people of the Eastern Highlands of PNG marked the social significance of menstruation through initiation practices that celebrated, as a group, the transformation of a non-reproductively active girl into a reproductively active one.

Salisbury's (1965) ethnographic account of the Siane indicated that "a girl's first menses are treated as a form of pregnancy . . . but giving birth to blood alone. As this is paternal blood, magical and practical precautions are taken to ensure that the 'birth' occurs on clan territory" (p. 72). The father of the girl prepares an herbal infusion to rub on his daughter and she is said to "give birth" in her mother's house, hidden behind a barrier of sweet-smelling branches erected by her eldest brother. Men from other villages come and sing songs for five nights running. These songs are said to protect her spirit. On the sixth day of her menarche she comes out from behind the seclusion partition and is led to the senior males of her lineage group who, "using techniques familiar from male initiation," prepare her for her new transformation—as wife and mother (p. 73). She is tossed a bundle of sugar cane to eat and told, "Eat the powdered skulls of your ancestors, their arms and legs. This will bar the road to enemies. Do not forget this" (p. 73). Salisbury tells us that this female ritual is parallel to male initiation in that it symbolically transfers ancestral spirit, it educates the young person in the duties of adult life, and it contains times of seclusion (p. 73).

The Siane smallest level of social grouping, as described by Salisbury, consists of about ten individuals who recognize one male as "oldest brother" (*yarafo*) and one as "oldest sister" (*atarafo*) (p. 52). When an *atarafo* first menstruates, she is recognized in the same ritual sequence as other young women but with an added feature. When she emerges from seclusion all the men from her clan hide in a limestone cave frequented by flying foxes.[4] For four days the men club flying foxes to death as the bats settle into the cave to sleep. The unmarried daughters of the hunters come and collect the carcasses of the bats. These animals are subsequently divided between the menstruating girl, the men's houses of the phratry, and the married and nonmarried sisters of the phratry. "Throughout the ceremony people assert that they are 'eating their ancestors' " (p. 75). The Siane are reported to say that "women see the *korova's* [spirits of the dead] skin" (p. 75), and Salisbury tells us that to the Siane, women are "the ultimate ideal of society" (p. 75). Also, in rituals to the spirits women pulled on strings, equated with the umbilical cord of mythical spirit birds, "thereby stressing the role of women in childbearing and as links to the spirit world" (p. 68) by this act of "pulling down" fertility.[5]

Salisbury's account stresses the positive and recognized significance of menstruation. This is set into the context of general ideas about blood and conditions of the human body (see Strathern and Stewart 1999a; Stewart and Strathern 2001a). Blood is one of the places where the Siane say the living human spirit (*oinya*) is located—in addition to the hair, sexual organs, and breath (Salisbury 1965: 56). The initiation of Siane boys involved the letting of their own blood from the nose and also the penis (p. 91). This was done to increase the balance of paternal blood so that more paternal blood and spirit was left in the youths. Girls and women were thought to retain their own paternal blood, which would be passed on to their children as the children's maternal blood, thus, perhaps, necessitating its subsequent removal through blood letting to symbolically retain clan fraternal allegiance, which would be of paramount importance in cases of hostile relations between groups. The society was therefore based on a recognition of the power of blood and on practices designed to manage its proportions in the bodies of women and men. Blood, in general, along with other substances, could make a person ill or enhance well-being. "Cold blood" signaled that a person had "become a spirit" and might die. This would require treatment such as giving hot foods, for example, meat mixed with salt and ginger, to the person and smearing red ocher clay on the body.

Salisbury's account shows the presence of a humoral system of ideas among the Siane. The general point regarding the first flow of menstrual fluid and menstruation is that it was regarded as signifying renewed fertility and was thus treated as a significant and powerful transition point in an individual's life with relevance for the group at large. A menstruating girl's first menses and seclusion were accompanied by collaborative male activities. Men from her own group were involved in one set of activities and men from another group came for another level of action. The Siane case can be suggestive for other groups, whether or not elaborate first menses rituals were conducted, since in all cases the transformation of a non-reproductively active girl to a potentially reproductively active woman was regarded as significant and was communicatively marked in various ways such as the first stay in a menstrual hut. The physical removal of a woman to the menstrual hut also signaled to the group at large her reproductive position, which was significant not just at the first occurrence but subsequently also as a marker of reproductive success, for example, when a woman did not visit the seclusion hut due to pregnancy, or, alternatively, as indicating the cessation of a sexually reproductive existence at menopause.

The final removal of a woman (at post-menopause) from the monthly ritual of menstruation could mark the transformation of a female and her passage to another phase of social action, such as occurred among the Hua. Meigs states that "the postmenopausal woman with three or more children was formally initiated, [and] took up residence in the men's house, where she was shown the secrets of male society, previously hidden from her on pain of death" (1984: 67). She goes on to state that women with fewer children were not initiated in this way.[6]

For the Hua menstruation was seen as a purification of the female body and it was thought to be the cause of the rapid growth of girls relative to boys (Meigs 1984: 55–58). Hua men practiced blood letting in "imitation" of menstruation. This was thought to "purify" the body and to be able to cure headache, toothache, and pain in the joints and elsewhere.

This treatment let blood from the stomach, navel, lower back, and buttocks. Meigs says that blood in general is not lexically differentiated from menstrual blood and that "blood let from the limbs of middle-aged men was eaten by other males to enhance growth and strength" (p. 57).[7] The Hua explanation for male blood letting applies widely to other Eastern Highlands cases, also to the Wogeo (Hogbin 1970). Far from blood letting being based on a separate ideology, it was in fact patterned on the model of female menstruation itself.

Thus, we see the powers of substances such as blood and the need to retain a balance or equilibrium of these substances (see Stewart and Strathern 2001a for further discussion on humors and substances in New Guinea cultures). In addition to the need for retaining a balance in bodily fluids, powerful substances must be handled "correctly" to avoid dangerous consequences. In the Pangia area (Southern Highlands of PNG), it was thought that a man could become pregnant if he got menstrual blood inside his body by inadvertently consuming it through his penis. The symptoms included a swollen abdomen, analogous to a state of pregnancy.

The cure for this was conducted by a ritual expert as well as the stricken man. This is what one ritual expert was reported to have done in his treatment: "The thing that is called menstrual blood in a woman's stomach he [the expert] takes and brushes it away with bird feathers, with feathers of the cockatoo, with feathers of the lorikeet, with feathers of the hornbill, with feathers of the *ōnio* bird, with the fur of the flying fox, with the hairy leaves of the *pepeyo* plant, he wipes and throws away the menstrual blood, he says. . . . The menstrual blood makes an egg to appear in the man's stomach, a bird's egg, and the expert takes this and reverses it in his spell [i.e., removes it]" (Strathern and Stewart 1999e: 81).

Here we see that one of the fears of male contact with menstrual blood was male pregnancy and thus losing male identity and becoming female through the transformative power of the menstrual fluid. This particular spell could be recited in the performance dedicated to the Pangia Female Spirit (Laiyeroa), but it was also used by expert healers to cure men inside the menstrual huts. The spell and cure can be seen as a ritual abortifacient to rid a man of a female condition that is dangerous to him since he has no uterus or vaginal opening to expel it. Thus, blood out of place can be dangerous in producing what we refer to as "sexual identity confusion." This underlying fear of confusion can be argued equally to be at the heart of menstrual taboos and practices in Hagen (Western Highlands, PNG) also, the more so since in the Female Spirit cult context men do take on ritually female roles (Strathern and Stewart 1999e).[8]

One expression used in the Pangia spell was "neke auwa-ne kamari toano dikoa angale pekakoa pianea." The meaning here is, "as your mother's blood does, so through words we reverse it," that is, the menstrual blood is likened to the blood of the mother that the man has in his body, a recognition of the powerful relationships of "giving birth' " that the mother and her kin have to her child in Pangia—a relationship that has to be recognized by "gifts for the body."[9] The same emphasis is found in the Laiyeroa Female Spirit cult dance when mother's kin lay claims on the wealth items, pearlshells carried by dance participants.

Among the Hua the condition of male pregnancy is called *kupa* (Meigs 1984: 52–62). The affected man's stomach is said to become progressively bigger and a mass of blood grows and develops fetal characteristics. Meigs states that "some informants even claim to have seen fetuses after their removal [of the mass] from men's bodies, an operation performed by non-Hua specialists" (pp. 47–48). Unless this procedure is undertaken it is said that the abdomen will burst open, causing death. Treatment for the condition "included bloodletting and the consumption of the eldest brother's wife's feces" (p. 52). Meigs states that these male "pregnancies" are said to be the outcome of "improper" practices such as ingesting menstrual blood or eating possum meat, which Hua males say is permitted only to uninitiated males or very old men (i.e., nonsexually functional males) (p. 52). The Hua believe that a fetus is formed primarily from "a large amount of menstrual blood and a small amount of semen. All the blood in the newborn, as in the adult, is the mother's" (p. 61).

The condition of male pregnancy was also reported by F. E. Williams (1969: 201–202) among the Keraki of the Trans-Fly area who used the consumption of lime as a "contraceptive" so as "to ensure that young men do not become pregnant." In this example it is thought that "male pregnancy" arose from sexual intercourse between men. Thus, the agent of conception in men in this case was thought to be semen, as opposed to female menstrual blood. Quite how the lime eating was supposed to counteract the effects of semen is not clear. Perhaps lime and semen were thought to have contrary powers.

Although much has been emphasized about the potential dangers of menstrual blood, we see that semen, in addition to other bodily substances, can be equally dangerous. In Hagen, for example, the postpartum taboo on intercourse was supported by the notion that the father's semen could be transmitted through the female body and enter into the breast milk of the mother. A cord system was thought to exist connecting a woman's uterus and her breasts (Stewart and Strathern 2001a: 92). If the woman's breast milk was contaminated in this way, it was thought that it could kill her baby if ingested. The same bodily substance that helped to make a child could kill it if it was ingested "improperly." Such an idea demonstrates that semen could be very dangerous in certain contexts while not so in others. This duality of "positive/negative" valuing of subtances is common. For example, *kopna* in Melpa is a term (literally "ginger") for a hot substance used in curative magic but it can also mean a poison with the ability to kill a person. A ritual curer could use such a substance to strengthen the body, while a sorcerer could use it to weaken the body. Contextual agency is thus most important in determining whether a substance acts "positively" or "negatively."

In Hagen it is thought that conception occurs when the blood in a woman's womb mixes with semen (see Strathern and Stewart 1998c: pp. 236–39), which is "positive." Likewise, among the Duna (Southern Highlands, PNG) female blood and male sexual fluid are thought to combine to produce a fetus (Strathern and Stewart 1999a: chapter 11), and this also is seen as "positive"; but in some contexts these mixed fluids can be very dangerous. In Duna, boys undergoing life-cycle transitions that involved their growth and maturation into adult males were, as we have seen earlier, segregated from others in their community. The boys stayed in seclusion huts in the forest so as to avoid contact with married and sexually active people of both genders. It was thought that contact with these individuals could impede the boys' maturation. The only female that the boys had putative contact with was the Female Spirit (Payame Ima) who served as instructor and helpmate to the bachelor ritual expert who looked after the boys in their seclusion.

The powerful nature of menstrual blood can be seen in another example from the Duna. Rituals of renewal that were practiced in the past sometimes used menstrual blood. In one ritual, the *kirao hatya*, a virgin's menstrual blood was collected into a bamboo tube and taken along a ritual trackway that was punctuated by sacred sites. At intervals along the ritual track sacred stones called *auwi* were supposed to have been found. These stones were thought to be the petrified hearts of ancestors that had risen from the earth and contained magical powers that could cure sickness if sacrifices were offered to them (Strathern and Stewart 1999a). The blood was then thrown into a hole where the ground-dwelling spirit (*tama*) was said to live. This action was said to appease the ground spirit and keep it from disturbing the ecological balance, by producing sickness, and reducing fertility of humans and animals (Strathern and Stewart 1998b). The girl was not allowed to enter into the human cycle of reproduction after her blood had been used in this ritual, but she remained an honored female in the social system.

In this example we see how the menstrual blood of a virgin could be used to appease a male spirit of the ground and so restore the earth to fertility, in a context of sacrifice. The same substance, however, obtained from a sister, could be used in a context of revenge—to kill an enemy. Both sacrifice and revenge here can be seen as different examples of the principle of restoring balance to social relations.

Duna speeches made to redress killings in which blood compensation needed to be made were an important aspect of this process of balancing socially upsetting events. An example of this genre follows. It deals with a case of death said to be caused by sorcery carried out with female blood (a fuller consideration of these speeches can be found in Stewart and Strathern 2000f).

In this Duna compensation speech (*tambaka*), the speaker is asking for compensation for the death of a man that putatively resulted from a sorcery attack carried out by means of the power in a woman's reed skirt (blood). Sorcery attacks against enemies were sometimes said to be facilitated by the power of a woman's pubic covering, as in this case, or by the use of a woman's menstrual blood (see also Stewart and Strathern 1999b, 2002). This kind of sorcery is called *tsome*. The *tambaka* follows:

1. *Hana ipapukumo pukwa*
   This man's face was like a waterfall
   Hongo rarono pukwa
   He wore a big band of nassa shells at his forehead
   Ita ngini ipuna mo pukwa
   He was like a well-fed favorite male piglet
   Yaripu mo pukwa
   Like the first rays of morning sun

5.   *Hona ka epana saiya kata yuna ima tele teka hani ranoa*
      This man whom you killed, the skirts of women covered him
      Iripu tyaka hani tanoa auwako tyako hani ranoa
      The skirts which grew as reeds in ponds covered him
      Penapu tyaka hani tanoa
      Those reed skirts covered him
      Hana ka koleta hoaino
      Remove his shell decoration and return it to me
      Hana no etona Ukurarokeyapa kunine sakondanya
      I will take it and put it with the bones of Ukurarokeyapa

10.   *Rumbiyalu kunine sakondanya*
      I will put it with the bones of Rumbiyalu
      Awira kunine sakondanya
      I will put it with the bones of Awira
      Pokopi ekenda tananaya
      I will put it in the cave at Pokopi
      Yawepi ekenda tananya
      I will put it in the cave at Yawepi
      Anopi ekenda tananya
      I will put it in the cave at Anopi

15.   *Atya ipa sapatya kuki suwananya*
      I will take this skull for the *kira* cult and drink water
      Koleta hua no kona
      Remove it and come with it
      Hameruana
      That is what I am saying
      Awa rapa ne ndupo mbaka mbaka tane
      Shells on his chest clink as he comes
      Hongo raro ndu po mbaka mbaka tane
      The shell forehead band on his head clinks as he comes

20.   *Ipi kitala hini paiyatana*
      The leaves of your pandanus tree flourished
      Upi kaya hini konane paiyatana
      The leaves of the swamp taro were large
      Tiki hinya kei paiyatana
      The leaves of the *tiki* sweet potato were healthy
      Alopi ngwa paiyatana
      The wild fowl made good new nests
      Hakuru hatya paiya kua kone
      Let it remain good like this

25.   *Koleta kuni hana no etono kuki yapi suwanda nya*
      Send the skull back to me, I will use it for my *kira* cult and drink water
      Pokopi kuki suwanda nya
      I will take it and drink it at Pokopi
      Anopi kuki suwanda nya
      I will take it and drink it Anopi

> *Kuni hana no koleta paiyano*
> Return this bone to me and make it good
> *A hana na naraiya nya no noma hota alopiaiya irinya*
> This bone does not belong to me, it is the bone of a wild fowl

30. *Apolema rokou irinya o*
    It is the feathers of the cassowary
    Waklauwa honi irinya
    It is the bone of the wild pig
    Hana kuni narainya
    It is not the skull of a man
    Yawa kuni naraiya-o
    The *yawa* grass has no bone
    Yaki kuni naraiya-o
    The *yaki* grass has no bone

35. *Ka yao kenoa wanda pe tirani*
    You had no reason for wanting us to try this
    Keno kendei ka hateta wanya
    We will try fighting this out with bows and arrows on the pathway.

Lines 1–4 praise the appearance and the shell decorations of the man who has died. Lines 5–7 explain that powerful magic was made against him by placing women's reed skirts on one of these decorations, his forehead band, associated with his adult male personhood. Lines 8–17 make a demand for the return of this decoration and of his skull so that these can be placed in the sacred secondary burial sites of the speaker's parish, up in the high forest above the areas of settlement. The speaker also wants the man's skull back so that it can eventually be propitiated in the *kira* cult (on this, see A. Strathern 1995; Stewart and Strathern 2001a). Before the skulls of forebears were ritually "fed" in this cult, the participants drank cooling water from bamboo tubes. Lines 18 and 19 hearken back recursively to lines 1–4 as a way of stressing the next point, lines 20–24, which is that the dead man's body has blessed the other side's gardens with fertility. Now it is time for the true owners of the skull and its shell decorations to get them back so that they can be integrated into the earth rituals of their own place. Lines 25–29 echo lines 9–17, saying that the speaker will drink cooling water at all the secondary burial sites. Such water from cool springs is associated with fertility and healing (see Strathern and Stewart 1999a).[10] Lines 29–34 take another approach, designed to appease the other side. The speaker now directly compares the dead man's bones to wild things of the forest that are not human, and ends with a conventional saying about grass and greens not having bones. The meaning here is that the speaker will not take vengeance if "the skull is returned" to him. This is a way of asking for compensation to be paid. Lines 35–36 end the speech with a threat. If the appeasement offered earlier and the request for compensation that goes with it are not honored, then the speaker's side is ready to fight, although he views this as

without foundation and unnecessary, and offers a peaceful balancing of relationships instead. The element of the killing by sorcery is not necessarily
attributed here to the agency of the woman herself. It is also set into a wide-
ranging and complex set of symbolic associations drawn from the environment and the social context, all of which point to an overall concern with
maintaining health, fertility, and moral relations as the basis for politics.

This same concern with cosmic context is found in the Hagen narrative
of the founding of the Female Spirit cult, as we have seen already. We cite
a few further details at this point.

The Central Melpa (Western Highlands, PNG) myth of how women became sexual reproductive partners is recounted in Vicedom and Tischner
(1943–48: vol. 3, 25–31) and Strauss and Tischner (1962: 436–37) (see
also Strathern and Stewart 1999e). In Vicedom's first version of the myth
the younger of a pair of bachelors who lived in the forest saw some large
red parrots (*köi nikint*), which often came to eat at fruit trees, and asked
his brother to shoot one of these birds. The brother did so but the bird
flew off. He followed after the bird but what he eventually found was a girl
whose upper arm was bandaged. She accepted his offer of a piece of meat.
He observed that she would leave her house and rub herself against a banana
tree stem. After seeing this, he took a fragment of shell and an axe blade
and inserted these into the tree where she rubbed herself. The next time
the girl rubbed herself in this way the objects slit her open, "making a
vagina." Later her sisters returned from where they had been staying, and
all except one, the youngest, entered the house, became hot, and after a
time went outside and rubbed up against the tree that had the sharp objects
embedded in it. The human man had tricked these Sky Sisters (Tei-Amb)[11]
into cutting their genitals open so that the man and his brothers could have
sexual intercourse with them. These "opened" women who had shed their
own blood thus became the ancestresses of humans. The one Sky Woman
who did not cut herself became the Female Spirit (Amb Kor). She, however,
became the spirit wife to many human men in the cult dedicated to her.

The man in the myth made aprons for all the girls, gave them cooked
meat, and took them to his home. He gave three of the girls to his younger
brother and kept four for himself as his wives. One day the man quarreled
with the girl whom he had first shot when she appeared as a "parrot" because she was infertile. The woman ran into her garden and cried. Then a
fierce storm blew up and the Amb Kor soon appeared in front of her. She
gave her "human sister" a bundle of dance decorations and red cordyline
plants, and told her to give these items to her husband and tell him to open
the bundle in the secret enclosure at the back of his men's house (Strathern
and Stewart 1997b). Thus, human men learned from a female spirit how to
enact the rituals to ensure fertility. In a sense this first human man tricked
the Sky Women into becoming "menstruating" human wives.

A similar myth exists among the Anganen of the lower Lai-Nembi Valley of the Southern Highlands Province of PNG (Nihill 1999). In this version a group of women with closed vaginas lived by themselves without men. "There were many of them, all dark except for one 'red' woman. . . . One day they were attacked by a group of men and fled. They climbed trees but the men noticed this and rubbed tree oil onto the trunk, causing the women to slip. At the base of the trees, men had placed their axes. When the women slipped they were cut and began to bleed. After this the women menstruated and had children . . . [one woman escaped being cut, and] she ran far away, later giving birth to a group of red people, the Australians" (p. 67).

Unlike the Hagen myth in which the escaping female becomes a female spirit, this Anganen myth depicts all the women as being cut open and the escaping female as giving birth to a category of spirit people. These were the Australians who were thought to be other than human when they entered into the lives of many Highlanders during the early days of exploration in New Guinea, the 1930s (Schieffelin and Crittenden 1991). These outsiders were often put into a category of spirit beings, one of which was the red-skinned spirits. The Anganen story confirms the association of Sky Women with light skin, which we have seen also from the Kewa area and is general throughout the Western and Southern Highlands and the Enga Province. The implication of this basic myth is that human women and Sky Women were originally related, and that since human men tricked the Sky Women into bleeding and becoming reproductively active, the remaining Sky Woman now offered men protection against the powers that menstruating women potentially have over men and offered women reproductive powers to procreate well.

Among the Telefolmin in the Ok region west of the Duna, Afek, a female creator figure similar to the Amb Kor in some aspects, is said in one myth to have generated all of the important cultural objects, including the netbag, from her vaginal secretions and menstrual blood. One of the uses that Afek put her netbag to was to wrap the bones of her husband/younger brother Umoin in prior to his funeral. The netbag, which has been equated with Afek's womb (externalized) (Stewart and Strathern 1997b), thus serves as a container of the human body at all stages of the life cycle, in which death at least partly recapitulates birth (MacKenzie 1991: 44–45). (See chapter 6 for a further discussion of netbags and other forms of bodily decoration and attire.) The womb from which menstrual blood flows, children are born, and into which male bodily substances enter is thereby expressed, in the example given here of Afek, as an arena of dynamic action, connecting the cosmologically cyclic ends of life and death. The elaborated forms of netbags also stand for the complementarity of men and women in the productive and reproductive realms.

For the complex of cases we have placed together from the western part of the Highlands of PNG, the particular widespread association of ideas about menstruation with a primal act of male trickery and with the transcendent powers of a female Sky Spirit brings sharply into focus those positive associations of the female domain and the essential dependencies and complementarities of men and women that we have summarized in our notion of collaboration and the Collaborative Model. For these societies, at least, the sensibilities associated with gender relations and with sexual activity are deeply infused with the values imparted through this cosmological dimension of ideas. In addition, the man's actions in the Hagen myth of cutting open the vaginas of the Sky Women may be seen either as a trick or as the working out of a kind of teleological process. Such an emphasis is not inconsistent with the finding that in these societies there are also strong notions of danger connected with menstrual blood. Indeed, the primal myth articulates female and male agency, humans and spirits, reproductive power and danger, all in a single narrative, versions of which are found from Mount Hagen to the Enga area (on Enga, see Wiessner and Tumu 1998: 181, 202, 207, 228–29, 269, 366, for references on the Sky people in general). These myths concerning the Sky Women also contain basic messages regarding the morality and psychology of interpersonal relations. The Female Spirit is thought of as powerful and beneficent, but at the same time as jealous and possessive if any aspect of her domain is infringed upon by inappropriate acts. This is the reason why in Hagen the Spirit is said to make human women who enter her cult area exit in confusion, with their front aprons twisted round to the back, exposing their genitals. In the Enga area, *sangai* traditions in the bachelors' cult attest to the notion that if one of the bachelors who is symbolically married to the Spirit should have incorrect contact with human women while in the seclusion area, the sacred *lepe* plants in bamboo containers in the cult area will turn white and wither because of her jealousy (Wiessner and Tumu 1998: 226). This stress on jealousy and the need to avoid it runs all the way through from esoteric mythology and ritual to the daily experience and sensibilities of people in the Hagen and Enga areas. Ideas about menstruation, its origins and significance, need to be seen in the same way.

That there is a moral dimension to notions about menstruation that goes beyond an explanation based on the concept of "pollution" as such can be inferred from the fact that the Highlands myth regarding the creation of the vagina and its flows of blood appears also in a different area, in the northern coastal part of Papua New Guinea, Pomio in East New Britain. There members of the Kivung Association in the late 1980s told Harvey Whitehouse that the story of creation in the Old Testament was broadly correct, but

that original sin had nothing to do with the eating of a forbidden fruit but consisted instead of sexual intercourse between Adam and Eve (Adam having been tempted by Satan to commit this sin). When God saw what his human creations had done, he put it into Adam's head to send Eve up a betel palm to fetch him some betelnut. While Eve was at the top, God caused Adam to lodge a piece of flint in the tree trunk so that, as Eve slithered down, the flint cut into her vagina, producing a strong flow of menstrual blood. This blood was imbued with supernatural energy, causing Eve to grow breasts and enabling her to bear children. But the blood was dangerous to Adam and he was prohibited from coming into contact with it when it flowed every month thereafter. (Whitehouse 1995: 56–57)

The part played in the story by the betel nut, which produces a red juice like blood, explains why Kivung members are prohibited from chewing this narcotic.

The concepts of God and sin have been woven into this narrative. Also, Adam and Eve are depicted as first having intercourse at the promptings of Satan. Such notions are extraneous to the Highlands myth, in which intercourse is said to follow the act of cutting, and this act is prompted simply by the desire to create a vagina in women. Otherwise, the narrative possesses exactly the same elements as appear in the indigenous versions of the Highlands. Missing from it, however, is the role of the Female Spirit and her transcendent powers, presumably because she has been displaced by God. We see, then, that the moral message in the indigenous myth is supplied by the interventions of this Spirit, who confers fertility on men's wives while guarding carefully her own domain. By the same token men learn to respect their own wives' feelings, on pain of suffering the consequences of not doing so. Men in the myth "create" menstruation, but their power is tempered by a more transcendent female power. Overall, therefore, a balance of power and the sensibilities that go with it are created.

The literature on gender in the Highlands has dealt variously with questions of the fluidity and stability of gendered bodies, with ideas of polarity, separation, antagonism, opposition, contrast, difference, and domination. Another stream of writings has concerned itself with matters of complementarity, balance, and collaboration. On the whole this stream has until recently been rather muted by comparison with the first. The total picture of gender relations must surely be concerned with both ways of thinking about the ethnographic materials, and with the realization that the elements involved are dialectically interrelated. Discussions of menstruation have been heavily weighted toward the first stream of writings, and we have therefore deliberately sought to draw on the perspectives we have established in earlier chapters in order to highlight the complementary and collaborative aspects of the practices at issue. We have also pointed out that the important messages conveyed through ideas of the powers of substances are about the morality of relationships and the sensibilities set up through such formulations of morality. These are the same themes that appear strikingly in Highlands folk tales, whose magical aura also surrounds the courting songs and ballads we have exemplified in earlier chapters.

NOTES

1. Knauft, for example, has demonstrated a method of looking at the complexities of gender relations in his study of South Coast New Guinea cultures (Knauft 1993: 86–116), and has examined issues of gender and modernity in Melanesia and Amazonia (Knauft 1999: 157–94). In the latter work Knauft has discussed several criticisms of "classic models of sexual antagonism in Melanesia and Amazonia," noting how these models tend toward static functionalism and universalism and fail to pay attention to female agency. Knauft also helpfully surveys ways in which gender relations are changing in today's world. It may be useful to add here that ethnographic accounts of the Highlands in the 1950s and 1960s were themselves dealing with societies heavily influenced by Christian mission teachings and by colonial pacification, so that we cannot simply treat those accounts as an ethnographic baseline from which to consider subsequent change. This observation applies to gender relations as well as to all other aspects of society. Nevertheless, we can gain glimpses of important pre-colonial historical processes of changing gender relations prior to Australian impact and consider these on a regional, comparative basis.

Although we have not ventured into the ethnographic region of Amazonia here, the following quotation from Michael Brown's work on the Aguaruna Jivaro of Peru strikingly indicates the possibilities of intriguing comparisons with Highland Papua New Guinea ideas about Female Spirits: "More than an abstract symbol of vitality, blood is a sign of women's fertility. . . . Menstrual blood is a manifestation of the mythical being Etse . . . whom myths describe as an extremely seductive woman with a scent so magnetic that men cannot resist having intercourse with her. . . . Etse, then, is more than a mythical being—She is a female essence, at once attractive, fecund, and dangerous to men. All of these qualities are reified in menstrual blood" (Brown 1986: 129).

2. This point can be extended to include the fluids of corpses, since these can be seen as having either lethal or beneficial powers, depending on context. In Hagen, for example, these fluids from a corpse were sometimes said to be drawn from the body in order to be used as "poison" in sorcery against those suspected of being responsible for the person's death. In the Duna area a corpse's fluids are thought to be beneficial to the general ecological system by renewing the soil's "grease" and fertility. Likewise, in Hagen, the "grease" (*kopong*) of the dead in general was held to benefit the earth in what A. Strathern called the "grease cycle" (1982).

3. The Hua ideas operate via the central concept of *nu*, the vital essence in food and people whose flow and balance with other substances have to be managed. The concept is similar to the Hagen idea of *kopong*, "grease"; but the Hua have developed it systematically with regard to gender in their own way. Males have a relatively small amount of *nu* when young and so grow slowly as adolescents and find it hard to maintain vitality as adults. Females have a greater endowment of *nu*, so they grow quickly and age slowly but because of an excess of *nu* suffer from too great a moistness of the body (Meigs 1984: 27). Sexual activity involves the transfer of *nu*, and males claim that it depletes theirs in favor of women's; but women counter this by saying that intercourse increases the dangerous flow of menstrual fluids (p. 41). Meigs provides a sophisticated exploration of notions of this kind.

4. Certain kinds of flying foxes are classified by the Siane as *korova* (spirits of the

dead), as are many objects, including the sacred bamboo flutes, the masks used in fertility ceremonies, and some *gerua* boards (Salisbury 1962: 32).

5. Compare this example with the theme of the cosmic umbilical cord that connects Sky and Earth in eastern Indonesian traditions, sometimes symbolized as a liana or as a python, as discussed in Strathern and Stewart (2000a: 60–65, 72–73). Closer to hand we may compare these Siane ritual actions with those O'Hanlon reports for the Wahgi area in which at a major *gol* dance two girls pull in a hand-over-hand way at strings attached to an effigy (O'Hanlon 1989: 106).

6. Meigs's argument at this point (p. 68) invokes states of "pollution" in these women but the argument might equally be made that the women who produced less for the group were not honored as highly as the ones who did more, thereby demonstrating the recognition by both women and men of the importance of reproduction as a common goal that is to be aimed at.

7. Knight (1991) asks, "If menstruation were necessarily emblematic of feminine weakness, why should men want to emulate it? I [Knight] suspected that . . . menstruation had been culturally constructed as a source (perhaps even *the* symbolic source) of ritual power" (p. 37).

8. Indeed, we may argue generally that rituals permit roles to be taken on by performers that would not normally be allowed outside of the ritual context, allowing contradictions to be expressed and mediated. Here our reference means simply that one section of the male dancers is said to represent the "women's house" (*amb-nga*), and all the dancers in a sense represent the Female Spirit by manifesting her presence in their performance. We do not imply transvestism on their part.

9. In Pangia a series of gifts is supposed to be made by paternal kin to maternal kin as payments for the skin/body of children (*tingine-ke mereko*). Matrilateral kin are called *opianango*, "the men who gave birth to one," and they retain mystical powers of health or sickness over the bodies of their sisters' children. The payments to them are made to ensure the growth of children and to keep them free of sickness that might be provoked by the anger of these kin: anger which in turn would be provoked by nonpayment.

10. See Strathern and Stewart 1999a and Stewart and Strathern 2001a for an in-depth discussion of this topic.

11. The Sky Folk (Tei-Wamb) were thought generally to have revealed themselves to the first founders of the Melpa tribes and to have laid down each tribe's divination substance or *mi* (see Strauss and Tischner 1962 on this concept). These Sky Sisters had first been seen by the human men as parrots (*köi nikint*). For the Kawelka group the *mi* substance is the cordyline plant (Stewart and Strathern 2001d), which also was supposed to have formed a part of the ritual package that the Female Spirit revealed to people in giving them the knowledge to perform her cult (or, at least, the red variety of the cordyline was involved).

Chapter 8

Conclusion

The investigation of sensibilities in gender relations has taken us from the realms of song, through folk tales, mythology, and ritual, to the intersection between these realms and everyday practice. Obviously practice does not simply instantiate mythico-ritual themes, but it is informed by them as these themes are also informed by practice. When we look at gender relations in New Guinea from this totalizing perspective we are able to understand better the human sentiments that come into play and thus to avoid various stereotypes about the region and its people. We are also able to provide an idea of the positive sensibilities at work in this area and how they vary. Our aim has thus been to present a picture of cultural ideas and practices that has not been highlighted previously because of an emphasis on restrictions (perceived and real) rather than on a nuanced emphasis on "sensibilities," which we have introduced as an alternative approach, drawing on the domain of expressive genres, including songs, in order to bring this model to life.

Obviously, one of the chief matters at issue in an exercise of this sort is the question of what kind of overall picture is being drawn of the cultural and social life of a people. In deploying the concept of sensibility, our intention has been to offer it as a conceptual tool for avoiding overgeneralizations about the Highlands societies of New Guinea we have discussed. The idea of sensibility resembles that of ethos, but with a shift toward the expression of feelings in practices and, on the other hand, without the claim that people's lives are pervaded by a single overall orientation or dominating set of values to the exclusion of others. To replace one stereotype with another would have been entirely counter to our aims here. People may have varying sensibilities about the arenas of their lives and conflicting values and tendencies may coexist uneasily or may come into play in different contexts or at different stages of the life cycle. Our overall strategy has been to approach the much contested and discussed topic of gender relations in the Highlands from a pathway not predominantly chosen before, a "road not taken" in Robert Frost's phrase (Frost 1969). This pathway has been the pathway of "expressive genres": songs, particularly courting songs, myths, folk tales, and ballads, from the popular to the esoteric realms of cultural knowledge and practice. This in turn has led us to a "clearing" (Jackson 1989) in which we have highlighted religious notions that are prominent in a number, though certainly not all, of these societies and center on concepts of female spirits and their powers and the theme of the spirit marriage. By giving the expressive genres their due, by making them central rather than peripheral to ethnographic discussion, we are better able to portray the sophistication and humanity of the Highlands people, and therefore to understand better both their past social forms and their orientations to current processes of change.

It is evident that our project in this book has not encompassed the whole topic of gender relations, still less its history either in anthropological theorizing or among the Highlanders of Papua New Guinea themselves. We have concentrated on what we call a "moment," but an important moment: the time of life when young people in the past entered into courtship and marriage. Through songs, rituals, and narratives we have traced a pathway of ideas about growth, attractiveness, desire, and emotions generally that constitutes a chart of sensibilities far removed from the themes of exploitation, dominance, and violence that sometimes have loomed large in older ethnographic accounts. We have also frequently encountered jealousy, trickery, anger, and revenge as counterparts of thwarted desire and attraction. Our main argument is that these materials should not be peripheralized in debates about gender, whether these be focused on "male cults" (see, e.g., Gregor and Tuzin 2001 for a recent set of discussions on this and other themes) or on notions of gendered complementarity. Above all, we have tried to give readers a glimpse into the expressive attractiveness of the Highlands genres themselves. If people were able to make these representations of themselves and their wishes, surely it tells us about their humanity and their subtlety in general.

As for the concept of sensibilities, the dominant tone of many of the genres is one that is at least partly grasped by the term "pathos." The Melpa term *kond* (Pangia *ela*) expresses this. *Kond* is a highly positive, if ambivalent, emotion, expressing how people feel bonded to one another yet recognize their separation. It acutely captures the uncertainties of the life phase of courtship and marriage; as well as the ultimate realities of life and death themselves.[1]

During the 1980s, as Marcus and Fischer pointed out (1986, 2nd ed. 1999), cultural anthropology in the United States and elsewhere went through a period of doubt and difficulty, signaled as the "crisis of representation." The crux of this crisis was the realization of the essential subjectivity of accounts and therefore of the indeterminacy of ethnographic descriptions and analyses, largely understood as a mark of post-modernism. How could anthropology claim to be an objective science if subjectivity and variation lay at its heart? The responses to this problem have been various. One has been to reaffirm the arenas in which at least partial objectivity can be claimed. Another has been to embrace the idea of subjectivity as one that can lead to the creative deployment of different ways of approaching ethnographic accounts: the "experimental moment" advocated also by Marcus and Fischer. Both responses are surely valid. Here, we have made use of the second one, bringing into view a range of materials in order to highlight an aspect of life not regularly made central in earlier accounts. We have been able to draw on a diverse set of trends and publications, however, that point in the same direction, or can be used comparatively. Our overall aim has been to let the re-theorization of our topic emerge through the materials rather than by casting around for theories to "apply" to "the data." Of course, in doing so we have been led by our own sense of the topic and our previous work on spirits, the spirit marriage, bodily humors and substances, and less directly, questions of religious change, all seen through a comparative lens in which ethnographies can "speak to one another" about interrelated themes, and a comparative phenomenology of sensibilities can emerge (Jackson 1996).

This book has in many ways been an exercise in reaching back, across historical time and a congeries of ethnographic accounts, for a descriptive pattern relating to Highlands cultures of New Guinea (largely Papua New Guinea) that would look different from the patterns that were produced by anthropologists in the 1960s and 1970s (see Langness 1999). Fundamental reorientations of those earlier patterns of writing have previously been broached in a number of ways, especially perhaps in the spheres of gender and personhood, topical arenas that we also have taken for discussion here. While we recognize the insights to be derived from this corpus of writings on the Highlands of New Guinea, we have been concerned here to reach for a separate consideration of themes, grounded first in questions of sensuous experience of the world and second in the genres of imaginative self-expression, which Highlanders made for themselves and glimpses of which appear in the ethnographic records that we have. Our focus therefore has been largely on the recent past of these Highlands cultures, with perhaps some implications for their pre-colonial history as well. We have not been concerned primarily with social changes, although we have not excluded them either, since life in the Highlands has been a continual tale of such changes. Nor have we, on the other hand, desired to establish any ethnographic "ground zero" point of commonality from which changes could then be reckoned historically.

Rather, our interest has lain in revealing some of the sensibilities of people in the realm of intimate gender relations, and by so doing to alter the tone of descriptions of these societies couched purely in terms of notions of domination and "pollution," especially with regard to cult practices. Since most of the cult activities involved were discontinued at some point in time after the colonial intrusions of the 1930s and 1950s, this has inevitably involved looking back to times now long gone from the lives of the people we have discussed. This does not mean, however, that such an exercise is irrelevant to the more recent past and the present of those peoples. Christian churches appealed to people in the Highlands partly because of the mythic and gnomic ways in which their proponents revealed their forms of "knowledge"; and there has been room for incorporating local ideas into Christian patterns that are ostensibly very different from indigenous ones (see Stewart and Strathern 2000g, 2001b, for example). The past is therefore not irrelevant, and in seeking to change the images of that past we have sought also to alter the opportunities of understanding the present and the future.

Our focus on sensibilities has been pluralistic in intention. We have not seriously sought to draw up society-wide generalizations or cross-societal comparisons in any hard and fast way, although obviously we do not maintain that all the Highlands societies were or are "the same" as one another. Within a given area, more than one sensibility may apply to gender relations, for example. A "romantic" or erotic set of attitudes in one modality may perfectly well coexist with forms of ambivalence or fear and with instances of cruel and aggressive behavior. Indeed the myths and folk tales we have often adduced themselves attest eloquently to these mysterious complexities in relationships and feelings, perhaps with a recognition of pathos, irony, and tragedy in them. The powerful Enga story of the spirit woman who tells her lover to cut off her two breasts, from which the sacred *lepe* plants (irises) will grow that will have the magical power to make youths into handsome attractive men, is surely an example of such a complexity, because the spirit is herself first killed by the very cohort of males to whom, out of her feelings for her lover and his people, she will endow the enduring powers of her female body: the power to make these youths grow into men because of their desire for the attractive quality of the female herself. Certainly, profound messages about relationality and interdependence are conveyed in this story (see Stewart and Strathern 2000b for a review of the literature on this concept).

Our focus has not simply been on myth, if this is defined as esoteric but important narratives known only to a select few. The messages of myth are conveyed also, refracted into many permutations, in popular folk tales and songs, repeated widely and known to people of different ages. The specific story of the origin of the Female Spirit cult in Hagen was not recited by any of the participants in this cult from the 1960s onward in the Dei Council area of Hagen. This was undoubtedly because the cult was only just making its way into the area, and its origin myths were "looked after" by people nearer to its apparent point of origin or dispersal far to the south in Tambul. However, the values and themes that underpinned the cult were expressed in a host of detailed behaviors and attitudes as well as being reflected in a corpus of popular folk tales in the area. From this point it is evident that the realm of myth extends into and informs everyday life and vice versa. Myth and everyday life are not entirely separate realms and we cannot test the one against the other to see which expresses the greater "truth" about a society. It is clear that myths may enunciate values that are not well maintained in practice. But we are talking of people's attitudes here, and their sensibilities; and we are arguing that sensibilities in particular are pervaded by values that also show in myth and narrative. A parallel exists in many cultures: the values associated with sex relations and marriage are not always realized in practice, yet people's aspirations and feelings still turn toward them, and they still remember moments and occasions when a partial realization took place, often centered on the idea of courtship.

Songs and ballads are a crucial part of the pathway by which we can enter into people's imaginative sensibilities. Concentrating on the phase of courtship, we have adduced songs from a number of areas and have given some idea of the rich depths of materials to be found in the epic or balladic traditions of the Hagen and Duna areas. Investigation of these materials provides an image of a lively, sensuous, dramatic set of sensibilities, full of the contrast between danger, excitement, and desire that is infused into the contexts of courtship. Clearly, by concentrating on this "moment" in gender relations within the life cycle we have given only a partial portrait of a wider domain. But it is a portrait that can take its place along with other perspectives on the broader theme of gender relations and their history.

In the course of following our materials it became more evident to us that a whole complex of ideas regarding Female Spirits was much more important and pervasive than was perhaps previously allowed, or certainly than would fit with other stereotypes of the Highlands societies. In terms of comparative ethnography and cultural history, this finding is significant enough in itself. The specific ways in which we have used the finding to engage further with the analysis of the Highlands societies are twofold: first, we find that the strength of men is imaged as dependent in part on the patronage of a female spirit; and second, relatedly, we see that the distinction between societies with and those without practices of male initiation dissolves, at least partially, when we realize that this syndrome of female power is important in varying degrees across the board. This re-imaging of religious cults thus constitutes a form of re-visioning of gender relations in general. It is also interesting to note here that ethnographers of Strickland-Bosavi cultures on the edges of the Highlands have all tended to give a poetic and expressive slant to their accounts; whereas the ethnography of the Highlands has concentrated more on politics, exchange, and descent in line with the preoccupations of the social anthropology of the 1960s rather than the American cultural anthropology of the 1980s. What we have done here, therefore, is to reveal the expressive and poetic side of the Highlands cultures themselves, making them in a sense more comparable with those on the edge of their region.

Our re-imaging exercise also, of course, involves our own sensibilities in relation to the materials, just as earlier images depended on the sensibilities of the ethnographers and their choices of people to work with and ways to describe those people in their ethnographic writings. Underlying this question is the tension between imaging people as "others" or as "like ourselves"—something that clearly depends on what "we ourselves" are like. The images produced in the 1960s, in line with the sense of entering a new world, tended to stress difference, and tended to pigeonhole people in terms of ideas such as menstrual "pollution" and male dominance. The views that ethnographers such as K. E. Read and Mervyn Meggitt held about gender relations in general would have greatly informed their writings and would differ from those of ethnographers nowadays who may have a very different set of ideas about male and female relations owing to different life experiences.

In contesting or modifying stereotypes from the older literature, we have not simply tried to replace them with a model of similarity. We are not saying that the cultural complexes of feelings regarding courtship and marriage are the same, or were the same, in the Highlands as in some mythical realm of the "the West" presented as "ourselves." That would be another exercise in stereotyping again. We have attempted to touch on, and point to, arenas of similarity or communicability. In this regard the songs, folk tales, and ballads we have cited have spoken most eloquently for themselves, even as, at the same time, to understand them requires a considerable amount of background exegesis. The genres of expression speak clearly across and through this background. The kinds of images that speak for themselves in this way can be well exemplified by the notions surrounding the Campnosperma oil, a source of perceived vitality and beauty that also turns out to have a mythological origin; or in the secret origins of the *lepe* plant in the Enga bachelors' cult of the *sangai*, shared by the Paiela, the Huli, and the Duna; or in the lines of the Hagen ballad of Miti Weipa and Kundila Rangkopa, where the singer praises and makes "glorious" the name of Rangkopa herself:

> Her face was like an iris flower,
> The woman of Kundila, Rangkopa.
> Her face was like a sweet-flag flower,
> The woman of Kundila, Rangkopa.

Bog-iris, sweet flag, *Acorus calamus*, the *lepe*, the *palena*, the secret at the heart of male initiation, are found here in the image of the face of Rangkopa, the woman of Kundila, whose name can also mean "the dawn."

We hope our efforts in this book will assist in the fuller understanding and appreciation of ethnographic materials from the Highlands of New Guinea. Much can be obtained by looking at them with an eye for the sensibilities of the people being studied and a careful consideration of their sophisticated forms of communication.

NOTE

1. Robert Gardner and Karl Heider (1974: 67) give us a snippet of creativity from the Dugum Dani of the Baliem Valley, Irian Jaya (West Papua), in the early 1960s. They write about boys' songs, referring to their sexual connotations (which they say do not otherwise enter much into ordinary Dani conversation). "Such tunes," they say, "are sung with great exuberance and humor." The boys sing to girls. In one example a boy sings to a girl, recalling that she said long ago, "I will go far away, I shall go far away." Another song runs as follows:

> You are sitting next to the poles of the fireplace.
> I don't want to buy nassa shells,
> I don't want to buy cowrie shells,
> Giluge girl, Yaiige girl.
> The blue sky up there, your hand grasped it.
> The white cloud down there, your foot stepped on it.

The song seems a perfect rendering of the *kond* complex, with its ambivalence, distancing, and sense of intimate regret. Materials of this kind, appearing here almost as an afterthought in the Dani ethnography, provide an important source of evidence about the kinds of shared sensibilities that have been our topic in this book. While writers on other parts of Papua New Guinea, as we have noted (for example, Feld 1982, Scoditti 1996), have explored this domain extensively, it has not been made central, on the whole, in the work of Highlands New Guinea ethnographers. This is the significant lacuna we have attempted to fill here.

References

Ackerman, Diane. 1990. *A Natural History of the Senses.* New York: Random House.

Allen, M. 1967. *Male Cults and Secret Initiations in Melanesia.* Melbourne: Melbourne University Press.

Appadurai, Arjun. 1996. *Modernity at Large: Cultural Dimensions of Globalization.* Minneapolis and London: University of Minnesota Press.

Ballard, Chris. 1998. The Sun by Night: Huli Moral Topography and Myths of a Time of Darkness. In L. R. Goldman and C. Ballard, eds., *Fluid Ontologies,* 67–86. Westport, Conn.: Bergin & Garvey.

Barth, Fredrik, ed. 1969. *Ethnic Groups and Boundaries. The Social Organization of Culture Difference.* Bergen: Universitets Forlaget.

Bergmann, W. n.d. (1969) *Die Kamanuku. Die Kultur der Chimbu Stämme. Eine Monographie.* Mimeographed (4 vols.).

Berndt, R. M. 1962. *Excess and Restraint. Social Control among a New Guinea Mountain People.* Chicago: University of Chicago Press.

Biersack, Aletta. 1982. Ginger Gardens for the Ginger Woman: Rites and Passages in a Melanesian Society. *Man* (n.s.) 17: 239–58.

———. 2001. Reproducing Inequality. The Gender Politics of Male Cults in the Papua New Guinea Highlands and Amazonia. In T. A. Gregor and D. Tuzin, eds. *Gender in Amazonia and Melanesia,* 69–90. Berkeley: University of California Press.

Blacking, John. 1977. Towards an Anthropology of the Body. In John Blacking, ed. *The Anthropology of the Body,* 1–28. Association of Social Anthropologists Monographs, 15. London: Academic Press.

Bloch, Maurice. 1989. *Ritual, History and Power: Selected Papers in Anthropology.* LSE Monographs in Social Anthropology, no. 58. London Athlone Press.

Bourdieu, Pierre. 1977. *Outline of a Theory of Practice*. Trans. Richard Nice. Cambridge: Cambridge University Press.

Bowden, Ross. 1983. *Yena. Art and Ceremony in a Sepik Society*. Oxford: Pitt-Rivers Museum Monograph, no. 3.

————. 1984. Art and Gender Ideology in the Sepik. *Man* (n.s.) 19: 445–58.

Brady, Ivan, ed. 1991. *Anthropological Poetics*. Lanham, Md.: Rowman and Littlefield.

Brenneis, Don, and Fred R. Myers, eds. 1991. *Dangerous Words. Language and Politics in the Pacific*. Prospect Heights, Il.: Waveland Press.

Bristow, Joseph. 1997. *Sexuality*. London and New York: Routledge.

Brooks, Peter. 1993. *Body Work. Objects of Desire in Modern Narrative*. Cambridge, Mass.: Harvard University Press.

Brown, Michael F. 1986. *Tsewa's Gift. Magic and Meaning in an Amazonian Society*. Washington, D.C., and London: Smithsonian Institution Press.

Brown, Paula. 1972. *The Chimbu. A Study of Change in the New Guinea Highlands*. Cambridge, Mass.: Schenkman Publishing Company.

Brumbaugh, Robert C. 1980. A Secret Cult in the West Sepik Highlands. Ph.D. diss., State University of New York at Stonybrook.

————. 1990. Afek Sang: The "Old Woman" Myth of the Mountain Ok. In B. Craig and D. Hyndman, eds. *Children of Afek*, 54–87. Oceania Monographs, no. 40. Sydney: University of Sydney.

Buckley, Thomas, and Alma Gottlieb, eds. 1988a. *Blood Magic. The Anthropology of Menstruation*. Berkeley: University of California Press.

————. 1988b. Introduction: A Critical Appraisal of Theories of Menstrual Symbolism. In T. Buckley and A. Gottlieb, eds. *Blood Magic. The Anthropology of Menstruation*, 1–54. Berkeley: University of California Press.

Burgin, Victor, James Donald, and Cora Kaplan, eds. 1986. *Formations of Fantasy*. London and New York: Methuen.

Bynum, W. F., and Roy Porter, eds. 1983. *Medicine and the Five Senses*. Cambridge: Cambridge University Press.

Caplan, Pat, ed. 1995. *The Cultural Construction of Sexuality*. London: Routledge.

Carucci, Laurence M. 1997. *Nuclear Nativity. Rituals of Renewal and Empowerment in the Marshall Islands*. DeKalb: Northern Illinois University Press.

Clark, Jeffrey. 1991. Pearlshell Symbolism in Highlands Papua New Guinea, with Particular Reference to the Wiru People of Southern Highlands Province. *Oceania* 61: 309–39.

————. 1999. Cause and After: Primal Woman, Bachelor Cults and the Female Spirit. *Canberra Anthropology* 22 (1): 6–33.

————. 2000. *Steel to Stone. A Chronicle of Colonialism in the Southern Highlands of Papua New Guinea*. Ed. Chris Ballard and Michael Nihill. Oxford: Oxford University Press.

Classen, Constance. 1993. *Worlds of Sense: Exploring the Senses in History and across Cultures*. London: Routledge.

Cohen, Anthony. 1994. *Self Consciousness: An Alternative Anthropology of Identity*. London: Routledge.

Csordas, Thomas J. 1990. Embodiment as a Paradigm for Anthropology. *Ethos* 18: 5–47.

————, ed. 1994. *Embodiment and Experience. The Existential Ground of Culture and Self.* Cambridge: Cambridge University Press.

Damasio, Antonio R. 1994. *Descartes' Error. Emotion, Reason, and the Human Brain.* New York: G. P. Putnam's Sons.

————. 1999. *The Feeling of What Happens: Body and Emotion in the Making of Consciousness.* New York: Harcourt Brace.

Descola, Philippe. 2001. The Genres of Gender: Local Models and Global Paradigms in the Comparison of Amazonia and Melanesia. In T. A. Gregor and D. Tuzin, eds. *Gender in Amazonia and Melanesia,* 91–114. Berkeley: University of California Press.

Donne, John. 1970. "The Relique" and "The Extasie." In H. Gardner, ed. *The Metaphysical Poets,* 77, 80–81. Harmondsworth: Penguin Books. (Reprint)

Dosedla, H. C. 1984. Kultfiguren aus Flechtwerk im zentralen Hochland von PNG (Papua Neuguinea). *Abhandlungen und Berichte des Staatlichen Museums für Völkerkunde Dresden* 41: 86–100.

Douglas, Mary. 1966. *Purity and Danger: An Analysis of the Concepts of Pollution and Taboo.* London: Routledge and Kegan Paul.

————. 1970. *Natural Symbols: Explorations in Cosmology.* New York: Pantheon Press.

Dwyer, Peter, and Monica Minnegal. 2000. El Niño, Y2K and the "Short, Fat Lady": Drought and Agency in a Lowland Papua New Guinean Community. *Journal of the Polynesian Society* 109 (3): 251–72.

Ekman, Paul. 1994. All Emotions Are Basic. In Paul Ekman and Richard P. Davidson, eds. *The Nature of Emotion: Fundamental Questions,* 15–19. New York: Oxford University Press.

Falk, Pasi. 1994. *The Consuming Body.* London: Sage Publications.

Feil, Daryl K. 1987. *The Evolution of Papua New Guinea Highlands Societies.* Cambridge: Cambridge University Press.

Feld, Steven. 1982. *Sound and Sentiment. Birds, Weeping, Poetics and Song in Kaluli Expression.* Philadelphia: University of Pennsylvania Press.

Foucault, Michel. 1990. *The History of Sexuality.* Vol. 1, *An Introduction.* New York: Vintage Books.

Frankel, Stephen. 1986. *The Huli Response to Illness.* Cambridge: Cambridge University Press.

Frost, Robert. 1969. "The Road Not Taken." In E. C. Lathem, ed. *The Poetry of Robert Frost,* 105. New York: Holt, Rinehart and Winston.

Gardner, Robert, and Karl G. Heider. 1974. *Gardens of War. Life and Death in the New Guinea Stone Age.* Harmondsworth: Penguin Books.

Geertz, Clifford. 1965. Religion as a Cultural System. In M. Banton, ed. *Anthropological Approaches to Religion.* ASA Monographs, no. 3. London: Tavistock.

Gewertz, Deborah, ed. 1988. *Myths of Matriarchy Reconsidered.* Oceania Monographs, no. 33. Sydney: University of Sydney.

Gibbs, Philip. 1978. The *Kepele* Ritual of the Western Highlands, PNG. *Anthropos* 73: 434–47.

Gillison, Gillian. 1980. Images of Nature in Gimi Thought. In C. MacCormack and M. Strathern, eds. *Nature, Culture, and Gender.* Cambridge: Cambridge University Press.

———. 1993. *Between Culture and Fantasy. A New Guinea Highlands Mythology.* Chicago: University of Chicago Press.

Glasse, Robert. 1968. *Huli of Papua. A Cognatic Descent System.* Paris: Mouton.

Godelier, Maurice. 1986. *The Making of Great Men. Male Domination and Power among the New Guinea Baruya.* Trans R. Swyer. Cambridge and Paris: Cambridge University Press, Editions de la Maison des Sciences de l'Homme.

Goldman, Laurence. 1983. *Talk Never Dies. The Language of Huli Disputes.* London and New York: Tavistock.

Goldman, L. R., and C. Ballard, eds. 1998. *Fluid Ontologies.* Westport, Conn.: Bergin & Garvey.

Goodenough, Ward. 1953. Ethnographic Notes on the Mae People of New Guinea's Western Highlands. *Southwestern Journal of Anthropology* 9: 29.

Gray, D. 1973. The Logic of Yandapu Enga Puberty Rites and the Separation of the Sexes. M.A. thesis, University of Sydney.

Gregor, T. A., and D. Tuzin, eds. 2001. *Gender in Amazonia and Melanesia.* Berkeley: University of California Press.

Harrison, Simon J. 1982. *Laments for Foiled Marriages. Love Songs from a Sepik River Village.* Port Moresby: Institute for Papua New Guinea Studies.

———. 1990. *Stealing People's Names. History and Politics in a Sepik River Cosmology.* Cambridge: Cambridge University Press.

Healey, Christopher. 1990. *Maring Hunters and Traders.* Berkeley: University of California Press.

Heider, Karl G. 1970. *The Dugum Dani. A Papuan Culture in the Highlands of West New Guinea.* Chicago: Aldine.

Herdt, Gilbert. 1997. *Same Sex, Different Cultures.* Boulder, Col.: Westview Press.

———. 1999. *Sambia Sexual Culture. Essays from the Field.* Chicago: University of Chicago Press.

Hogbin, Ian. 1970. *The Island of Menstruating Men. Religion in Wogeo, New Guinea.* London and Toronto: Chandler.

Howes, David, ed. 1991a. *The Varieties of Sensory Experience.* Toronto: University of Toronto Press.

———. 1991b. Sensorial Anthropology. In D. Howes, ed. *The Varieties of Sensory Experience*, 167–191. Toronto: University of Toronto Press.

Jackson, Michael. 1989. *Paths toward a Clearing. Radical Empiricism and Ethnographic Inquiry.* Bloomington and Indianapolis: University of Indiana Press.

———, ed. 1996. *Things as They Are: New Directions in Phenomenological Anthropology.* Bloomington and Indianapolis: University of Indiana Press.

Jenkins, Carol, et al. 1994. National Study of Sexual and Reproductive Knowledge and Behaviour in PNG. Goroka: PNG Institute of Medical Research.

Johnston, Victor S. 1999. *Why We Feel. The Science of Human Emotions.* Reading, Mass.: Perseus Books.

Jones, Ernest. 1925. Mother-Right and the Sexual Ignorance of Savages. *International Journal of Psychoanalysis* 6: 109–30.

Josephides, Lisette. 1982. Kewa Stories and Songs. *Oral History* 10 (2).

Kagl, Toby Waim. 1984. *Kallan.* In A Strathern, ed. *Two Highlands Novels* by Michael Yake Mel and Toby Waim Kagl. Port Moresby: Institute of Papua New Guinea Studies.

Kasaipwalova, John, and Ulli Beier, eds. 1978. *Yaulabuta. The Passion of Chief Kailaga*. Port Moresby: Institute of Papua New Guinea Studies.

Kelly, Raymond. 1976. Witchcraft and Sexual Relations. In P. Brown and G. Buchbinder, eds. *Man and Woman in the New Guinea Highlands*, 36–53. Washington, D.C.: American Anthropology Association.

———. 1993. *Constructing Inequality. The Fabrication of a Hierarchy of Virtue among the Etoro*. Ann Arbor: University of Michigan Press.

Kidd, Stephen W. 2000. Knowledge and the Practice of Love and Hate. In J. Overing and A. Passes, eds. *The Anthropology of Love and Anger*, 114–132. London and New York: Routledge.

Kilage, Ignatius. n.d. *My Mother Calls Me Yaltep*. Port Moresby: Institute of Papua New Guinea Studies.

Knauft, Bruce. 1985. *Good Company and Violence. Sorcery and Social Action in a Lowland New Guinea Society*. Berkeley: University of California Press.

———. 1993. *South Coast New Guinea Cultures*. Cambridge: Cambridge University Press.

———. 1996. *Genealogies for the Present in Cultural Anthropology*. New York and London: Routledge.

———. 1999. *From Primitive to Post-Colonial in Melanesia and Anthropology*. Ann Arbor: University of Michigan Press.

Knight, Chris. 1991. *Blood Relations. Menstruation and the Origins of Culture*. New Haven and London: Yale University Press.

Kuipers, Joel. 1991. Matters of Tastes in Weyewa. In D. Howes, ed. *The Varieties of Sensory Experience*, 111–127. Toronto: University of Toronto Press.

Kyakas, A., and P. Wiessner. 1992. *From Inside the Women's House: Enga Women's Lives and Traditions*. Brisbane: Robert Brown.

Lacey, Roderic. 1975. Oral Traditions as History: An Exploration of Oral Sources among the Enga of the New Guinea Highlands, Ph.D. diss. University of Wisconsin.

Lakoff, George, and Mark Johnson. 1999. *Philosophy in the Flesh*. New York: Basic Books.

Lamb, Sarah. 2000. *White Saris and Sweet Mangoes. Aging, Gender, and Body in North India*. Berkeley: University of California Press.

Lambek, Michael. 1991. Foreword. In D. Howes, ed. *The Varieties of Sensory Experience*, ix–xi. Toronto: University of Toronto Press.

Lambek, Michael, and Andrew Strathern, eds. 1998. *Bodies and Persons. Comparative Perspectives from Africa and Melanesia*. Cambridge: Cambridge University Press.

Langness, L. L. 1967. Sexual Antagonism in the New Guinea Highlands. A Bena Bena example. *Oceania* 37: 161–177.

———. 1999. *Men and "Woman" in New Guinea*. Novato, Calif.: Chandler & Sharp.

Larson, Gordon F. 1987. The Structure and Demography of the Cycle of Warfare among the Ilaga Dani of Irian Jaya. Ph.D. Dissertation, University of Michigan.

Lattas, Andrew. 1989. Trickery and Sacrifice: Tambarans and the Appropriation of Female Reproductive Powers in Male Initiation Ceremonies in West New Britain. *Man* (n.s.) 24 (3): 451–469.

———. 1998. *Cultures of Secrecy.* Madison: University of Wisconsin Press.

Lazarus, Richard S. 1991. *Emotion and Adaptation.* New York: Oxford University Press.

Leach, Edmund R. 1954. *Political Systems of Highland Burma.* London: Bell.

Leach, Jerry. 1981. A Kula Folktale from Kiriwina. *Bikmaus* 2 (1): 50–92.

Leavitt, Stephen C. 2001. The Psychology of Consensus in a Papua New Guinea Christian Revival Movement. In C. Moore and H. F. Matthews, eds. *The Psychology of Cultural Experience.* 151–172. Cambridge: Cambridge University Press.

Lederman, Rena. 1986. *What Gifts Engender.* Cambridge and New York: Cambridge University Press.

LeRoy, John, ed. 1985a. *Kewa Tales.* Vancouver: University of Vancouver Press.

———. 1985b. *Fabricated World. An Interpretation of Kewa Tales.* Vancouver: University of Vancouver Press.

Lindholm, Charles. 1998. The Future of Love. In V. C. de Munck, ed. *Romantic Love and Sexual Behavior,* 17–32. Westport, Conn.: Praeger.

Lipset, David. 1997. *Mangrove Man. Dialogics of Culture in the Sepik Estuary.* Cambridge: Cambridge University Press.

Londono-Sulkin, Carlos David. 2000. "Though It Comes as Evil, I Embrace It as Good": Social Sensibilities and the Transformation of Malignant Agency among the Muinane. In J. Overing and A. Passes, eds. *The Anthropology of Love and Anger,* 170–186. London and New York: Routledge.

Lord, Albert Bates. 1991. *Epic Singers and Oral Tradition.* Ithaca: Cornell University Press.

Lyons, William. 1985. *Emotion.* Cambridge: Cambridge University Press.

MacKenzie, Maureen. 1991. *Androgynous Objects. String Bags and Gender in Central New Guinea.* Philadelphia: Harwood Academic Publishers.

Malinowski, B. 1929. *The Sexual Life of Savages in North-Western Melanesia.* London: Routledge.

———. 1955. *Sex and Repression in Savage Society.* New York: Meridian Books. (First pub. 1927)

Maori Kiki, Albert, and Ulli Beier. 1969. Women of Orokolo. *Journal of the Papua and New Guinea Society* 3 (1): 14–21.

Marcus, George, and Michael Fischer. 1999. *Anthropology as Cultural Critique: An Experimental Moment in the Human Sciences.* 2nd ed. Chicago: University of Chicago Press.

Marx, Katina. 1994. Blood, Semen, and Fears: Body Substance Ideologies and Gender in New Guinea. M.A. thesis, University of Hawaii.

Meggitt, M. J. 1964. Male-female Relationships in the Highlands of Australian New Guinea. *American Anthropologist* 66: 204–224.

Meigs, Anna. 1984. *Food, Sex and Pollution: A New Guinea Religion.* New Brunswick, N.J.: Rutgers University Press.

Modjeska, C. Nicholas. 1977. Production among the Duna. Ph.D. diss., Australian National University.

———. 1995. Rethinking Women's Exploitation: The Duna Case and the Material Basis of Big-man Systems. In A. Biersack, ed. *Papuan Borderlands,* 265–80. Ann Arbor: University of Michigan Press.

Munck, Victor C. de, ed. 1998. *Romantic Love and Sexual Behavior: Perspectives from the Social Sciences.* Westport, Conn.: Praeger.

Myers, Fred. 1986. *Pintupi Country, Pintupi Self: Sentiment, Place, and Politics among Western Desert Aborigines.* Washington, D.C.: Smithsonian Institution Press.

Nihill, Michael. 1999. Time and the Red Other: Myth, History and the Paradoxes of Power in Anganen. *Canberra Anthropology* 22 (1): 66–87.

O'Brien, Denise. 1970. The Economics of Dani Marriage. Ph.D diss., Yale University.

O'Hanlon, Michael. 1989. *Reading the Skin: Adornment, Display, and Society among the Wahgi.* London: British Museum Publications.

———. 1993. *Paradise. Portraying the New Guinea Highlands.* London: British Museum Publications.

Ortner, Sherry B., and Harriet Whitehead. 1981a. Introduction: Accounting for Sexual Meanings. In S. B. Ortner and H. Whitehead, eds. *Sexual Meanings,* 1–28. Cambridge and New York: Cambridge University Press.

———, eds. 1981b. *Sexual Meanings. The Cultural Construction of Gender and Sexuality.* Cambridge and New York: Cambridge University Press.

Overing, Joanna, and Alan Passes, eds. 2000. *The Anthropology of Love and Anger. The Aesthetics of Conviviality in Native Amazonia.* London and New York: Routledge.

Paia, Robert, and Andrew Strathern. 1977. *Beneath the Andaiya Tree.* Port Moresby: Institute of Papua New Guinea Studies.

Parker, Richard G., and John H. Gagnon, eds. 1995. *Conceiving Sexuality. Approaches to Sex Research in a Postmodern World.* New York and London: Routledge.

Pert, Candace B. 1997. *Molecules of Emotion. Why You Feel the Way You Feel.* New York: Scribner.

Pugh-Kitingan, Jacqueline. 1981. An Ethnomusicological Study of the Huli of the Southern Highlands, Papua New Guinea. Ph.D. diss., University of Queensland.

Rappaport, Roy A. 1999. *Ritual and Religion in the Making of Humanity.* Cambridge: Cambridge University Press.

Read, Kenneth E. 1954. Nama Cult of the Central Highlands, New Guinea. *Oceania* 23: 1–25.

———. 1965. *The High Valley.* New York: Columbia University Press.

———. 1980. *Return to the High Valley: Coming Full Circle.* Berkeley: University of California Press.

Reay, Marie O. 1959. *The Kuma: Freedom and Conformity in the New Guinea Highlands.* Melbourne: Melbourne University Press. (Published by Cambridge)

Rumsey, Alan. 2001. *Tom Yaya Kange*: A Metrical Narrative Genre from the New Guinea Highlands. *Journal of Linguistic Anthropology* 11 (2): 1–46.

Salisbury, R. F. 1962. *From Stone to Steel.* Melbourne: Melbourne University Press.

———. 1965. The Siane of the Eastern Highlands. In P. Lawrence and M. J. Meggitt, eds. *Gods, Ghosts and Men in Melanesia,* 50–77. New York: Oxford University Press.

Schieffelin, E. 1976. *The Sorrow of the Lonely and the Burning of the Dancers.* New York: St. Martin's Press.

Schieffelin, Edward L., and Robert Crittenden. 1991. *Like People You See in a Dream. First Contact in Six Papuan Societies.* Stanford: Stanford University Press.

Schneider, David M. 1984. *A Critique of the Study of Kinship.* Ann Arbor: University of Michigan Press.

Scoditti, Giancarlo M. G. 1996. *Kitawa Oral Poetry: An Example from Melanesia.* Pacific Linguistics Series D-87. Canberra: Australian National University.

Sexton, Lorraine. 1986. *Mothers of Money, Daughters of Coffee.* Ann Arbor: UMI Research Press.

Shaw, R. Daniel. 1990. *Kandila. Samo Ceremonialism and Interpersonal Relationships.* Ann Arbor: University of Michigan Press.

Shweder, Richard A. 1994. "You're Not Sick, You're Just in Love." Emotion as an Interpretive System. In P. Ekman and R. J. Davidson, eds. *The Nature of Emotions,* 32–44. New York: Oxford University Press.

Shweder, Richard A., and Edmund J. Bourne. 1984. Does the Concept of the Person Vary Cross-culturally? In R. A. Shweder and R. A. Levine, eds. *Culture Theory: Essays on Mind, Self, Emotion,* 158–199. Cambridge: Cambridge University Press.

Sillitoe, Paul. 1985. Divide and No-one Rules: The Implications of the Sexual Division of Labour in the New Guinea Highlands. *Man* (n.s.) 20: 404–522.

———. 1988. From Head-dresses to Head-messages: The Art of Self-decoration in the Highlands of Papua New Guinea. *Man* (n.s.) 23 (2): 298–318.

———. 1993. A Ritual Response to Climatic Perturbation in the Highlands of Papua New Guinea. *Ethnology* 32: 169–185.

———. 1996. *A Place against Time.* Amsterdam: Harwood Academic Publications.

Sillitoe, Stewart, and A. Strathern. 2002. *Highlands New Guinea Horticulture.* Ethnology Monograph Series, no. 18.

Spiro, Melford E. 1982. *Oedipus in the Trobriands.* Chicago: University of Chicago Press.

Stanner, W.E.H. 1962. Foreword. In R. F. Salisbury, ed. *From Stone to Steel.* Melbourne: Melbourne University Press.

Stewart, Pamela J. 1998. Ritual Trackways and Sacred Paths of Fertility. In J. Miedema, C. Odé, and R.A.C. Dam, eds. *Perspectives on the Bird's Head of Irian Jaya, Indonesia,* 275–290. Amsterdam: Rodopi.

Stewart, Pamela J., and Andrew Strathern. 1997a. Female Spirit Cults as a Prism of Cultural Performance in the Hagen, Pangia, and Duna Areas of Papua New Guinea, 1–41. *Okari Research Group Working Paper,* no. 1.

———. 1997b. Netbags Revisited: Cultural Narratives from Papua New Guinea. *Pacific Studies* 20 (2): 1–30.

———. 1997c. Sorcery and Sickness: Spatial and Temporal Movements in Papua New Guinea and Australia. *JCU, Centre for Pacific Studies Discussion Papers Series,* School of Anthropology and Archaeology, James Cook University of North Queensland, no. 1, pp. 1–27.

———. 1998. Life at the End: Voices and Visions from Mt. Hagen, Papua New Guinea. *Zeitschrift für Missionswissenschaft und Religionswissenschaft* 82 (4): 227–44.

———. 1999a. Female Spirit Cults as a Window on Gender Relations in the Highlands of Papua New Guinea. *The Journal of the Royal Anthropological Institute*. 5 (3): 345–60.

———. 1999b. "Feasting on My Enemy." Images of Violence and Change in the New Guinea Highlands. *Ethnohistory* 46 (4): 645–669.

———. 1999c. Politics and Poetics Mirrored in Indigenous Stone Objects from Papua New Guinea. *Journal of the Polynesian Society* 108 (1): 69–90.

———. 1999d. Self-decoration in Hagen and Duna (PNG): Display and Disjuncture. Paper presented at the 1999 AAA meetings, "Embodying Modernity and Postmodernity in Melanesia," Sandra Bamford, session organizer.

———, eds. 2000a. *Identity Work: Constructing Pacific Lives.* Pittsburgh: Pittsburgh University Press.

———. 2000b. Introduction. Narratives Speak. In Pamela J. Stewart and Andrew Strathern, eds. *Identity Work: Constructing Pacific Lives*, 1–26. Pittsburgh: Pittsburgh University Press.

———. 2000c. Power and Placement in Blood Practices. Paper presented at the 2000 AAA meetings, "Blood Mysteries," Janet Hoskins, session organizer.

———. 2000d. Naming Places: Duna Evocations of Landscape in Papua New Guinea. *People and Culture in Oceania* 16: 87–107.

———. 2000e. Dreaming: When the Spirit Takes a Walk on the Wild Side, 1–28. *Okari Research Group Working Paper*, no. 9, 1998.

———. 2000f. *Speaking for Life and Death: Warfare and Compensation among the Duna of Papua New Guinea.* Senri Ethnological Reports no. 13. Osaka, Japan: National Museum of Ethnology.

———, eds. 2000g. *Millennial Countdown in New Guinea.* Special Issue of *Ethnohistory* 47 (1).

———. 2001a. *Humors and Substances. Ideas of the Body in New Guinea.* Westport, Conn., and London: Bergin & Garvey.

———. 2001b. The Great Exchange: Moka with God. Special issue, Pentecostal and Charismatic Christianity in Oceania, edited by Joel Robbins, Pamela J. Stewart, and Andrew Strathern. *Journal of Ritual Studies* 15 (2): 91–104.

———. 2001c. The Ultimate Protest Statement: Suicide as a Means of Defining Self-worth among the Duna of the Southern Highlands Province, PNG, 1–24. *Okari Research Group Prepublication Working Paper*, no. 18

———. 2001d. Origins versus Creative Powers: The Interplay of Movement and Fixity. In Alan Rumsey and James Weiner, eds. *Emplaced Myths: Space, Narrative, and Knowledge in Aboriginal Australia and Papua New Guinea Societies*, chapter 5, pp. 79–98. Honolulu: University of Hawai'i Press.

———. 2002. *Re-Making the World: Myth, Mining and Ritual Change among the Duna of Papua New Guinea.* Washington, D.C.: Smithsonian Institution Press.

———. n.d. *Colonial Compressions: [Pangia] Papua New Guinea.* (Manuscript in preparation)

Stocker, Michael, with Elizabeth Hegeman. 1996. *Valuing Emotions.* Cambridge: Cambridge University Press.

Stoller, Paul. 1989. *The Taste of Ethnographic Things: The Senses in Anthropology.* Philadelphia: University of Pennsylvania Press.

———. 1997. *Sensuous Scholarship.* Philadelphia: University of Pennsylvania Press.

Strathern, Andrew. 1971. *The Rope of Moka*. Cambridge: Cambridge University Press.

———. 1974. *Melpa Amb Kenan*. Collected and trans. by A. Strathern. Port Moresby: Institute of Papua New Guinea Studies.

———. 1977. *Myths and Legends from Mount Hagen*. Trans. of G. F. Vicedom, *Die Mbowamb*, vol. 3. Port Moresby: Institute of Papua New Guinea Studies.

———. 1982. Witchcraft, Greed, Cannibalism and Death: Some Related Themes from the New Guinea Highlands. In M. Bloch and J. Parry, eds. *Death and the Regeneration of Life*, 111–133. Cambridge: Cambridge University Press.

———. 1985. A Line of Boys: Melpa Dance as a Symbol of Maturation. In P. Spencer, ed. *Society and the Dance*, 119–39. Cambridge: Cambridge University Press.

———. 1989. Flutes, Birds and Hair in Hagen (PNG). *Anthropos* 84: 81–89.

———. 1993. *Voices of Conflict*. Ethnology Monographs, no. 14. Pittsburgh: Department of Anthropology, University of Pittsburgh.

———. 1996. *Body Thoughts*. Ann Arbor: University of Michigan Press.

Strathern, A., and Pamela J. Stewart. 1997a. Ballads as Popular Performance Art in Papua New Guinea and Scotland. *JCU, Centre for Pacific Studies Discussion Papers Series*, School of Anthropology and Archaeology, James Cook University of North Queensland, no. 2, pp. 1–17.

———. 1997b. The Efficacy-Entertainment Braid Revisited: From Ritual to Commerce in Papua New Guinea. *Journal of Ritual Studies* 11 (1): 61–70.

———. 1997c. Introduction: Millennial Markers in the Pacific. In Pamela J. Stewart and A. J. Strathern, eds. *Millennial Markers*, 1–17. Townsville: JCU, Centre for Pacific Studies, March.

———. 1998a. Seeking Personhood: Anthropological Accounts and Local Concepts in Mount Hagen, Papua New Guinea. *Oceania* 68 (3): 170–88.

———. 1998b. Embodiment and Communication: Two Frames for the Analysis of Ritual. *Social Anthropology* 6, part 2: 237–51.

———. 1999a. *Curing and Healing: Medical Anthropology in Global Perspective*. Durham, N. Car.: Carolina Academic Press.

———. 1999b. *Collaborations and Conflicts. A Leader through Time*. Fort Worth: Harcourt Brace College Publishers.

———. 1999c. Objects, Relationships, and Meanings: Historical Switches in Currencies in Mount Hagen, Papua New Guinea. In David Akin and Joel Robbins, eds. *Money and Modernity: State and Local Currencies in Melanesia*, 164–91. ASAO (Association for Social Anthropology in Oceania) Monograph Series, No. 17. Pittsburgh: University of Pittsburgh Press,

———. 1999d. Outside and Inside Meanings: Non-verbal and Verbal Modalities of Agonistic Communication among the Wiru of Papua New Guinea. *Man and Culture in Oceania* (15): 1–22.

———. 1999e. *"The Spirit is Coming!" A Photographic-Textual Exposition of the Female Spirit Cult Performance in Mt. Hagen*. Ritual Studies Monograph Series, monograph no. 1. Pittsburgh: Department of Anthropology, University of Pittsburgh.

———. 1999f. Cults, Closures, and Collaborations. Paper presented at the 1999 ASAO meetings, "Women in Male Rituals in New Guinea," Hilo, Hawai'i, Pascale Bonnemére, session organizer.

————. 2000a. *The Python's Back: Pathways of Comparison between Indonesia and Melanesia.* Westport, Conn.: Bergin & Garvey.

————. 2000b. *Arrow Talk: Transaction, Transition, and Contradiction in New Guinea Highlands History.* Kent, Ohio, and London: Kent State University Press.

————. 2000c. *Stories, Strength and Self-Narration: Western Highlands, Papua New Guinea.* Barthurst, Australia: Crawford House Publishing.

————. 2000d. Further Twists of the Rope: Ongka and Ru a Transforming World. In Pamela J. Stewart and Andrew Strathern, eds. *Identity Work: Constructing Pacific Lives,* ASAO (Association for Social Anthropology in Oceania) Monograph Series, no. 18. Pittsburgh: 81–98. University of Pittsburgh Press.

————. 2000e. Dangerous Woods and Perilous Pearl Shells: The Fabricated Politics of a Longhouse in Pangia, Papua New Guinea. *Journal of Material Culture* 5 (1): 69–89.

————. 2000f. Melpa Ballads as Popular Performance Art. In *Ivilikou: Papua New Guinea Music Conference and Festival,* 76–84. Edited by Don Niles and Denis Crowdy. Boroko, PNG: Institute of PNG Studies.

————. 2001. Rappaport's Maring: The Challenge of Ethnography. In Ellen Messer and Michael Lambek, eds. *Ecology and the Sacred: Engaging the Anthropology of Roy Rappaport,* 277–90. Ann Arbor: University of Michigan Press.

————. n.d. (Manuscript in preparation) *Hagen and Duna Ballads.*

Strathern, M. 1988. *The Gender of the Gift.* Berkeley: University of California Press.

Strauss, Hermann, and H. Tischner. 1962. *Die Mi-Kultur der Hagenberg Stämme.* Hamburg: Cram, de Gruyter and Co.

Talyaga, Kundapen. 1975. *Modern Enga Songs.* Trans. K. Talyaga. Port Moresby: Institute of Papua New Guinea Studies.

Tomkins, Silvan S. 1961. *Affect, Imagery, Consciousness.* Vol. 1, *The Positive Affects.* New York: Springer Publishing Co.

Trompf, Garry W. 1991. *Melanesian Religion.* Cambridge: Cambridge University Press.

————. 1994. *Payback. The Logic of Retribution in Melanesian Religions.* Cambridge: Cambridge University Press.

Turner, Bryan S. 1992. *Regulating Bodies: Essays in Medical Sociology.* London and New York: Routledge.

Turner, Victor 1977. *The Ritual Process. Structure and Anti-Structure.* Chicago: Aldine.

Vicedom, G. F., and H. Tischner. 1943–48. *Die Mbowamb.* 3 vols. Hamburg: Friederichsen, de Gruyter and Co.

Wagner, Roy. 1972. *Habu. The Innovation of Meaning in Daribi Religion.* Chicago: University of Chicago Press.

————. 1978. *Lethal Speech.* Ithaca, N.Y.: Cornell University Press.

Weiner, James F. 1988. *The Heart of the Pearl Shell.* Berkeley: University of California Press.

————. 1991. *The Empty Place. Poetry, Space, and Being among the Foi of Papua New Guinea.* Bloomington and Indianapolis: Indiana University Press.

————. 1995. *The Lost Drum. The Myth of Sexuality in Papua New Guinea and Beyond.* Madison: The University of Wisconsin Press.

Whitehouse, Harvey. 1995. *Inside the Cult. Religious Innovation and Transmission in Papua New Guinea.* Oxford: Clarendon Press.

———. 2000. *Arguments and Icons. Divergent Modes of Religiosity.* Oxford: Oxford University Press.

Wiessner, Polly, and Akii Tumu. 1998. *Historical Vines.* Washington, D.C.: Smithsonian Institution Press.

Williams, F. E. 1969 (1936). *Papuans of the Trans-Fly.* London: Oxford University Press.

Wood, Michael. 1982. Kamula Social Structure. Ph.D. diss., Macquarie University.

Index